Are We Neglecting a Great Salvation?

An Exposition of the Book of Hebrews

MIKE O'DOWD

WestBow
PRESS®
A DIVISION OF THOMAS NELSON
& ZONDERVAN

WestBow Press books may be ordered through booksellers or by contacting:

WestBow Press
A Division of Thomas Nelson & Zondervan
1663 Liberty Drive
Bloomington, IN 47403
www.westbowpress.com
844-714-3454

For my lovely wife Lucia, my "good thing" I found by God's grace, my best friend, and my soul companion and fellow traveler unto eternity and the eternal dwelling we will share in Christ.

Contents

Preface

In *The Lord of the Rings*, Tolkien writes of Bilbo sharing some sage advice to Frodo: "It's a dangerous business, Frodo, going out your door. You step onto the road, and if you don't keep your feet, there's no knowing where you might be swept off to."[1] As a Christian writer, I never feel comfortable going too far afield in my writing away from the biblical text. After all, there's no knowing where I (and my readers) might be swept off to! God's Word is a lamp to my feet and a light to my path. It's not some general and varying form of illumination that occasionally shines in my direction. Therefore, when I write, I make it a point to bind my points to the text of the scriptures. At least this is an assertion of my conviction, but I pray that as you read, this assertion proves to be true for you to our mutual edification. And if my assertion is true, then I would encourage you to read the pages that follow with a copy of the scriptures open as you go in whatever format you choose to read it. And as you go, I pray the Lord will bless you richly in the reading of the pages that follow, all by His grace.

Introduction

Neglect. How do you feel when you're neglected? Maybe it's an experience you've had at work. You've worked hard and made meaningful contributions in your workplace, yet you feel like you have no value there and no hope for an opportunity to advance within the company or organization where you work. You've become something less than the status quo because you're convinced your absence or departure would have no effect on the status quo. Maybe you've experienced this in a friendship where you seem to be "the disposable" friend. As a pastor, I've seen neglect take root in marriages as other relationships or commitments rise above love and devotion to a spouse. Sometimes substitutes for love and devotion come into the marriage, but over time, the money from hard work or the stuff money brings or whatever the substitute may be fails to satisfy the deeper need for love and devotion. Eventually, the substitutes only serve as a bitter reminder of what's missing, of what has been neglected. And for many, neglect brings a great distance in the relationship that can't be bridged. More often than not, *neglect is attitude and action toward something precious that is lost through neglect.* In other words, neglect can be dangerous, especially in our life in Christ.

The book of Hebrews is well known for its warning passages and the challenge of interpreting those passages. I'm not going to address those challenges here beyond making an assertion about the first warning passage in Hebrews 2:1–3. But before I make the assertion, let's briefly consider the passage first. The text reads, "Therefore we must pay much closer attention to what we have heard, lest we drift away from it. For since the message declared by angels proved to be reliable, and every transgression or disobedience received a just retribution, how shall we escape *if we neglect such a great salvation?*" The concern raised here is that the readers have been at least somewhat inattentive to the message of God's new covenant in Christ, and there is a risk of drifting away from the truth of the message if they continue such a half-hearted trend. The author of Hebrews (hereafter referred to as "the author") shows his concern by noting that the old covenant message was reliable, and disobedience to it brought God's justifiable retribution upon the transgressors. And if that's true as a consequence of the old covenant, then "how shall we escape if we neglect such a great salvation?"

This "great salvation" is the salvation believers have now and eternally by grace through faith in Christ, and it is "great" (both now and eternally) and can be neglected. We can make it something less than love and devotion to Christ in our relationship with Him, and we can introduce substitutes into this most precious of all relationships we have. And this neglect can have consequences that may be inescapable. So then, here is my assertion. This first warning against neglecting "such a great salvation" is the author's principal spiritual concern toward his readers; and his desire, like a faithful undershepherd to the Lord, is to turn his readers from the danger of their neglect and its consequences while there may yet be time for God's grace to permit such a turn. And if this is so, then the rest of Hebrews, including all the warning passages, is a message to *believers who have salvation* in Christ but risk the consequences of the loss of blessings and rewards of life in Christ, both now and in eternity. And if this is what is at stake, then a vital question for believers today is "How were the original readers of Hebrews neglecting 'such a great salvation'?"

As we move together through the book of Hebrews, we'll see their forms of neglect in detail, but in a general sense, the neglect came in the form of embracing competitors to Jesus Christ in their relationship with God, likely for the purpose of avoiding the hardships that come with faithfulness to Christ. Yet as we look at the forms of neglect in the faith and practice found in the text of Hebrews, we would be guilty of the worst form of neglect if we failed to discern and address the parallel forms in the church today: "And this we will do if God permits" (Hebrews 6:3).

1

Getting Your Attention

(HEBREWS 1:1–4)

Many of you might be old enough to remember the commercials from the American stock brokerage firm EF Hutton. The firm's TV commercials were best known for the phrase "When EF Hutton talks, people listen." An EF Hutton commercial usually involved a *young professional* remarking at a dinner party that his broker was EF Hutton, which caused the loud party to stop all conversation to listen to him. Why? Well, the implication was that EF Hutton was so reputable that only a fool would neglect their message on financial matters. Hebrews 1:1–4 begins the message of the book of Hebrews by saying, essentially, "When the Son of God talks, He's worth listening to" because, among other things, He created this majestic universe and, by the very power of His spoken word, He upholds—He sustains—this very universe He created. He is worthy of our attention. He is worthy above all others of our attention. This introductory passage is an attention-getter, both for us and the original audience. God has spoken to us "at many times and in many ways," and the climax of His message to us has been given in one very significant and final way: "By His Son." And as if to anticipate that one might be uncertain about why the Son of God merits our undivided attention, the author gives us a brief yet compelling résumé for Jesus to make the point right from the start that Jesus is a matchless voice who should have no competitors in gaining our attention and commanding our obedience. When Jesus has spoken, God has spoken.

God Has Spoken

"Long ago, at many times and in many ways, God spoke to our fathers by the prophets, but in these last days he has spoken to us by his Son" (Hebrews 1:1–2). The book begins dramatically, like a story. Three adverbs are strung together: *many times, many ways, long ago*. And in the Greek text of verse 1, the author uses alliteration, choosing five words that begin with the *p* sound. He clearly wants to begin dramatically. And by breaking down God's revelation to us through His Word into two parts—first through the prophets and then through His Son—the author shows both the continuity of God's message in His Word and the progress of His message. And it is a progress from promise to fulfillment—that a right understanding of what was promised by the prophets is fulfilled through the Christ.

We get a good look at both the continuity in God's Word and the progress toward fulfillment later in Hebrews 11:37–40, where the author, speaking of the Old Testament saints, writes,

> They were stoned, they were sawn in two, they were killed with the sword. They went about in skins of sheep and goats, destitute, afflicted, mistreated—of whom the world was not worthy—wandering about in deserts and mountains, and in dens and caves of the earth. And all these, though commended through their faith, did not receive what was promised, since God had provided something better for us, that apart from us they should not be made perfect.

But there is no progression beyond the teaching of Christ in God's spoken message to us. Jesus is the final word, and in both His coming and His teaching, we are no longer in the days of the promise of His coming. We are "in these last days," a phrase the author uses in verse 2, which literally renders the Hebrew phrase used in the Old Testament to denote the age when the words of the prophets would be fulfilled. *Both we and the original audience from the book of Hebrews are in the same time*: the age of fulfillment. We have heard the final word, and the Son of God is worthy above all to be God's final word.

Jesus Is God's Final Word

The author concludes his brief introduction with seven declarations about the Son of God intended to point to His greatness and to show us why the revelation given to us by Him is the highest and greatest that God can give. Therefore, without further ado, let's consider each declaration and ponder the awe and wonder of each, beginning with the fact that He has been "appointed the heir of all things." We see this in the second part of verse 2, and "all things" means "all things"—particularly the lasting things that will endure for all eternity. Jesus Christ is the Father's appointed heir of an infinite universe, which will be made forever new and forever good in an endless eternity. Not too shabby an opening statement for a résumé.

But not only does He stand to inherit "all things"; "all things" were created through Him. Verse 2 concludes, speaking of Jesus, "Through whom also he created the world." Your translation might say He created "the universe" or "the worlds" here. The Greek word literally means "ages" but can have the sense of all that has been created in the time and space in which the ages have occurred. And the fact that all things were created by Jesus is well attested in the scriptures. For example, in John 1:3, John writes, "All things were made through him, and without him was not any thing made that was made"; and in Colossians 1:16, Paul writes, "For by him all things were created, in heaven and on earth, visible and invisible, whether thrones or dominions or rulers or authorities—all things were created through him and for him." Jesus, the Son of God, demonstrated the mighty power of God in creating everything in this infinite universe, and in so doing, He shows us something wonderful.

Jesus perfectly displays God's glory. Verse 3 states, "He is the radiance of the glory of God." The word *radiance* indicates a light shining forth from its source. When moonlight shines on us, we receive the reflected light from a source: the sun. But when sunlight shines on us, we bask in the light of the source itself. Jesus is not some secondary source of God's glory, but rather, in Himself, He reveals the very glory of God. As John describes Him in John 1:14, "And the Word became flesh and dwelt among us, and we have seen his glory, glory as of the only Son from the Father." And Jesus perfectly displays God's glory because of a profound aspect of His nature.

Jesus is the exact representation of God's nature. Verse 3 continues by declaring Jesus as "the exact imprint of his nature." In other words, Jesus, in and of Himself, precisely possesses every aspect of God's nature and perfectly reveals God's character. Being fully

God is who He is and has always been who He is. Being fully God is not something He had to become nor is it something He is ever at risk of not becoming. So then, the man Jesus Christ could reprimand Philip in John 14:9 by saying, "Have I been with you so long, and you still do not know me, Philip? Whoever has seen me has seen the Father." But if you're still not convinced of Jesus's credentials as the foremost voice in the universe to heed, the author then weighs in on a crucial line in Jesus's résumé.

Jesus's very Word sustains the universe: "He upholds the universe by the word of his power" (verse 3). The Word translated *upholds* here in this sense means "to sustain." Your translation may read "sustain" rather than "upholds," and I prefer *sustain* because *upholds* conjures the image of the mythical Atlas holding up the deadweight of the world. What Jesus is described as doing here is much more awe-inspiring. Not only do we know from the scriptures that He spoke the universe into existence—incomprehensible enough—but here we see that He sustains the very universe He spoke into existence by the mighty power of His Word as well. In Matthew 8:24–27, Jesus was in a boat with His disciples in the midst of a deadly storm, which threatened to kill them. Jesus was asleep during it all, so His disciples, terrified, woke Him and pleaded for His help. "Then he rose and rebuked the winds and the sea, and there was a great calm. And the men marveled, saying, 'What sort of man is this, that even winds and sea obey him?'" (8:26–27). He is the sort of man Who can not only command the winds and sea by His spoken word but also sustain an infinite universe by that very same word. And this very same Son of God humbled Himself to save us from sin's power.

Suddenly, in the middle of this breathtaking description of the matchless cosmic power of the Son of God, the author writes, "After making purification for sins" (verse 3). He shifts from displays of the Son of God's cosmic power to His personal relationship with humankind. He shifts to Jesus's work as His people's high priest, which is a major focus in the message of Hebrews. The wisdom and power that created the universe and sustains it will certainly produce in us a sense of awe and wonder, but the grace that has provided the remedy for our sin through a life freely offered up to God on our behalf evokes a sense of personal indebtedness that the contemplation of divine cosmic power could never evoke. Jesus has made "purification for sins," not only saving us from sin's consequences but saving us from its corrupting and defiling power as well. And just like everything else presented in Jesus's résumé thus far, this is a mighty work none other than God Himself could accomplish. And this accomplishment leads to the proper conclusion one ought to come to based on the remarkable things we've read thus far.

His name is as great as the Majesty on high for "he sat down at the right hand of the Majesty on high, having become as much superior to angels as the name he has inherited is more excellent than theirs" (verses 3–4). The language here indicates the absolute exaltation and supremacy of Christ. As Paul writes in Philippians 2:9–11, "Therefore God has highly exalted him and bestowed on him the name that is above every name, so that at the name of Jesus every knee should bow, in heaven and on earth and under the earth, and every tongue confess that Jesus Christ is Lord, to the glory of God the Father."

So then, this is Jesus's résumé; the credentials of the One the author will now appeal to in his exhortation to his readers to "press on to maturity" (Hebrews 6:1 NASB). Theologian F. F. Bruce sums up these seven declarations about Jesus this way:

> Thus the greatness of the Son of God receives sevenfold confirmation, and it appears, without being expressly emphasized, that he possesses in himself all the qualifications to be the mediator between God and the human race. He is the Prophet through whom God has spoken his final word; he is the Priest who has accomplished a perfect work of cleansing for his people's sins; he is the King who sits enthroned in the place of chief honor alongside the Majesty on high.[2]

So then, like the master of ceremonies at a great event, the author has given us a grand introduction as if to ask his readers, "Are you ready?"

Are You Ready for God's Final Word?

Are you ready for a message from the Majesty on High? In Hebrews 2:1–3, the author seems to be asking this question in so many words when he writes,

> Therefore we must pay much closer attention to what we have heard, lest we drift away from it. For since the message declared by angels proved to be reliable, and every transgression or disobedience received a just retribution, how shall we escape if we neglect such a great salvation? It was declared at first by the Lord, and it was attested to us by those who heard.

In other words, we need to heed God's Word. God's Word is reliable in its entirety, but the fullness of what it has promised has now been made known to us by Jesus Christ, the final word, and passed on to the church by those who learned from Him. In John 10:27, Jesus declared, "My sheep hear my voice, and I know them, and they follow me." Do you hear His voice? Is it really His direction from His Word that you follow?

Many times have I sat down and counseled Christians who are determined to live according to a set of convictions that contradict God's Word. And in the most distressing instances, counsel from God's Word falls on deaf ears. Christians can clearly heed a voice that is not the voice of their Shepherd. Do you hear His voice? Are you following Him? Or do your convictions and the life that proceeds from those convictions have another source? Your college professor? Your peers? Your advanced degree? Fox News or CNN? Your boss who promoted you through the ranks of your organization? Your political party and its candidate's agenda? Your children who have rejected the Lord or wandered from Him and so your life now revolves around keeping their favor and defending their choices? A former church that espoused a lot of rules but never bothered to get around to finding a sound biblical basis for them?

Jesus commands His church to teach His disciples "to observe all that I have commanded you" (Matthew 28:20). This is a tall order from Jesus Christ, the Majesty on High. The author was concerned his audience would favor competing voices instead. As a pastor of a church, I share this concern with respect to the congregation I've been called to shepherd. And as a writer to Christ's followers in the church universal, my concern carries over to you. So as we begin this journey, count the cost and ask yourself the questions, "Am I ready for a message from the Majesty on High," and "Am I ready to heed it?"

Neglect Connections

One of the purposes for the author making His very over-the-top and very true introduction of Jesus is to establish in the minds of his readers exactly who it is they're neglecting. It seems to me as well that he is, at the same time, making the implicit point that neglecting Jesus in favor of lesser things is the very height of folly, and a costly folly. The author may be alluding to the great cost of neglecting Jesus when he states in verse 2 that Jesus is "the heir of all things," and this fact has great bearing on believers for Paul writes in Romans 8:16–17 "That we are children of God, and if children, then heirs—heirs of God and fellow heirs with Christ, *provided we suffer with him in order that we may also be glorified with him.*"

A thread that runs throughout Hebrews is that neglecting Christ and His call upon their lives was motivated, at least in part, by a desire to be free from the persecution and trials that came with devotion to Christ and His calling. Jesus is "the heir of all things," and we are "fellow heirs with Christ, *provided we suffer with him.*" As the church in a Western culture that has all but institutionalized freedom from suffering for faith in Christ (and called this good), the hard question twenty-first-century Western believers need to ask is, "Are we neglecting a great salvation?" Like the original readers of Hebrews, have we embraced a different gospel that foregoes suffering with Christ?

2

This Seat Is Taken!
(HEBREWS 1:5–14)

Jesus "sat down at the right hand of the Majesty on high, having become as much superior to angels as the name he has inherited is more excellent than theirs" (Hebrews 1:3–4). Jesus is much superior to angels. This is the case the author makes in this next passage in Hebrews 1, which is plain to see from the text. What is not so evident is "Why is he making this case?" I believe the need for him to do this will become more evident as we move through the book, but as a bit of a preview to an answer to the why question, the author makes the point in verse 2 of chapter 2, "the message declared by angels proved to be reliable." What message did angels declare?

Well, angels declare many messages in the scriptures, but the reference in Hebrews 2:2 is to a "message," singular. In Galatians 3:19, speaking about the law of Moses, Paul indicates the law "was put in place through angels by an intermediary." In other words, God's means of communicating the law to Moses was through angels. So then, given that we're going to discover that a key spiritual problem of the original readers of the book of Hebrews was a tendency to fall back into a reliance upon the law as the means to live out their relationship with God, the nature of the authority of the angels and their message that put the law in place needs to be rightly understood in light of the nature of the authority of Jesus Christ and His message. So then, the author of Hebrews quotes from seven Old Testament passages to ensure that his readers keep angels in their proper place with respect to God's final word "spoken to us by his Son." And to cap off his case for the superiority of Jesus, the author comes back to the point he made in Hebrews 1:3 as to where Jesus is presently seated by quoting a Psalm in Hebrews 1:13 and the Father's statement to His Son to "sit at my right hand." There's only one seat at the Father's right hand. It is the seat of the one exalted to equal standing with the Father. And, folks, this seat is taken!

We have already seen that the credentials of the Son of God are matchless; therefore He is a matchless voice in all the universe for us to hear and heed. He has no real competitors; the only competitors to His message are those voices we choose to make His competitors. And since we *do* tend to make other voices His competitors, the author takes on the task of tackling those competitors, beginning with the angels. He does so, not because the angels have made themselves Christ's competitors, but because the people the author is addressing may be tempted to give them such a place out of their desire to step back into old practices, practices that Christ has made obsolete through His life, death, resurrection, ascension, and ongoing ministry as the mediator of the new covenant. So as we move through this passage, we're going to see the author make the case that Christ is superior to angels for three very important reasons.

Jesus Is Superior to Angels because He Is the Son

First, Christ is superior to angels because He is the Son of the Father (verses 5–6). The author begins this point by quoting Psalm 2:7 in verse 5, writing, "For to which of the angels did God ever say, 'You are my Son, today I have begotten you'?" As students of the scriptures, you may be aware that there are times when the scriptures refer to angels collectively as "the sons of God," but the point being made here is the particular status of *the* Son. The Old Testament scriptures thoroughly develop and speak of a particular person— the Messiah or the Christ—whom God would bring into the world. The Christ would come to fulfill an everlasting role of exercising prerogatives in God's plan of redemption and restoration, and in Jesus, we come to understand that the Christ is none other than the eternal Son of God who has come into the world, taken on human form, and fulfilled all the works prophesied of the Christ. And in fulfilling all the works of the Christ, Jesus has entered into the full exercise of the role and prerogatives of the Christ in accordance with the scriptures. So when the Father says in Psalm 2:7, "You are my Son, today I have begotten you," He is declaring the time when the Son, having finished the works of the Son, now receives the Father's appointment into the roles of the Son.

So for example, in Psalm 2:8, the next thing the Father says to the Son after He says "today I have begotten you" is "Ask of me, and I will make the nations your heritage, and the ends of the earth your possession." And why can the Son ask this? Because the Father has appointed the Son "heir of all things" as we saw in Hebrews 1:2. "Begotten today" is not a reference to a son being born as is often mistakenly understood. It is a reference to the Son's divine appointment by the Father, in the case of Psalm 2:7, to serve in the role reserved for the Messiah to rule all the nations of the earth forever. You see this meaning of the Father's statement in Psalm 2:7 indicating the Father's divine appointment for the Son to exercise the role of the Christ later in Hebrews 5:5 where the author writes, "So also Christ did not exalt himself to be made a high priest, *but was appointed by him* who said to him, 'You are my Son, today I have begotten you.'"

The author continues in verse 5 to make the case for Jesus as the One who fulfills the works of the Son and enters into the role reserved for the Son when he quotes 2 Samuel 7:14, saying, "Or again, 'I will be to him a father, and he shall be to me a son.'" This is God's promise to David concerning David's successor Solomon, but the promise goes on to an extent that Solomon could not possibly fulfill when God tells David in 2 Samuel 7:16, "And your house and your kingdom shall be made sure forever before me. Your throne shall be established forever." But we know from Gabriel's pronouncement to Mary in Luke 1:32–33 that Jesus would be the fulfillment of this promise as Gabriel says, "He will be great and will be called the Son of the Most High. And the Lord God will give to him the throne of his father David, and he will reign over the house of Jacob forever, and of his kingdom there will be no end."

Finally, in verse 6, the author quotes from Deuteronomy 32:43 when he writes, "And again, when he brings the firstborn into the world, he says, 'Let all God's angels worship him.'" Interestingly, this call for the angels to worship in Deuteronomy is a call to worship God. So then, in using this verse in this way, he's telling his readers by implication that the worship due to the God of Israel is due also to His incarnate Son because He too is worthy of worship, something the angels will never be worthy of. Rather, the angels are called to render worship to the Son because He is "much superior to angels" as the Son who has fulfilled all that was prophesied for Him to accomplish and has entered into His exalted and appointed role as a result. But the author isn't done making his case for Christ's superiority.

Jesus Is Superior to Angels because He Is the Everlasting God

We see this point made in two important ways in verses 7–12. First, in verses 7–9, Jesus is the everlasting King. In verse 7, the author quotes Psalm 104:4 to essentially make a point about angels that he'll revisit in verse 14, that they are ministering spirits created to serve, but in comparison to angels, he writes in verses 8–9, "But of the Son he says, 'Your throne, O God, is forever and ever, the scepter of uprightness is the scepter of your kingdom. You have loved righteousness and hated wickedness; therefore God, your God, has anointed you with the oil of gladness beyond your companions.'" This is a quotation from Psalm 45:6–7, and the reference is to One who can be referred to as a King who is God ("Your throne, O God, is forever and ever"). And yet, because of His perfectly righteous character, He can be described by the statement, "Therefore God, your God, has anointed you with the oil of gladness beyond your companions."

Which King can possibly have an eternal reign and be both God and yet receive an anointing from God? Only the eternal Son of God who is the Christ, the Messiah. And we who have placed our faith and trust in Him are His companions as we see in Hebrews 2:10–11: "For it was fitting that he, for whom and by whom all things exist, in bringing many sons to glory, should make the founder of their salvation perfect through suffering. For he who sanctifies and those who are sanctified all have one source. That is why he is not ashamed to call them brothers." Jesus Christ, the Son of God, is the everlasting King, but another mark of His superiority to angels is that He is the everlasting Lord as well.

Still referring to the Son, the author quotes Psalm 102:25–27 in verses 10–12. These verses describe God's work as creator, and the fact of His eternal nature means He will remain after the work of renewing His creation—making all things new—is complete. Without any debate, as he has already affirmed the Son's work in creating the universe, the author applies these verses to the Son and inserts the word *Lord* into the quotation (verse 10). The angels are ministering spirits. Jesus Christ is the everlasting King and Lord. That is a particular and exalted place in God's eternal plan and eternal work that cannot be shared with anyone, much less with angels, a point driven home in the author's closing argument.

Jesus Is Superior to Angels because He Is Exalted

Christ is superior to angels because He alone is exalted to the place of highest favor (verses 13–14). The clinching point in the argument revisits the closing point in the introduction of the book in verses 3–4. Jesus has "sat down at the right hand of the Majesty on high," an appointment that proclaims His superiority as the One whom "God has highly exalted … and bestowed on him the name that is above every name" (Philippians 2:9), even above the angels. To back up his assertion in verses 3–4, the author quotes Psalm 110 in verse 13, a psalm that will also play a central role throughout the book of Hebrews: "And to which of the angels has he ever said, 'Sit at my right hand until I make your enemies a footstool for your feet.'" In Mark 12:35–37, Jesus quotes this psalm as well, but more fully. "And as Jesus taught in the temple, he said, 'How can the scribes say that the Christ is the son of David? David himself, in the Holy Spirit, declared, "The Lord said to my Lord, 'Sit at my right hand, until I put your enemies under your feet.'" David himself calls him Lord. So how is he his son?'" Jesus's point was that if the Christ is referred to by David as "Lord" under the inspiration of the Holy Spirit, then He is more than just a human descendant of David. He is Lord. So when "the Lord said to my Lord 'sit at my right hand,'" then as the author is indicating here, this is the message of the Father to the Son, the Son who is seated at the right hand. This is the seat of favor, the seat for the one who is on equal footing to the one who has given Him the right to sit there. This is an exclusive seat, reserved solely for the one who has perfectly accomplished every work of the Christ set forth in the scriptures. This is an exclusive seat—and this seat is taken.

In comparison to Jesus, the argument closes in verse 14, saying of the angels, "Are they not all ministering spirits sent out to serve for the sake of those who are to inherit salvation?" In verse 2, the author declared the Son has been "appointed the heir of all things." As we've already considered, Paul writes, "The Spirit himself bears witness with our spirit that we are children of God, and if children, then heirs—heirs of God and *fellow heirs with Christ*" (Romans 8:16–17). Christians are fellow heirs of all things: the fullness of our salvation that we stand to inherit with Christ and solely because of Christ. In the order of God's plan for eternity, not only are the angels not superior to Christ, but their appointed role is also to serve us, those "who are to inherit salvation."

So then, in this passage, the author has aimed to dispel any convictions that the message of angels merits consideration on par with what has been revealed to us through Christ. As we'll see in the next passage, the prophetic message declared by angels to God's people under the old covenant "proved to be reliable," but must be understood in light of the message of the great salvation we have in Jesus Christ as John writes in Revelation 19:10: "For the testimony of Jesus is the spirit of prophecy." But interestingly, John made this statement after one of his "not-so-great" moments in an encounter with an angel, which leads me to this closing thought to ponder on matters of our own neglect, not unlike the neglect of the author's original readers.

Neglect Connections

Does the message of angels pose a threat to the spiritual well-being of the church today? I believe so in three ways. First, by our mishandling of a reliable message. I hope you have discerned a key point in the message of this passage. The author has in mind the message and ministry of faithful angels in this passage. He isn't disparaging these angels in their role; he's warning against how his audience may respond in an unedifying way to angels as they faithfully serve. The angels have clearly played a role in bringing the message of God's Word to His people, particularly the law. Exalting the law, and those whom God used to communicate the message (which also includes Moses as we'll see in chapter 3), independent of what we know about the law through the revelation given to us by Christ, is spiritually dangerous. This remains a perennial challenge to the church, and it is the responsibility of the church to ensure the whole counsel of God's Word is accurately handled.

A second way in which the message of angels poses a threat is in the fact that not all angels and their messages are created equal. We know that there are many angels who followed Satan in his rebellion and are in league with him still. I believe it was such a twisted messenger that Paul may have had in mind when he wrote in Galatians 1:8, "But even if we or an angel from heaven should preach to you a gospel contrary to the one we preached to you, let him be accursed." Paul teaches in Galatians 1 that there is one Gospel, and it is from Christ, and warns against embracing any distortion of the Gospel even if the messenger is angelic. We have a tendency, given the power and glory angels presently possess with respect to us, to regard them in ways well beyond their due.

In Revelation 19:10 (mentioned earlier), John describes his response to an angel communicating a message for him to write down in this way: "Then I fell down at his feet to worship him, but he said to me, 'You must not do that! I am a fellow servant with you and your brothers who hold to the testimony of Jesus. Worship God.'" This is one of two instances in Revelation where John records himself wrongly worshipping an angel and being corrected for it. When you combine our tendency to exalt angels when we encounter them with the warning Paul gives that heeding a distorted angelic message leads to being accursed, this too is a timeless danger. Just as an aside, two great religions in the world—Islam and Mormonism—are both deadly distortions of the truth of the Gospel, and both trace their origins to angelic revelations. No small threat indeed.

Lastly, our culture exalts pleasant fiction about angels. Joseph Loconte, an associate professor of history at the King's College in New York City, notes that many people today are still obsessed with angels, particularly angelic beings who seem tailor-made to meet our every need. He cites a book by metaphysician Doreen Virtue who describes angels this way: "They look past the surface and see the godliness within all of us … So angels aren't judgmental, and they only bring love into our lives. You're safe with the angels, and you can totally trust them." One of the ways she espouses the practical helpfulness of angels is with our travel plans. They help you get an extremely nice, warm, friendly, and competent customer-service representative when calling an airline to book reservations. They help you avoid lines at check-in and work with sweet and competent personnel. They let you sail through airport security without being searched. They protect and deliver your baggage so that your suitcases are the first ones on the luggage carousel when you're there to collect it. With her appearances on *CNN*, *Oprah*, and *The View*, Virtue's message, shared by many other authors in her field, clearly has a large audience: "I've discovered that the quickest and most efficient route to happiness is through connecting with the angels."[3]

So then, these are three potential threats angelic messages and messengers represent to the spiritual well-being of the church. We can and do distort a reliable angelic message in the law by failing to accurately handle it. We can and do embrace false messages such as a false gospel delivered by a fallen angel. And we can and do delight in pleasant fictions about angels, nearly to the point of making this a cultural pastime. And with this last threat, the message of angels becomes rooted in whatever you want, making it, perhaps, the greatest danger of the three.

3

Neglecting a Great Salvation

(HEBREWS 2:1–4)

During the latter 1970s, while living a reclusive life in New York City, the former Beatle John Lennon experienced a brief period where he claimed to be a born-again Christian. Apparently, Lennon became an avid viewer of Billy Graham and Pat Robertson on TV and, during an Easter series of messages by Pat Robertson, had a joyful and ecstatic conversion experience. For a few months thereafter, Lennon claimed to be born again, and phrases like "Praise the Lord" and "Thank you, Jesus" became regular parts of his conversation. Lennon also began attending church services and even called *The 700 Club* help line to request prayer for his health and troubled marriage. But John Lennon's experience clashed with, and faltered in the face of, the new age views of his wife Yoko Ono; and his born-again experience was short-lived. John Lennon lived out the rest of his days living a life dictated by astrologers, numerologists, clairvoyants, psychics, herbalists, and tarot card readers. He had a brief taste of Jesus Christ and then drifted away to the song of different voices.[4]

Genuine faith in Jesus Christ is not a life adrift. As theologian D. A. Carson writes,

> People do not drift toward holiness. Apart from grace-driven effort, people do not gravitate toward godliness, prayer, obedience to Scripture, faith, and delight in the Lord. We drift toward compromise and call it tolerance; we

drift toward disobedience and call it freedom; we drift toward superstition and call it faith. We cherish the indiscipline of lost self-control and call it relaxation; we slouch toward prayerlessness and delude ourselves into thinking we have escaped legalism; we slide toward godlessness and convince ourselves we have been liberated.[5]

To drift is to neglect a purposeful sense of direction, and we have no more purposeful sense of direction than a life driven by the Gospel message of our salvation. Hebrews 2:1–4 is the first of five warning passages in the book of Hebrews, and it's a warning against neglecting "such a great salvation" (verse 3). The warning reflects a pastoral concern of the author that such neglect may be a problem among the audience he's writing to. In fact, as the title of this book indicates, I believe this is the author's foremost concern in the book of Hebrews with all that follows serving as an impassioned teaching to believers who are neglecting their salvation in ways particular to their spiritual life and harmful to their spiritual life. Therefore, in keeping with the author's purpose, let's begin considering the question, "Are we neglecting such a great salvation?" along with its implications for our spiritual lives.

Are We Careless with the Truth of the Gospel?

In this passage, there are two key attitudes the author points to that serve as indicators of such neglect, and they both pertain to attitudes toward the message of our salvation: the Gospel of Jesus Christ. We see the first of these attitudes in verse 1, the attitude of carelessness. Are we careless with the truth of the Gospel, which we have heard? The author writes in verse 1, "Therefore we must pay much closer attention to what we have heard, lest we drift away from it." He begins with "therefore," which refers back to the case he makes in Hebrews 1 that Jesus and His message are much superior to angels and their message; and if that's the case, then we must "pay much closer attention" to Jesus's message of salvation. The author actually isn't finished making His case that Jesus is much superior to angels; he's going to pick that train of thought back up in 2:5. But here in verses 1–4, he pauses to warn his readers of the implications of neglecting Jesus's message in light of the case he's made for the preeminence of Christ thus far.

We'll see this "pause for warning" approach four more times in Hebrews, a few of which we'll preview shortly, and I see a pastor's concern in this approach. He knows his readers are on the cusp of spiritual danger and so in the midst of urging them to press on to maturity (also a dominant concern in Hebrews), we'll see these frequent pauses where he warns them of the consequences of failing to press on to maturity. Today's passage is his first "warning shot across the bow," the warning to not neglect "such a great salvation," which he indicates here in verse 1 begins by drifting away.

The phrase "drift away" here has the sense of someone being carried along by a current and doing nothing to correct course away from the potential danger of doing so. When I was in seminary, I owned a boat and lived very conveniently near a large lake. On nice days when I didn't have class, I used to love to take the boat out into the middle of the lake, cut the motor, and drift. I would then take out my schoolwork and immerse myself in it. I can't tell you how many panicked moments I had doing that kind of thing, drifting toward a hazard or into a busy channel or toward the shallows of the shore. I was often careless as I was adrift, and dangers were often the result.

This is the spiritual concern here, an awareness of potential danger in drifting away from the truth of the Gospel, yet not caring enough to do something to correct it. The antidote for this is spelled out in verse 1: "Pay much closer attention," which includes not only carefully listening to Christ's message but also heeding it. So are we neglecting "such a great salvation"? It begins with growing careless with the Gospel as we cease to grow in our understanding of the Gospel and so our conformity to Christ. This is a spiritual concern Peter also warns against when he writes, "For it is time for judgment to begin at the household of God; and if it begins with us, what will be the outcome for those *who do not obey the gospel of God*?" (1 Peter 4:17). But being careless still implies that a sense of urgency can be restored to our walk. But what happens when we cease to care?

Have We Ceased to Care about Such a Great Salvation?

Are we unconcerned about the great salvation we've received? The spiritual digression the author shows us is the digression from carelessness to not caring. In verse 1, his antidote for reversing carelessness was to radically shift our attention back to Jesus's message of salvation and the exclusive driving force it should be in our lives. But as carelessness becomes a lack of concern altogether, the author begins to draw upon the antidote by drawing attention to an important lesson learned from the law in verse 2. In essence, he's asking his readers the question, "Do we realize God's former covenant with His people Israel proved to be reliable?"

The author writes in verse 2, "For since the message declared by angels proved to be reliable, and *every transgression or disobedience received a just retribution.*" In verse 2, the author is giving the first part of a further explanation as to why "we must pay much closer attention to what we have heard." Because "the message declared by angels proved to be reliable," and we know from the warning context of this passage that he's not simply making the point that God's Word given in the law was reliable. It was reliable in a particular way and meant to help us understand an important aspect of God's nature: that "every transgression or disobedience received a just retribution." Whether it's the vivid instances of God acting at a point in time to bring judgment on the rebellious among His people in the book of Numbers or God acting in His time to bring the curses of covenant disobedience to His people as he promised in Deuteronomy 28, the law proves God was faithful to ensure that "every transgression or disobedience received a just retribution." The law, in the mind of the author, serves a purpose of helping us anticipate God's faithfulness in acting according to His promises in covenant relationship, *whether those promises entail blessing or judgment.* And if that's the case, then with His new covenant people, it's as if the author is asking his readers the question in verses 3–4, "Do we realize how *much more* reliable His new covenant will prove to be?"

His focus is still upon reliability in judgment as he indicates by his question in the first part of verse 3, "How shall we *escape* if we neglect such a great salvation?" The author comes back to this point later in Hebrews 12:25 when he writes, "See that you do not refuse him who is speaking. For if they did not *escape* when they refused him who warned them on earth, much less will we *escape* if we reject him who warns from heaven." The first escape he refers to in Hebrews 12:25 is a reference to those who rebelled against God in the wilderness and were destroyed after refusing to heed His warnings to them. The second escape refers to those of us today who refuse to heed the warning of "him who warns from heaven." Those who were destroyed in the wilderness ceased to care about the warnings. The same end awaits those who cease to care today, an attitude captured by the word *neglect* in the phrase in verse 3, "neglect such a great salvation."

The Greek word translated *neglect* means "to have no care for, to be unconcerned";[6] and in a chilling sense of this word, the author uses it again in Hebrews 8:9 where, in contrasting the old covenant with the New, he writes, "Not like the covenant that I made with their fathers on the day when I took them by the hand to bring them out of the land of Egypt. For they did not continue in my covenant, and so *I showed no concern* for them, declares the Lord." So then, another way in which we could state verse 3 would be to say, "How shall we escape if we *show no concern* for such a great salvation?" How indeed!

But there remains an antidote. It began in verse 2 by reminding his readers that God's faithfulness in judgment in the old covenant is a cautionary lesson to learn from, and in verses 3–4, he essentially says how much more should this lesson be applied given the message of salvation has a much superior source than the proven, reliable message "declared by angels." To begin with, the message of salvation was declared at first by the Lord as we see in verse 3. The significance of this point is captured well by F. F. Bruce in his commentary on verse 3 when he writes,

> The great salvation proclaimed in the gospel was brought to earth by no angel, but by the Son of God himself. To treat it lightly, therefore, must expose one to sanctions even more awful than those which safeguarded the law ... our author was afraid that his readers, succumbing to more or less subtle pressures, might become liable to those sanctions—if not by an overt renunciation of the gospel, then possibly by detaching themselves increasingly from its public profession until *it ceased to have any influence upon their lives.*"[7] (my emphasis)

And just as "the message declared by angels proved to be reliable," so too the message declared by the Lord further proved to be reliable as it was attested to by those who heard from the Lord. "It was attested to us by those who heard" (verse 3), so then, neither the author nor his audience was an eyewitness to the Lord's ministry. They learned from those who were eyewitnesses, and it proved reliable in the process. The word translated in verse 3 as *attested* is the verb form of the adjective *reliable* in verse 2. The teaching of the Lord Jesus was faithfully handed down to the church by those disciples who learned directly from Him, and so their message bears the authority and truth of the Savior's message just as He promised them in John 14:26 when He said, "But the Helper, the Holy Spirit, whom the Father will send in my name, he will teach you all things and bring to your remembrance all that I have said to you." But if that is not emphatic enough to convince us that we should not "neglect such a great salvation," the author gives a third and very compelling reason for us to reverse course. The message of our great salvation was confirmed by God through the mighty works of His power.

Simultaneously with Christ's message being "attested to us by those who heard," the author writes in verse 4, "God also bore witness by signs and wonders and various miracles and by gifts of the Holy Spirit distributed according to his will." Just as God did in the wilderness with His people Israel, He endorsed the authority and reliability of His messengers with mighty works of His power through His messengers. Signs, wonders, miracles, and spiritual gifts are never given for the sake of exalting or glorifying God's messengers; they're given for the sake of endorsing the messengers and their message as authentic. And because God endorsed His message as authentic in the three-fold way the author presents here (His own declaration, the faithful attestation of witnesses, and the confirmation of His mighty works of power), the early church was able to distinguish between His inspired and authoritative message to be taken as scripture and those messages that did not merit such consideration.

We have the Lord Jesus's reliable message—all of it as He indicates in John 14:26—passed on to the church "by those who heard." It is a reliable message of "such a great salvation" from the singular source of our Lord Jesus Christ that we must not neglect. Neither carelessness nor an "I could care less" attitude should ever encroach upon the heart, mind, and will of the believer. And it starts with a drift. And as I think I've already demonstrated, drifting leads to danger, not deliverance.

Neglect Connections

A 2014 *Wall Street Journal* article drew attention to a fast-growing trend in the US athletic apparel market—people are buying sports clothing without actually practicing the sport. The article projected that the US athletic apparel market would increase by nearly 50 percent by 2020 with only a marginal increase in people's participation in the very things the apparel is designed to foster. But the purchase of such apparel does foster something as indicated by this sentiment expressed by one buyer of athletic apparel who enjoys wearing yoga pants around town but who seldom has time to work out. She says, "When you put on your workout apparel, you think, 'Huh, maybe I should think about working out today.'"[8]

If you don't think you're capable of drifting away from the life the Gospel calls us to, think for a moment about this phenomenon in athletic apparel. It allows someone to think about what the apparel indicates they *should do* as a substitute for actually doing it, and it allows people to appear to be something without actually having to "be" that something.

That's a pretty relevant example to illustrate how many of us can and have drifted in our Christian walk. Thinking about who we should be and what we should do as followers of Jesus Christ or appearing to be so has become our pleasant substitute for the holy and dedicated life Christ calls us to. This is us drifting, and it leads to danger, not deliverance. The author is going to come back to this spiritual danger by way of warning several times. When we come to them, we'll consider them fully. But given that this is the first such warning passage in the book, I think it's appropriate to preview some of the others. Here they are without further comment.

> For it is impossible, in the case of those who have once been enlightened, who have tasted the heavenly gift, and have shared in the Holy Spirit, and have tasted the goodness of the word of God and the powers of the age to come, and then have fallen away, to restore them again to repentance, since they are crucifying once again the Son of God to their own harm and holding him up to contempt. For land that has drunk the rain that often falls on it, and produces a crop useful to those for whose sake it is cultivated, receives a blessing from God. But if it bears thorns and thistles, it is worthless and near to being cursed, and its end is to be burned. (Hebrews 6:4–8)

> For if we go on sinning deliberately after receiving the knowledge of the truth, there no longer remains a sacrifice for sins, but a fearful expectation of judgment, and a fury of fire that will consume the adversaries. (Hebrews 10:26–27)

And lastly,

> For you have not come to what may be touched, a blazing fire and darkness and gloom and a tempest and the sound of a trumpet and a voice whose words made the hearers beg that no further messages be spoken to them. For they could not endure the order that was given, "If even a beast touches the mountain, it shall be stoned." Indeed, so terrifying was the sight that Moses said, "I tremble with fear." But you have come to Mount Zion and to the city of the living God, the heavenly Jerusalem, and to innumerable

angels in festal gathering, and to the assembly of the firstborn who are enrolled in heaven, and to God, the judge of all, and to the spirits of the righteous made perfect, and to Jesus, the mediator of a new covenant, and to the sprinkled blood that speaks a better word than the blood of Abel. See that you do not refuse him who is speaking. For if they did not escape when they refused him who warned them on earth, much less will we escape if we reject him who warns from heaven. At that time his voice shook the earth, but now he has promised, "Yet once more I will shake not only the earth but also the heavens." (Hebrews 12:18–26)

4

How Great Is Our Salvation?

(HEBREWS 2:5–18)

In Hebrews 2:6, the author quotes Psalm 8, which includes the question, "What is man, that you are mindful of him, or the son of man, that you care for him?" In Psalm 8, the phrase "son of man" clearly refers to humanity, but the author has a particular purpose for quoting this verse. "Son of man" is a phrase that not only unquestionably applies to someone who is human, but was also Jesus's favorite way of referring to Himself—some eighty-two times in the Gospels. In other words, Jesus was emphatic in letting people know He was every bit as human as they were. The author has already made the case that Jesus is much superior to angels because He is fully God, and now he's going to resume that case with a twist in his train of thought, which, at first glance, seems to make no sense: that Jesus is much superior to angels because "for a little while [He] was made lower than the angels" (Hebrews 2:9). He became a son of man. But how does becoming human, and therefore lower than the angels (at least in the present age), make Jesus much superior to angels? Here's the answer in a nutshell: because *only a human being* can accomplish all the works of the Christ that has brought us "such a great salvation."

If you've ever wondered why refusing to believe Jesus Christ is fully God *and* fully man is heretical, in other words, why it is absolutely necessary for Him to be fully man as well as fully God, then the message from this passage should go to great lengths to offer an explanation as it answers the question "How great is our salvation?" while explaining to us why *Jesus must be a son of man to save us*. And we're going to see why He must be a son of man and how great our salvation is in three ways: because Jesus, the "son of man," has restored our inheritance, restored our place in the family of God, and has delivered us from Satan's authority, power, and control. Jesus Christ, the one who is and always has been the eternal Son of God, fully sharing with the Father a status far above the angels, humbled Himself and chose to come down to our level. It was a rescue mission, but it was not just a rescue mission: it was a mission to restore our inheritance as well.

Jesus Came to Restore Our Inheritance

Let's start to unpack this point in verse 5: "For it was not to angels that *God subjected the world to come, of which we are speaking.*" The topic the author's been addressing is the world to come and who it is that will exercise authority over it. So then, the "great salvation" we see in Hebrews 2:3 entails the life of exercising authority over the world to come. Exercising authority over the world to come is what awaits "those who are to inherit salvation" mentioned in Hebrews 1:14. Our salvation in its final and fullest sense is our inheritance of the world to come, not unlike what Jesus says in Matthew 5:5, "Blessed are the meek, for they *shall inherit the earth.*" Or when John writes in Revelation 21:1 and 7 (NASB), "Then I saw a new heaven and a new earth; for the first heaven and the first earth passed away … He who overcomes *will inherit these things.*" And these things are *all things* because Jesus has been "appointed the heir of all things" (Hebrews 1:2) and we are "*heirs of God and fellow heirs* with Christ" (Romans 8:17). This is our "great salvation," and it is God's great purpose for creating humanity: a point the author supports by quoting Psalm 8 in verses 6–8. "For a little while," we have been made "lower than the angels," yet "you have crowned him with glory and honor, *putting everything in subjection under his feet.*"

In Psalm 8, David is reflecting upon God's purpose for creating us as expressed in Genesis 1 before the fall, but the author draws attention to a really obvious point at the end of verse 8: "At present, we do not yet see everything in subjection to him." Why is that? Because we failed in living out our purpose. In Genesis 3, we joined Satan in his rebellion against God and so ceded our dominion to him. We lost the promise of glory and dominion because of our sin. But as both David and the author knew, our failure was not the end of the story. There remains a time when our great purpose will be restored, when God brings to pass our "great salvation," the inheritance of all things. And it will

not be because of us. You see, there is a "son of man" (verse 6) who has been "crowned …
with glory and honor" (verse 7), who, as our fully human representative, has perfectly
succeeded in accomplishing God's will on our behalf. Therefore, He has been "appointed
the heir of all things" (1:2) on His own merits as a "son of man," and by God's grace and
mighty power, we receive, along with Him, what He alone deserves.

This is our inheritance—our "great salvation"—and Jesus has won it for us as our
representative because He became one of us, yet without sin. So then, Daniel prophesies
of a day still to come in Daniel 7:13–14:

> I saw in the night visions, and behold, with the clouds of heaven there came
> *one like a son of man*, and he came to the Ancient of Days and was presented
> before him. And to him was given dominion and glory and a kingdom,
> that all peoples, nations, and languages should serve him; his dominion is
> an everlasting dominion, which shall not pass away, and his kingdom one
> that shall not be destroyed.

And so Jesus promises His fellow heirs in the church at Thyatira in Revelation 2:26–27:
"The one who conquers and who keeps my works until the end, to him I will give authority
over the nations, and *he will rule* them with a rod of iron, as when earthen pots are broken
in pieces, *even as I myself have received authority* from my Father." This is a promise Jesus can
make to those to whom God has "subjected the world to come" (verse 5) because Jesus, the
son of man, has overcome our failure and restored our inheritance. But there's a second
aspect of restoration Jesus brings that we see in this passage.

Jesus Came to Restore Our Place in the Family of God

Jesus did this through His obedience to the Father, submitting Himself to suffering and
death, something He had to become a "son of man" to accomplish. In verses 9–10, the
author writes, "But we see him who for a little while was made lower than the angels,
namely Jesus, crowned with glory and honor because of the suffering of death, so that by
the grace of God he might taste death for everyone. For it was fitting that he, for whom
and by whom all things exist, in bringing many sons to glory, should make the founder of
their salvation perfect through suffering."

For the first time in Hebrews, Jesus is referred to by the name He was given when He came into the world, when He "for a little while was made lower than the angels." As Paul teaches in Philippians 2, His name has been exalted above every name; and in verse 9, we see that the reason He has been exalted is because He suffered death, and not just any death, but a death that pays the wages of sin for everyone by the power of God's grace. In other words, *just as the promise of our inheritance is restored because of the merits of Jesus Christ, so too the merits of His death serve as a substitute for our death and the judgment against us because of our sin.* His death on our behalf brings a perfect and complete salvation as we see in verse 10.

The Father has made "the founder of [our] salvation perfect through suffering." The word *perfect* here doesn't suggest Jesus had imperfections to work out. It's a word that conveys something that has been brought to completion, and it indicates here that Jesus perfectly did the Father's will in accomplishing all the works of the Christ, of which the foremost of the Christ's works was His death and suffering on our behalf and for our salvation. As Paul writes, "For our sake he made him to be sin who knew no sin, so that in him we might become the righteousness of God" (2 Corinthians 5:21). And because our Savior accomplished a perfect work for our sakes, as we see in verse 10, He brings many sons to glory. And how can He bring us to glory? Because His perfect work will have a perfect result: Jesus will bring us to glory by imparting to us the righteousness He modeled, thus making us fit to be daughters and sons of the Father. As the New Living Translation renders verse 11, "So now Jesus *and the ones he makes holy* have the same Father. That is why Jesus is not ashamed to call them *his brothers and sisters.*"

The power of Jesus's life made complete in His resurrection is a life that has the power to make us holy and will make us holy, which is why we are adopted into God's family as sons and daughters of God without shame because our character will no longer be cause to bring shame upon the Father's name. The work of sanctification being done in us now will progress to its completion. As F. F. Bruce writes in his commentary on verse 11, "For sanctification is glory begun, and glory is sanctification completed."[9] So then, our life in glory is the life of family as brothers and sisters of Jesus Christ, the Son of God. Through His perfect saving work as the son of man, Jesus has restored our place in the family of God forever. Finally, through His perfect saving work, Jesus delivers us from a family doomed to destruction.

Jesus Has Delivered Us from Satan's Authority, Power, and Control

Before Jesus saved us, Satan held evil sway over us in two ways, but Jesus has delivered us from Satan's sway in each of these ways; first, by delivering us from slavery to the power of death. Verses 14–16 read, "Since therefore the children share in flesh and blood, he himself likewise partook of the same things, that *through death he might destroy the one who has the power of death*, that is, the devil, and deliver all those who through fear of death were subject to lifelong slavery. For surely it is not angels that he helps, but he helps the offspring of Abraham." First, notice once again that Jesus had to become human—to "share in [our] flesh and blood"—to destroy Satan's power over us and so deliver us from that power. One more reason why denying the full humanity of Jesus is heretical: if He's not fully human, then His death does not deliver us from Satan's power.

And the real source of Satan's power is the fear of death. It is the fear of death that compels us to place our faith and trust in what life in this world promises and to cling to those promises at all costs. This fear-driven mindset is at the heart of Satan's will for you. The fear of death becomes a tyrannical force in your life and becomes a great source of terror to those who recognize that their death is the penalty of sin just as the author later indicates in 10:26–27. "For if we go on sinning deliberately after receiving the knowledge of the truth, there no longer remains a sacrifice for sins, but a fearful expectation of judgment, and a fury of fire that will consume the adversaries." But since death did not have the last word with Jesus since he rose victorious over it, the death of we who are in Christ takes on the character of His death.

Our death is no longer a fearful final step to judgment, but a sure and certain next step to glory. So then, if death itself cannot separate those who are in Christ from God's love, which has been revealed in Him, then it can no longer be held over our heads by the devil or any other malignant power as a means of intimidation. Jesus has delivered us from the sway Satan once held over us through the fear of death. But there is a second way in which Satan once held sway over us.

Even though delivered from the fear of death, we need help to live this life in Christ and we can be assured we have all the help we need through Christ as verse 11 indicates, "For surely it is not angels that he helps, but he helps the offspring of Abraham." And His help to us is a present help in time of need for He has delivered us from our powerlessness to face temptation. Verses 17–18 state, "Therefore *he had to be made like his brothers in every respect*, so that he might become a merciful and faithful high priest in the service of God, to make propitiation for the sins of the people. For because he himself has suffered when tempted, he is able to help those who are being tempted." Once more, we see why Jesus must be both fully man as well as fully God. He was made like us in every respect, yet He lived His life without sin as we've already seen. And because He is a sinless *human*, Jesus is our propitiation: a word that essentially teaches that Jesus's death perfectly satisfies all of the Father's righteous demands to act in judgment against our sin. Yet His sinless life did not keep Him from a full understanding of how sin brings struggle and temptation into our lives. Rather, it enables Him to be merciful and faithful toward us as our high priest, always acting to make intercession for us. *Satan no longer has unchallenged authority and power to lead us into temptation* and so to devour our lives. Rather, Jesus is always on the job and at the ready to help us when we are tempted to stray against God's will and sin. But do we believe this? Do we believe His help is real?

In His book *Prayer*, Christian author Philip Yancey recalls how Jesus prayed for Peter as Peter faced temptation, and he makes the point that this gives us a picture of Jesus's present help to us by His intercession for us at the Father's right hand.[10] If the prayer of a righteous person avails much as the scripture teaches, how much more does the prayer of the Son of God on our behalf avail to us? Here's the incident that Yancey refers to in Luke 22:31–34:

> "Simon, Simon, behold, Satan demanded to have you, that he might sift you like wheat, but *I have prayed for you that your faith may not fail.* And *when you have turned again, strengthen your brothers.*" Peter said to him, "Lord, I am ready to go with you both to prison and to death." Jesus said, "I tell you, Peter, the rooster will not crow this day, until you deny three times that you know me."

A couple of points to take from this passage about the nature of the help our high priest, Jesus Christ, gives us in the face of temptation: (1) Peter was under attack by Satan, (2) Jesus prayed that Peter's "*faith may not fail,*" (3) notice Jesus prays for Peter *before* he fails in the moment of temptation, (4) Jesus knows His prayer will be effective to restore Peter to faithful ministry, and (5) all these things indicate Jesus is Lord over our temptations and those who tempt us *even if in the moment, we fail.* Because He is our great high priest and the author of so great a salvation, if we are His, then in the end, our faith will not fail. As Paul teaches in Romans 14:4, "Who are you to pass judgment on the servant of another? It is before his own master that he stands or falls. And he will be upheld, *for the Lord is able to make him stand."* This is the help of Jesus Christ, the son of man and our great high priest who delivers us from the power of Satan and delivers us into "such a great salvation." So then, let's come back to the question I believe this passage in Hebrews 2 does so much to help us answer.

Neglect Connections

How great is our salvation? Well, as we've just learned, it restores our inheritance to us: the promised eternal life of meaningfully serving the Father, exercising His full authority over His creation, which will be made forever new and forever good. And as we do so, this great salvation brings us back into the family of God as His sons and daughters who are currently being transformed into the likeness of Jesus and will be resurrected as finished works who perfectly bear His righteousness. And until that day, this great salvation delivers us from Satan's power and frees us to live our lives by the power of God because the power of the life of Jesus Christ is an ever-present help in our weakness. But what else does our salvation entail?

It would take a while to list it all from the scriptures (if I even could), but here are a few more facts about this great salvation Jesus has won for us. The righteousness of God is credited to us (Romans 4:3). We have peace with God and bold access to His presence (Romans 5:1–2). We no longer face the prospect of condemnation by God (Romans 8:1). The eternal life promised to us is one we already possess (John 5:24). Our sins have been forgiven (Ephesians 1:7). The Holy Spirit dwells within us as our helper and as a guarantee that all of God's promises to us will come to pass (Ephesians 1:13–14). And we now possess the ability to do the good works "God prepared in advance for us to do" (Ephesians 2:10). I could go on at length, but this is a taste of what makes our salvation great, and knowing how great it is should serve as a great motivation for us to not neglect it. But have you been taught about the greatness of the salvation we have in Christ?

I lament the content of the "gospel" many churches feed people, leading them to profess faith in Christ on the flimsiest of grounds. A robust Gospel faithful to the truth of God's Word focuses on Jesus, begging *and answering* the question "Who is Jesus?" A watered-down gospel is most often rooted in a watered-down Jesus. In 1 Corinthians 15:3, Paul begins a very concise expression of the Gospel message, writing, *"Christ died for our sins in accordance with the Scriptures."* What does it mean for Jesus to be the Christ *in accordance with the scriptures?* You can write volumes on the topic, but far too many Christians can squeeze out nary a word in answer to it. Paul continues to concisely state the Gospel in 1 Corinthians 15:4, writing, "He was raised on the third day." I have seen many a preacher give an invitation after a Gospel message that both waters down Jesus and outright neglects to mention His resurrection, and when Christ's resurrection is mentioned, it's an afterthought without any explanation of its significance—like our inheritance and our place in the family of God, etc.

In Acts 17, Luke records Paul's evangelistic efforts in Thessalonica, describing it this way in verses 2–3. "And Paul went in, as was his custom, and on *three Sabbath days he reasoned with them from the Scriptures,* explaining and proving that it was necessary for the Christ to suffer and to rise from the dead." Perhaps we need to take a cue from Paul. Perhaps we need to cease and desist treating the Gospel like a spiritual drive-by shooting. How do we stop neglecting a great salvation? Maybe we need to stop neglecting the fullness of the Gospel of the author of so great a salvation. What if from time to time, we choose to devote some extensive time reasoning, explaining, and proving (for our sakes) the necessity of Jesus the Christ, His death, and His resurrection?

5

"Think Carefully about This Jesus"
(HEBREWS 3:1–6)

In Hebrews 3:1, the author gives his very first command to his readers, which the NLT renders, "Think carefully about this Jesus." Think carefully. It's a command that foreshadows the approach the author will once again take in much of chapters 3 and 4: a warning against failing to "think carefully about this Jesus," a warning to not be careless in our consideration of Him.

In the latter half of the nineteenth century, a lighthouse was constructed on a large peninsula jutting into the Tasman Sea in southern Australia. It stood for forty years and was notorious for leading ships to shipwreck because its site was poorly selected. And the reason it was poorly selected was because the Colonial architect, Alexander Dawson, was more interested in the ease of construction rather than providing a good site to aid navigation. For four decades, the poorly sited lighthouse was responsible for some two dozen shipwrecks until it was replaced in 1899.[11] The main thing of concern in this matter was to site and construct a lighthouse that would provide safe navigation, but the architect didn't *keep the main thing the main thing*, a careless distraction that brought great harm to many. To "think carefully about ... Jesus" is to keep Him the main thing, to keep Jesus's message as our preeminent guide and to judge every other guide by their conformity to His message. To fail to do so will result in great harm; therefore, let's dig into the first command to the reader of the book of Hebrews.

Think Carefully about This Jesus

Once again, the author will address the dangers his audience faces should they make other voices a competitor to Jesus, even a voice as revered as Moses. Christ and His message must be valued, and as Augustine once taught, "Christ is not valued at all, unless he is valued above all." And when we carefully consider this truth about Jesus and His message, then we should come to the conclusion that Jesus truly has no competitors, even if the competition is someone as great as Moses. But given Moses's well-deserved special place in the life of the people of Israel, the author begins to make his case that Jesus is superior to Moses in a diplomatic way, not with a stark contrast but with the favorable comparison that thinking carefully about Jesus should lead us to conclude that He was just as faithful in His ministry as Moses was.

Hebrews 3:1–2 states, "Therefore, holy brothers, you who share in a heavenly calling, *consider Jesus*, the apostle and high priest of our confession, who was faithful to him who appointed him, just as Moses also was faithful in all God's house." Looking first at verse 1, as I mentioned earlier, we see the first command in the entire book directed toward the reader. "Consider Jesus" ("think carefully about this Jesus," NLT). And the command is given to "holy brothers … who share in a heavenly calling." This is a reminder to the reader that they have been set apart by God to live in this world focused on eternal matters. Paul writes similarly in Colossians 3:2 to "set your minds on things that are above, not on things that are on earth." And the thing about Jesus that we're called to set our minds on is His role as "the apostle and high priest of our confession."

The word *apostle* refers to one who is sent as a representative bearing a message, and the role of a high priest is the role of one who makes intercession on behalf of the people so that they may remain in God's favor. So then, Jesus is God's representative bearing His message, and He is the one who intercedes on our behalf so that we may remain in God's favor; in verse 2, we see that Jesus was faithful to God in these roles God appointed Him to. This is important for us to know, but the author is drawing attention to these roles, not so much to instruct His readers, but to remind them that this is part of who they confess Jesus to be. And in reminding them of this role as one who is sent bearing God's message and making intercession for us, the author makes the favorable comparison to Moses who was also sent by God to bear His message and who made intercession for the people of Israel throughout his ministry. And Moses also did so faithfully. It's a thoughtful and favorable comparison between Jesus and the revered Moses that creates a gracious opening to the next step in the author's train of thought, which he previews at the end of verse 2 when he writes, "In all God's house." *House* here is a reference to the people of God, His household, which, in Moses's ministry, was the people of Israel. And it is in their relative places within God's household that the train of thought moves from Jesus and Moses considered on equal terms to Jesus being exalted to His proper place with respect to Moses.

Jesus's Greater Glory

Thinking carefully about Jesus should lead us to conclude that He is worthy of much more glory and honor than Moses because Jesus is the builder of, and heir to, God's household. The contrast introduced here in verses 3–4 is pretty straightforward. As a practical everyday analogy, a house has a certain amount of honor, but that honor pales in comparison to the honor bestowed upon the builder. The point to the reader is pretty plain. As great as Moses's ministry was, it is inferior to the ministry of the new covenant that Christ has brought to pass, and in verse 4, the author applies his everyday analogy in verse 3 to the eternal significance of the analogy. Relying upon points about Jesus's glorious résumé, which he has already presented and supported, Jesus Christ, the Son of God, through whom all things were made and who has been appointed the heir of all things, is both the builder and inheritor of the household. So then, Jesus is worthy of much more glory and honor than Moses because He is the builder of, and heir to, God's household and also, as we see in verses 5–6, because Jesus's status as *Son over* God's household is greater than Moses's status as a *servant in* God's household.

Once again, Moses is justifiably commended for his faithfulness in verse 5, but he's commended for his faithfulness as a servant "*in … God's house.*" In other words, as you look back to the relative honor due to the house and its builder in verse 3, Moses isn't even "the house"! He's a servant in it, and his message only has meaning when understood in light of how it points us to Christ as the text indicates at the end of verse 5. Moses's message testified "to the things that were to be spoken later." This is very much Jesus's point in John 5:45–47 when He says to a Jewish audience, "Do not think that I will accuse you to the Father. There is one who accuses you: Moses, *on whom you have set your hope.* For if you believed *Moses,* you would believe me; for *he wrote of me.* But if you do not believe his writings, how will you believe my words?" As we see in verse 6, as the Son, Jesus is Lord over God's household while Moses is merely a servant in it. And Moses knew this and knew that his message found its great worth in that it pointed to the hope that could be found only in Christ as the author reveals later in 11:26 when he writes of Moses, "He considered the reproach of Christ greater wealth than the treasures of Egypt, for he was looking to the reward."

Moses understood and embraced his proper place in God's household, especially with respect to the Christ who would come into the world and be given the name Jesus. Moses understood his place; however, the author feared that his audience would not. Just as he feared his readers might exalt the message of angels above Jesus, so he feared they might fall back into exalting the message of Moses above Jesus. If you remember the message from chapter 1 about his concern over his readers' view of the message of angels in relation to Jesus's message, I applied that to us with the question, "Whose voice are we listening to?" And so as the author revisits this concern with respect to Moses, let me likewise revisit that concern with us through some insightful questions for us to consider from Kevin DeYoung: pastor, author, theologian, and chairman of the Gospel Coalition.

Kevin asks these questions in light of his pondering over how we might answer Jesus's question to His disciples in Matthew 16:15—"Who do you say that I am?" You see, we're not as likely to replace Jesus with Moses or angels in our faith and confession, but we're very susceptible to putting the words of others in Jesus's mouth and making those words our strongest convictions. Here are some examples Kevin DeYoung gives of how we answer Jesus's question "Who do you say that I am?" today.

There's *the Republican Jesus* who is against tax increases and activist judges and for family values and owning firearms. There's *Democrat Jesus* who is against Wall Street and Walmart, and for reducing our carbon footprint and printing money. There's *Therapist Jesus* who helps us cope with life's problems, heals our past, tells us how valuable we are and not to be so hard on ourselves. There's *Starbucks Jesus* who drinks fair trade coffee, loves spiritual conversations, drives a hybrid, and goes to film festivals. There's *Open-minded Jesus* who loves everyone all the time no matter what (except for people who are not as open-minded as you). There's *Touchdown Jesus* who helps athletes run faster and jump higher than non-Christians, and determines the outcomes of Super Bowls. There's *Martyr Jesus*, a good man who died a cruel death so we can feel sorry for him. There's *Gentle Jesus* who was meek and mild, with high cheekbones, flowing hair, and walks around barefoot, wearing a sash while looking very German. There's *Hippie Jesus* who teaches everyone to give peace a chance, imagines a world without religion, and helps us remember that "all you need is love." There's *Yuppie Jesus* who encourages us to reach our full potential, reach for the stars, and buy a boat. And there's *Spirituality Jesus* who hates religion, churches, pastors, priests, and doctrine and would rather have people out in nature, finding "the god within."[12]

So who's your Jesus? If you claim to follow Him, take care what you declare in His name because whatever cause or agenda or philosophy you bind Him to with your words is what you'll bind yourself and a watching world to—a tragedy for both you and that watching world that needs the truth found in God's Word and not some substitute. But as the author will say in Hebrews 6:9, with a pastor's heart, "Though we speak in this way, yet in your case, beloved, we feel sure of better things." And so with the same sense of balance between caution and exhortation, the author closes this passage by telling his readers we are God's household "if indeed we hold fast our confidence and our boasting in our hope" (verse 6).

Hold Fast to What We Believe

This concern for holding fast to what we believe is the dominant theme for the rest of chapter 3 through 4:13. But "holding fast" is also a theological assertion that permeates the book as a whole. For example, Hebrews 3:14 states, "For we have come to share in Christ, if indeed *we hold our original confidence firm to the end.*" But is the author out of step with the rest of the scriptures in the way he binds life lived a particular way to a particular outcome? Well, consider Jesus's very similar statements in Revelation 2:26 and Matthew 10:22: "The one who conquers and who *keeps my works until the end*, to him I will give authority over the nations" and "But the one who *endures to the end will be saved.*" Or even Paul's statement in Colossians 1:21–23 where he writes, "And you, who once were alienated and hostile in mind, doing evil deeds, he has now reconciled in his body of flesh by his death, in order to present you holy and blameless and above reproach before him, *if indeed you continue in the faith, stable and steadfast, not shifting from the hope of the gospel that you heard*, which has been proclaimed in all creation under heaven."

This is not a perseverance in the faith that saves you but the teaching throughout the scriptures that *the truly saved persevere*, as F. F. Bruce teaches in his comments on verse 6. Bruce writes, "We find [in the book of Hebrews] such repeated insistence on the fact that continuance in the Christian life is the test of reality. The doctrine of the final perseverance of the saints has as its corollary the salutary teaching that the saints are the people who persevere to the end."[13] So as we move into the next couple of passages and through the book as a whole, remember this well-justified assertion from the scriptures: *genuine* faith in Jesus Christ will be reflected by a faith that perseveres, not because of our innate ability to do so, but because "he who began a good work in you will bring it to completion" (Philippians 1:6). The Holy Spirit will be effective and will persevere in His work in the lives of those He indwells through faith in Jesus Christ. And it is on the basis of this confidence and hope that we "press on to maturity" (Hebrews 6:1 NASB).

Neglect Connections

Once more, I'll ask the question, "Whose voice are we listening to?" In John 10:27, Jesus declares without qualification, "My sheep hear my voice … and they follow me." If you are Jesus's sheep, then you hear His voice and heed what He is saying because your hearing leads to following Him. You obey His word (Matthew 28:20). You walk in this world "in the same way in which he walked" (1 John 2:6). You think carefully about who Jesus is because His life was lived for us as "an example, so that you might follow in his steps" (1 Peter 2:21).

I once had a lengthy engagement with a gentleman in the area I live in who was adamant that I join my church with a confederation of churches in the region he was seeking to put together for the purpose of uniting the wider church in an uprising against our government. His conviction is that the church's mission in this present age is to overtake—essentially conquer—the dominion of human government, a perspective on the church that dovetails with broader current political agendas in the United States. This man's Jesus fell in line with what Kevin DeYoung calls "Republican Jesus" or "Democrat Jesus." I found his views impossible to substantiate from the scriptures, particularly in the way they distorted the Great Commission, the Gospel, the explicit commands in the scriptures governing the church's orientation toward human government, and most importantly, the example of Jesus Himself. In a funny yet tragic moment, when I pointed him to the scriptures' teaching to believers to follow Jesus's example (including the verses I refer to above), the gentleman told me I was being "intellectually dishonest" for using Jesus as an example to follow. In each case, I validated my objections to his views exhaustively from the scriptures, and in each case, he defended his views by citing the likes of Sir Edmund Burke, Thomas Paine, and Dietrich Bonhoeffer. Truth be told, I don't believe this man had the ability to make the distinction between Jesus's voice and the voices of those in the world whose views he had passionately embraced. He conflated Jesus with other voices, resulting in a Jesus that sounded like other voices.

Paul had concerns for the church at Corinth as they too had, at least in part, embraced a Jesus defined by powerful forces in their culture. On the basis of that subtle yet deadly exchange, Paul gave a warning to the church at Corinth and to us today, writing, "But I am afraid that as the serpent deceived Eve by his cunning, your thoughts will be led astray from *a sincere and pure devotion to Christ*. For if someone comes and proclaims *another Jesus* than the one we proclaimed, or if you receive *a different spirit* from the one you received, or if you accept *a different gospel* from the one you accepted, *you put up with it readily enough*" (1 Corinthians 11:3–4). Don't put up with another Jesus or a different gospel. "Think carefully about this Jesus" (Hebrews 3:1 NLT) and follow *this* Jesus.

6

Genuine Faith Finishes the Race Part 1

(HEBREWS 3:7–19)

T he previous chapter included the theological assertion that genuine faith in Jesus Christ will be reflected by a faith that perseveres. It's a position that can be well supported by the scriptures, and it's an assertion the author makes repeatedly, an example of which we see again in verse 14 of chapter 3 when he writes, "For we have come to share in Christ, if indeed we hold our original confidence firm to the end." But to make the case that sharing in Christ entails holding firm to Him to the end, the author uses the historical example of Israel's journey from being led out of slavery in Egypt to being led into the land of promise: an illustration he teaches that serves as a pattern for genuine faith in the one true God in every age. And in doing so, he's not alone.

The New Testament writers clearly saw Israel's experience in the exodus, wilderness wanderings, and deliverance into the land God promised as a portrait of the Christian experience. We are delivered from slavery to sin. As Israel was baptized into Moses, so too we are baptized into Christ. As Israel was led by Christ in the wilderness, we also are led by Him through this life. As Israel was supernaturally fed bread and water from heaven, we also are sustained by Jesus Christ, the bread of life: the true bread from heaven. And as the author will assert in the first half of chapter 4, just as the people of Israel entered their rest into the land promised as their inheritance, there also remains a rest we enter into—as those who share in Christ—which will come with our eternal inheritance. But if we accept Israel's example as a portrait of our life in Christ, then we must at least consider Israel's example fully. And in this passage "fully" includes the author's point that Israel's example teaches us that God will put our faith to the test to prove that it is genuine, and that genuine faith proves itself in obedience that holds firm to the end.

The backdrop to this passage is the instances of rebellion against God recorded in Exodus and Numbers and, particularly, Israel's rebellion against God and Moses when they refused to enter into the Promised Land and take possession of it in Numbers 14. This rebellion was very much a last straw; the tenth in a series of refusals by the people of Israel to heed the Lord's voice. These refusals tested His patience, mercy, and grace and brought each to an end as He declared His judgment upon them in Numbers 14:35, saying "I, the LORD, have spoken. Surely this will I do to all this wicked congregation who are gathered together against me: in this wilderness they shall come to a full end, and there they shall die." Israel's unbelief was proven by their disobedience, and a judgment was conferred upon them as a result. Yet in this historical example, we also learn, through the examples of Joshua and Caleb, that genuine faith is proven true by obedience and that this obedience persists until the faithful enter God's promised destination for them. And in using this example from Israel's history, the author teaches that the very same principles of faith and unbelief applies to us today.

Professed Faith in God Will Be Put to the Test of Obedience

In verses 7–11, the author quotes from Psalm 95:7–11 where the psalmist focuses on using Israel's failure by repeated rebellion against God in the wilderness as a historical example for *the people of Israel in his* (the psalmist's) *time to learn from*. So interestingly, the author is using Psalm 95 in the very same way the psalmist did, but as an example in his time for *the church to learn from*. So let's see what we can learn from this psalm *in our time*. First, notice in verse 7, right before he quotes from Psalm 95, he writes, "As the Holy Spirit *says*." Present tense. It is the Spirit who inspires the writer of Psalm 95, and He is still speaking to us today, for the quote then begins in verse 7 with, "*Today*, if you hear his voice." This message is still for us *today*, and this word still represents the voice of the Spirit *today*, still coming with the sense of urgency to hear and heed His voice *today*—not tomorrow or next week or next year. And the voice of the Spirit teaches us *today* that we learn from Israel's experience in essentially two ways.

The first is that unbelief will be revealed through testing by its persistent disobedience. We see this first in verse 8, which reads, "Do not harden your hearts as in the rebellion, on the day of testing in the wilderness." This is a reference to several instances in Israel's wilderness wanderings when their faith was put to the test and the response of many was repeatedly rebellion rather than obedience. The testing occurred in the wilderness, a place God deliberately led His people into. A place where self-reliance was of no worth. A place where water, food, and direction could only come from God, and a place where this experience would have been relatively brief if their faith in Him proved genuine, if they demonstrated in their actions that they truly trusted in Him to provide all those things and to deliver them into a land that was beautiful and occupied by enemies they could not possibly drive out in their own strength. But instead of proving faithful through testing in the wilderness, the Spirit says in verse 9 that the wilderness was the place "where your fathers *put me to the test* and saw my works for forty years."

And they repeatedly put the Lord to the test through disobedience as the Lord indicates in Numbers 14:22–23 when He tells Moses, "None of the men who have seen my glory and my signs that I did in Egypt and in the wilderness, and yet have *put me to the test these ten times and have not obeyed my voice*, shall see the land that I *swore* to give to their fathers." Rather than receiving the promise the Lord "*swore* to give to their fathers," the Spirit instead says in verse 11, "As I *swore* in my wrath, 'They shall not enter my rest.'" Unbelief will be revealed through testing by its persistent disobedience, and the consequence for Israel—and people today whose faith fails to prove to be genuine—will be the Lord's refusal to welcome them into His promised rest, whether that promised rest is in the inheritance of land in Israel or in the great salvation we stand to inherit. Conversely, genuine faith will persist in obedience.

The author makes this assertion once again, and on the basis of Israel's historical example, in verse 14 when he writes, "For we have come to share in Christ, if indeed we hold our original confidence firm to the end." And if that's so, and if Israel remains the example to support his assertions, then we ought to see this in the accounts of Israel's time in the wilderness. And we do, in Numbers 14 where Israel's foremost act of rebellion against God occurred: their refusal to trust in Him to bring them into the land of promise. In Numbers 14, the people of Israel refuse to heed God's direction to enter into the land He has promised to give them by going before them to drive out the formidable enemies in the land. They rebel against Moses and Aaron; express a great desire to return to Egypt, the land of their enslavement; plot to choose a leader who will bring them back there; and then communicate their intentions to kill anyone who would argue against this plan.

But in contrast with most of the people, Caleb and Joshua stand out as models of genuine faith. We see this in Numbers 14:6–9 where, in response to the people's rebellion against God, the scripture says,

> And Joshua the son of Nun and Caleb the son of Jephunneh, who were among those who had spied out the land, tore their clothes and said to all the congregation of the people of Israel, "The land, which we passed through to spy it out, is an exceedingly good land. If the LORD delights in us, he will bring us into this land and give it to us, a land that flows with milk and honey. Only do not rebel against the LORD. And do not fear the people of the land, for they are bread for us. Their protection is removed from them, and the LORD is with us; do not fear them."

And in response to Joshua and Caleb's commitment to obey the Lord's command to enter the land, the Lord would go on to say that unlike those who rebelled against Him and would die in the wilderness,

> My servant Caleb, *because he has a different spirit and has followed me fully,* I will bring into the land into which he went, and his descendants shall possess it ... your dead bodies shall fall in this wilderness, and of all your number, listed in the census from twenty years old and upward, who have grumbled against me, not one shall come into the land where I swore that I would make you dwell, except Caleb the son of Jephunneh and Joshua the son of Nun. (Numbers 14:24, 14:29–30)

This then is the lesson and the standard for us to affirm and follow: genuine faith will persist in obedience. Or, as the Lord says of Caleb, "because he has a different spirit and has followed me fully, I will bring [him] into the land into which he went." If we truly have a different spirit—one born again as a new creation who has "come to share in Christ"—then we will follow Him fully to the end.

The Church Must Exhort One Another to Walk in Obedience

Exhortations to obedience entail both an individual and a corporate dimension. From an individual perspective, we do this through individual self-examination. Verse 12 reads, "Take care, brothers, lest there be in any of you *an evil, unbelieving heart*, leading you to fall away from the living God." The lesson from the wilderness still applies here, and it is the lesson of the condition of the heart. Are we inclined to respond to God's direction to us in His Word and to heed His leading in our lives by the Holy Spirit? In particular, does our life reflect a willingness to trust Him in a place of testing? A place He brings us to in our lives where He calls us to be obedient to a course of action when all of our understanding tells us it makes no sense. For example, does it make sense to pick up and leave your longtime home, church, friends, most of family, and a steady job to move to Michigan and trust the Lord to provide all those things for you in the place He's called you to? It made sense to my good friends Steve and Sherry whom the Lord led to relocate from their longtime home and family connections in New York's Hudson Valley to live in Michigan, a place otherwise foreign to them. To do otherwise in such instances would begin to build a testimony to your own conscience that you may actually have a heart that is "leading you to fall away from the living God."

This verb "fall away" is an active one as indicated by the NET with its rendering "unbelieving heart that *forsakes* the living God." This is a willful decision made under the lens of testing as Jesus uses the very same verb in the parable of the soils in Luke 8:13 when He says, "And the ones on the rock are those who, when they hear the word, receive it with joy. But these have no root; they believe for a while, *and in time of testing* fall away." You see, there is a form of belief that does not rise to the level of saving faith, and it will be revealed as such in a time of testing when the one tested forsakes the living God rather than heeding His voice and walking in obedience. When we're told to "take care brothers" at the beginning of verse 12, it is the first command in the passage, and it's a command to look carefully at ourselves through the light of God's Word, as the author will later say, down to the division "between soul and spirit, between joint and marrow" as His Word "exposes our innermost thoughts and desires." This should be our routine as individuals as well as our routine as a believing community.

The second and final command in this passage is to "exhort one another every day" in verse 13. As we strive to live, mindful of the standard that genuine faith holds firm to the end, we have a responsibility to encourage one another to that same standard. There is no such thing as a lone-wolf or self-enlightened follower of Jesus Christ. Where there is isolation, we succumb. Subtle temptations overtake us. Rationalizing against faith and obedience becomes a pattern that dulls our conscience and blurs our sense of right and wrong. Sin truly is deceitful by its very nature, and all of this may be an indication of a life that truly has no share in Christ and needs to turn to Him—today. But a life that truly has a share in Christ is drawn to fellowship with His people, and so we should encourage one another to hold to this standard of faith and do so with the same vigor the author teaches when he writes, "Let us hold fast the confession of our hope without wavering, for he who promised is faithful. And let us consider how to stir up one another to love and good works, not neglecting to meet together, as is the habit of some, but encouraging one another, and all the more as you see the Day drawing near" (Hebrews 10:23–25). When we do this, the subtlety and deceitful rationalizations of sin are called out and turned from. We walk together to keep our path straight and narrow. We walk together so that our weakness can be remedied in a fellowship that exercises a watchful and unremitting care for one another, moving us to stand firm, and so to be strengthened. And we do this every day while there is still time for a "today" because of what's at stake.

The Disobedience of Unbelief Will Not Lead to His Rest

In verse 15, the text imparts a sense of urgency in light of the tragic implications of our disobedience: "As it is said, 'Today, if you hear his voice, do not harden your hearts as in the rebellion.'" The author repeats his quote of Psalm 95 from verses 7 to 8 and, in so doing, comes back *a third time* to his emphasis on "today," and he comes back to a condition of the heart for *the fourth time* in the passage: a heart that is rebellious, hardened, evil, and unbelieving. And then he asks a series of questions in verses 16–18, the answers to which pertain to this same group of people—the rebellious in the wilderness—while moving the reader sequentially through their spiritual journey. Their journey began as they "left Egypt led by Moses" (16). They "provoked [the Lord] for forty years" and died in the wilderness (17). And so the Lord swore "they would not enter his rest" (18). It's the same group of people, from beginning to end, with a common experience and fate. They were, as verse 18 indicates, "those who were disobedient." And this leads to the conclusion and explanation we see in verse 19: "So we see that they were unable to enter because of unbelief." *Unbelief is not a failure to make a profession of belief or faith.* In fact, this group described in these verses is part of the same group of people of which it is said of in Exodus 14:31, "Israel saw the great power that the LORD used against the Egyptians, so the people feared the LORD, and *they believed in the LORD and in his servant Moses.*" Yet it was the Lord who would later say of them at the time of their rebellion against His command to go into the land: "How long will this people despise me? And how long will they *not believe in me*, in spite of all the signs that I have done among them?" (Numbers 14:11). So then, it is neither an expression of belief nor belief for a time in miraculous signs that proves faith to be genuine. *It is obedience that proves faith to be genuine.*

We see this by inference in verses 18–19 because the author equates disobedience with unbelief. But we also see this in the structure of his line of reasoning for, you see, verses 15–19 are his explanation to support his point in verse 14 when he writes, "For we have come to share in Christ, if indeed we hold our original confidence firm to the end." We are fellow heirs with Christ and will enter the promised rest of our inheritance—*so great a salvation*—"if indeed we hold our original confidence firm to the end." Those who do not are, like the rebellious among the people of Israel, those whose unbelief will be revealed by their persistent disobedience in times of testing. "Those who, when they hear the word, receive it with joy. But these have no root; they believe for a while, *and in time of testing fall away*" (Luke 8:13).

Neglect Connections

Genuine faith finishes the race, but we're not done seeing this point in Hebrews because the author isn't done making this point! As a further exhortation, the author continues his train of thought in 4:1, saying, "Therefore, while the promise of entering his rest still stands, let us fear lest any of you should seem to have failed to reach it." We may have a tendency to balk at the suggestion that Israel's experience may serve as a true and applicable teaching illustration for what constitutes genuine faith in Jesus Christ, but as 4:1 indicates, the author clearly believes Israel's example is relevant, that it directly applies to our life of faith. Genuine faith truly does finish the race, and the author's going to come back to the fact that we have more than ample help from Jesus Christ as we run it. But before he does, the author is going to make the point that Christ's help will be fully effective in leading many sons and daughters to glory along a path of obedient lives and a faith that remains "firm to the end" (3:14).

This is what the Gospel of our Lord Jesus does! It does; just as Paul teaches in Romans 1:16, writing it is "the power of God for salvation to everyone who believes." This includes God's present work in us through His power as Paul indicates when he describes the Gospel to the Corinthians as "the gospel I preached to you, which you received, in which you stand, and by which you are *being saved, if you hold fast to the word I preached to you*" (1 Corinthians 15:1–2). We can water down the Gospel by watering down the message, but we can also water down the Gospel by watering down our expectations of what the Gospel does. We are far too comfortable accepting a person's profession of faith when the changed life the Gospel brings through a genuine profession is absent from their testimony. A profession is a wonderful thing, *but it didn't save the multitudes who professed belief in the wilderness.* John writes in 2 John 4, "I rejoiced greatly to find some of your children *walking in the truth*, just as we were commanded by the Father." Perhaps our greater rejoicing should be reserved for when we see a brother or sister walking in the truth as our Lord Jesus did.

7

Genuine Faith Finishes the Race Part 2

(HEBREWS 4:1–13)

n 1 Corinthians 9:24–27, Paul appeals to our understanding of athletics to make a point about our Christian life. He writes,

> Do you not know that in a race all the runners run, but only one receives the prize? So, run that you may obtain it. Every athlete exercises self-control in all things. They do it to receive a perishable wreath, but we an imperishable. So, I do not run aimlessly; I do not box as one beating the air. But I discipline my body and keep it under control, lest after preaching to others *I myself should be disqualified.*

The point is this: no one could rightly claim to be an athlete in competition while being aimless in the undertaking. You train and compete like the prize you seek demands your devoted discipline to obtain it. For athletes, the prize is perishable, but Paul really isn't talking about athletes here. He's talking about followers of Jesus Christ whose purpose is to obtain an imperishable prize: such as a great salvation. And from Paul's own perspective, he runs this race with such zeal and determination out of a concern that "I myself should be disqualified." The word translated *disqualified* here is used in the scriptures for the dross that is skimmed off molten metal to purify the metal. Paul's concern is that his Christian life may prove to not be the real thing, but rather may prove to be the worthless stuff that needs to be separated from the real thing. Paul lived his Christian life with the healthy fear that he needed to keep watch over his life, lest he be disqualified, lest he prove to not be the real thing. Just as we know what a genuine athlete looks like in competition, Paul knew what genuine faith looked like from beginning to end and strived to live every day accordingly. Paul knew that genuine faith finishes the race.

We've just seen the author use the historical example of Israel's deliverance from bondage, wilderness wanderings, and journey into the promised land to teach lasting spiritual principles about our Christian life, yet focusing primarily on one principle in particular: that Israel's failure teaches us that genuine faith is a life that persists in obedience to God's Word to the end.

That's the history lesson, and in 4:1–13, he then applies the history lesson to his readers in two ways: (1) by charging them to have a healthy fear of failing in the way Israel failed and (2), in light of the motivation of that healthy fear, to make every effort *not* to follow their example. This is the second of five warning passages in Hebrews, and the stakes couldn't be higher because following Israel's pattern will preclude us from entering the Father's eternal rest just as Israel's failure precluded many of them from entering the promised land. This section of Hebrews is clearly a warning against a false or vain faith, but in these warnings, I believe we're meant to find great sources of assurance in our great salvation as well—if our faith is genuine. And as the scriptures so often teach, the fear of God is the beginning of genuine faith, and I don't think this healthy fear is ever meant to disappear from our Christian walk but rather must purposefully remain.

Assurance of Salvation and a Healthy Fear of God Go Hand in Hand

Many Christians struggle with the book of Hebrews, seeing in it a message that leads people to call into question the assurance of their salvation. I think this understanding of Hebrews is skewed by a common thinking within the evangelical church often referred to as "easy believism," a view that believes that one is saved merely by an intellectual agreement with the Gospel and a profession of faith in Christ. "Easy believism" rejects the idea that any evidence (life change) of God's saving work is necessary or should even be expected in the life of the one who professes belief, and it further believes that such expectations of life change rob the "believer" of their "assurance" of salvation. But does our assurance in Christ come as a result of our intellectual claim to be a Christian through mere profession? On the contrary, if there is no evidence of the change Christ has promised to bring into the lives of His followers, then we have anything *but* assurance as the author asserts when he writes in 10:26–27, "For if we go on sinning deliberately after receiving the knowledge of the truth, there no longer remains a sacrifice for sins, but a fearful expectation of judgment, and a fury of fire that will consume the adversaries." A "faith" limited to what we know and claim to be doesn't lead to assurance; it leads to "a fearful expectation of judgment." Let me briefly illustrate this point.

When I was involved in training people for combat, the worst thing I could do to a person would be to give them the false assurance that they're something they're truly not. Real assurance in this case, and in the Christian life, is grounded in knowing you truly are who you claim to be. And as we've already seen with Paul, real assurance in the Christian life comes in knowing that in yourself, you see the qualifying work of the Holy Spirit rather than the disqualifying work of the flesh and its deeds while always being mindful with a healthy fear that as Paul writes in Romans 2:9–11, "There will be tribulation and distress for every human being *who does evil* ... but glory and honor and peace for everyone *who does good* ... For *God shows no partiality*." And in the case of the historical example of the people of Israel, the author begins to make the point with respect to God's impartiality that our assurance of salvation and a healthy fear of God go hand in hand because the Gospel brings no benefit to the disobedient.

Hebrews 4:1–2 reads, "Therefore, while the promise of entering his rest still stands, let us fear lest any of you should seem to have failed to reach it. For good news came to us just as to them, but the message they heard did not benefit them, because they were not *united by faith with those who listened*." In the Greek text, verse 1 purposefully begins with "let us fear." The NLT translates "we ought to tremble with fear." Why? As we'll see, the author takes the historical example of the people of Israel's efforts to enter into their rest in the promised land and applies their example to the Christian life. For the faithful, the promise of resting from our labors in this life to enter into God's promised eternal rest for us still stands for the faithful, but the cause for fear is that "any of you should seem to have failed to reach it." And how might we seem to fail to reach it? Because just as many in Israel failed to respond faithfully to the good news of God's promises to them, so too we might fail to respond faithfully to the Gospel. And what does failure look like? "Not [being] united by faith with those who listened."

Notice he doesn't say united with those who "believed" but "those who listened."

And he's not talking about those who simply heard, but those who heard and heeded. For example, parents, do we chastise our kids for not "listening" because they didn't hear us or because they heard but didn't do what we told them to do? Genuine faith and obedience are two sides of the same coin: one cannot be present without the other. As F. F. Bruce once again affirms in his comments on verses 1–2, "The practical implication is clear: it is not the hearing of the gospel by itself that brings final salvation, but its appropriation by faith; and if that faith is a genuine faith, it will be a persistent faith."[14] And it is in the life of those who possess such faith that the author now positively shifts to, teaching that assurance of salvation and obedience go hand in hand because we enter into the promise of His rest *now* through the obedience of faith.

The author makes this point, but he does so in the midst of an extensive validation of what the scripture means in Psalm 95:11 when the Lord says, "They shall not enter *my rest.*" In verse 3, he repeats this quote from Psalm 95 that he first made in 3:11; and then in verses 3–4, he makes the point that we understand what *"my rest"*—"God's rest"—entails on the basis of the creation account in Genesis 1–2. He then comes back to the Psalm 95 quote— "They shall not enter *my rest"*—to make the logical point that the rest God enjoys is, and from the beginning of creation, has been a rest that is available to mankind. Therefore, as he says in verses 6–7, "It *remains* for some to enter it." This is just as true "today" as it was true in David's time when he wrote of the promise of God's rest centuries *after* the people of Israel had their experiences in the wilderness. And here is the great assurance to the faithful. In verse 3, the author writes, "For we who have believed enter that rest," and *enter* is in the present tense. Although the promise of God's eternal rest remains, in the fullest sense, a future reality for the believer, in a very real sense, we enter into it the moment we believe. But again, as we see in verse 6, this faith that enters His rest is an obedient faith. The life that perseveres in faith to the end doesn't earn that rest. Rather, it proves that we are as predestined for it (Romans 8:29–30) as the dedicated athlete is for the finish line because the course of faith continues to the finish line.

As he moves on to verse 8 of chapter 4, the author makes one more point about the nature of the "rest" he's speaking of when he writes, "For if Joshua had given them rest, God would not have spoken of another day later on." Again, Israel's example of their wilderness experience and journey into the land teaches us spiritual truths about genuine faith, but the promise of God's rest being spoken of here is not the experience of rest the people of Israel had as Joshua led them into the land, an experience marked just as much by failure and frustration as by victory. Rather, just as God Himself enjoyed (and still enjoys) a Sabbath rest when He had finished his work of creation, so too God's faithful people, when their earthly work of serving him is duly completed, can look forward to joining Him in His heavenly rest. We see a beautiful picture of this reality in Revelation 14:13 as John writes, "And I heard a voice from heaven saying, 'Write this: Blessed are the dead who die in the Lord from now on.' 'Blessed indeed,' says the Spirit, 'that they may rest from their labors, *for their deeds follow them!*'" These are the deeds of genuine faith that finishes the race.

Therefore, Let Each of Us Make Every Effort to Finish the Race

Running the race goes hand in hand with our deep engagement with God's Word. In our every effort, we need to respond obediently to the deep conviction God's Word brings. Verse 11 reads, "Let us therefore strive to enter that rest, so that no one may fall *by the same sort of disobedience.*" Notice he writes, "Let us." We run this race together, striving like athletes to reach a finish line of rest and qualified for the prize. And we know what disqualifies us: "The same sort of disobedience" we see from the faithless among Israel in the wilderness. A life marked by repeated rebellion against God and His Word. Paul teaches that the likes of these will be found in the church in Titus 1:15–16 when he writes, "To the pure, all things are pure, but to the defiled and unbelieving, nothing is pure; but both their minds and their consciences are defiled. *They profess to know God, but they deny him by their works.* They are detestable, disobedient, *unfit* for any good work." Notice here that Paul essentially declares that a profession of faith is *worthless* if it's not joined to the obedient works of the faithful. How worthless? The word *unfit* is the same word Paul uses in 1 Corinthians 9:27 to describe what he makes every effort to prove he is not: "disqualified." The "unfit" dross skimmed off molten metal, the worthless stuff that needs to be separated from the real thing in order to preserve the purity of the real thing. But the great assurance genuine faith has is when it finds (verse 12) "the word of God is living and active, sharper than any two-edged sword, piercing to the division of soul and of spirit, of joints and of marrow, and discerning the thoughts and intentions of the heart."

Is the Word of God a two-edged sword in your life? Does it pierce through the resistance of your will? Does it cast its light down to the innermost recesses of your being, challenging your thoughts, attitudes, and convictions you've kept hidden in the dark, sometimes even unawares to you? Until the light of a test or trial is cast upon you and you discover something in you that needs to be cast out. This can be unpleasant, but it is a source of great assurance to us when we see God's Word "not returning to Him empty, but rather, accomplishing His purpose in us" (Isaiah 55:11). And it can be unpleasant because a two-edged sword is a weapon of war, and as Paul indicates in Galatians 5, the Spirit is at war in us, using the Word of God to battle the desires of our flesh, putting those desires to death and bringing to pass instead a life led by the Spirit. So then, even this battle is a source of assurance as it confirms the Spirit's presence in our lives that can only come through genuine faith in Jesus Christ. But it is a battle nonetheless; therefore, surrender to the mastery God seeks to have over you through the power of His Word.

Verse 13 reads, "And no creature is hidden from his sight, but all are naked and *exposed* to the eyes of him to whom we must give account." This statement concludes this second warning passage in the book of Hebrews that runs from 3:7 to 4:13, and it is a vivid conclusion. The word translated *exposed* here literally means to "lay bare." It's a term borrowed from the sport of wrestling and was used to describe the action of taking an opponent by the throat, thus putting you at his mercy. Given the description of God's Word as a deadly form of a sword, another way to take the author's point here may be that your opponent has laid you bare with a sword at your throat; you're fully at His mercy. It's at this point in the contest, in the battle, where surrender is the only reasonable recourse and, in this instance, to surrender to the one "to whom we must give account." And to me, although this is clearly a warning, I once again find assurance in this, assurance that comes if my life is lived every moment of every day with that healthy fear of God that motivates me to live in such a way that I will be found by Him on the day of my accounting, not as one "disqualified," but as one who is "blessed; who has rested from my labors, for my deeds follow me" (Revelation 14:13).

Neglect Connections

Don't seek assurance in your salvation "by grace ... through faith" (Ephesians 2:8) by denying or failing to understand what "grace" does. The grace by which you are saved is "training us to renounce ungodliness and worldly passions, and to *live self-controlled, upright, and godly lives in the present age*" (Titus 2:12). The effectiveness of God's grace through the power of His Gospel to change us, transform us, is thoroughly testified to in the scriptures.

In James chapter 2, James describes a faith with no works as "useless" (verse 20) for "even the demons believe—and shudder!" (verse 19). One way such *a* faith proves itself as useless is by *effectively denying the object of your faith*. Back in 2016, twenty-one people were trapped on a stalled amusement park ride 148 feet in the air. Because of this height, the only option for the firefighters was to lower each passenger from 148 feet in the air, harnessed to a single rope.

It was a terrifying proposition, but after affirming the passengers that the firefighters could be trusted in the task of saving them, all twenty-one passengers ultimately heeded their direction and were lowered safely to the ground.[15] Is there any truth in saying you trust in the firefighters unless you actually heed their directions? Is there any truth in saying you trust in Jesus Christ unless you heed His Word?

Another way faith with no works proves itself to be "useless" is in how it *denies the purpose and power of God*. Paul writes in 2 Corinthians 3:18, "And we all … are being transformed into the same image from one degree of glory to another. For this comes from the Lord who is the Spirit." If we are Christ's, then we are being progressively transformed into the likeness of His character by the Holy Spirit. *This reality will confirm who we claim to be.* Christian author Randy Alcorn, while teaching on how God uses suffering to bring this transformation in us, uses an illustration of mountain climbers. He writes, "Mountain climbers could save time and energy if they reached the summit in a helicopter, but their ultimate purpose is conquest, not efficiency." He goes on to describe that shortcutting the process like this doesn't make you a mountain climber. What makes you a mountain climber is the prolonged commitment to the life of a mountain climber where discipline is cultivated, endurance is built, and patience and skill are developed. And when failure comes, one improves and excels by recognizing it, receiving correction, learning from it and being transformed—into a mountain climber.[16]

No one can rightly claim to be a mountain climber because they took a helicopter ride to the top; that claim can come only from one who has faithfully followed a mountain climbers' course with the tools and skills of a mountain climber. "Therefore, since we are surrounded by so great a cloud of witnesses, let us also lay aside every weight, and sin which clings so closely, and let us run with endurance the race that is set before us, looking to Jesus, the founder and perfecter of our faith" (Hebrews 12:1–2). Genuine faith finishes the race by His grace. This is what grace does. It is the good work He began in us and He brings to completion.

8

Help in Time of Need Is Always Near

(HEBREWS 4:14–5:10)

How confident are we in our ability to live according to God's Word (and therefore, His will) when we are faced with the temptation to sin? Do we possess the strength of will to do so, or do we need help? Back in 2009, Dr. Loran Nordgren of Northwestern University conducted a study to evaluate the human ability to exercise self-control in tempting situations and concluded that we have a tendency toward what she calls "restraint bias." In other words, we tend to overestimate how much self-control we will have against temptation when we're not in the "heat of the moment" and that those who are most confident about their self-control are the most likely to give in to temptation.[17] Coming at this same issue of whether or not we possess the innate power to resist the temptation to sin from a Christian perspective, Bill Thrall, Bruce McNicol, and John Lynch write in their book *TrueFaced*, "Understand this: The intention not to sin is not the same as the power not to sin. God did not design us to conquer sin on our own. To think we can is an incalculable undervaluing of sin's power combined with a huge over valuing of our own willpower!"[18]

So how do we close this gap that our lack of willpower creates? The message in Hebrews thus far has greatly impressed upon us that a genuine faith in Christ is an obedient faith, but if we're doomed to fail because we're doomed to sin when we're tempted, then what hope do we have? We have the hope that help in time of need is always near. In Jesus Christ, we have all we need or, as Hebrews 4:14 reads, "we have a *great* high priest." We have seen the author make comparisons between Jesus and angels and Jesus and Moses in order to strongly urge his readers away from the temptation to put their faith in something far lesser than Jesus. He's about to do so once again by comparing Jesus's high priesthood with the high priests of the Old Testament to make the point that unlike the priests of the law, it is through Jesus that "we may receive mercy and find grace to help in time of need" (4:16). And our times of need include the times when we're tempted to sin because we lack the power to be faithful in those times.

We Can Always Come to Christ Confident in His Help in Time of Need

Back in Hebrews 3:1, the author refers to Jesus as the "high priest of our confession" as part of a validation that Jesus, His message, and His ministry are far superior to Moses and his message and ministry. Once again, here in verse 14, he returns to our confession of Jesus as our high priest, writing, "Since then we have a great high priest who has passed through the heavens, Jesus, the Son of God, let us hold fast our confession." One of the principal aspects of the law given to Moses by angels (2:2) was the priesthood of Aaron and his descendants. The highest privilege of these earthly high priests of Aaron's line was to pass once a year through the inner veil into the holy of holies in a temporary earthly sanctuary, appearing for a few moments once a year before the Lord on behalf of their people to offer an atoning sacrifice for their sins. The implied contrast in verse 14 (which the author will more thoroughly develop later in the book) is that Jesus has passed through the true sanctuary in heaven, having offered Himself as our atoning sacrifice for sin once for all and now permanently ministers on our behalf in the Father's presence. Jesus's high priestly ministry on our behalf is above any other, and our confession of Him as such is worth holding fast to. But if Jesus, the perfect offering for our sin, is so far exalted above us (so far from us?), then how does this seemingly great separation give us the confidence to draw near to Him for help in our time of need? Perhaps because Jesus has drawn near to us in a powerful way in every way.

In verse 15 of chapter 4, we learn that Jesus has fully shared our experience without sharing our failure. "For we do not have a high priest who is unable to sympathize with our weaknesses, but one who in every respect has been tempted as we are, *yet without sin.*" God, by nature, is omniscient. He knows everything including the knowledge of the fact that we are vulnerable to the powerful forces of temptation. But by His nature, God

Himself is not vulnerable to such powers. To experience the forces of temptation, as the author teaches in 2:17, "he had to be made like his brothers in every respect" so that as we see in verse 15, he could be "one who *in every respect* has been tempted as we are, *yet without sin.*" So then, Jesus becoming fully human teaches us that it's part of being truly human to feel the lure of that which is wrong, to feel the lure of sin's power. Just as we do, Jesus doesn't just *know* this is true about us; He knows exactly what it feels like in every way. He has walked the extra mile in our shoes. He can truly sympathize with us in our struggles, but unlike us, he knew the powerful lure of temptation without giving in to it and disobeying the Father. Therefore, His human life (and He is still fully human) both knows our needs in every way and has the power to help us overcome our temptation to sin in every possible way we can be tempted. We can come to Christ with confidence for help in time of need because the fullness of God's mercy and grace now comes to us through Him.

Verse 16 reads, "Let us then with confidence draw near to the throne of grace, that we may receive mercy and find grace to help in time of need." This verse begins with "Let us then," indicating that what we learn in verses 14–15 is the basis for this confidence we should have to come into the very presence of God, knowing that in our time of need, His boundless mercy and grace helps us in such times. And what do we see in verses 14–15? We see the two essentials for the perfect high priest: to be in the position of ultimate authority with the Father in heaven and yet also to have the intimate personal knowledge of our human condition. And in keeping with a dominant theme in the book, Jesus is superior above all because no *earthly priest* could be in the position of ultimate authority with God in heaven, and no *angel* can have the intimate personal knowledge of our human condition. *But in Jesus, we have both.*

Therefore, there can be no barrier to the "confidence" or lack of inhibition with which we can approach God (and stay!). And it's important to understand and recognize these themes of contrasting Jesus with competitors in order to demonstrate His superiority over them. The author's pastoral concern is that some segment of his readers may be proving themselves "disqualified" in their faith because their faith may be proving to be in the wrong thing, in other words, not Jesus, but rather, a lesser competitor with no power to save or to "help in time of need." And as I've suggested to you, the author's line of argument gives us every indication that the competitor his readers are being tempted to trust in is the law of Moses. And so, as the message of the book unfolds, we'll see that the author chooses to focus on the role of the high priest (both Jesus's role and the role of the earthly high priest under the law) as the primary contrast he pursues to convince his readers of the folly of forsaking faith in Christ for the law as an alternate or better source of salvation. So then, in Hebrews 5:1–10, he essentially compares and contrasts Jesus's high priesthood with the high priesthood of the law to urge his readers to choose wisely.

Hold Fast to the Confession that Jesus Is the Source of Our Salvation

In Hebrews 5:9, the author writes that Jesus "became the source of eternal salvation to all who obey him," and He became that source by the very life He lived. Because Jesus lived a life of perfect obedience to the Father, *His life has the power to impart such a life to us*, something the earthly high priest's ministry could never impart. But the nature of the earthly high priest's ministry, per the scriptures, sets important qualifications for the role of high priest, which *Jesus had to meet*. In other words, our confession of Jesus as our high priest has to conform to these standards because God has prescribed the qualifications of those who can act as a high priest on humanity's behalf in verses 1–4 of chapter 5.

Let's quickly look at these qualifications. In verse 1, we see that a high priest acts on behalf of humanity as one who is chosen from among humanity, and his actions on humanity's behalf are meant to satisfy God's expectations of humanity in their relationship with Him. So then, it is necessary for a high priest to be fully human and able to satisfy the role God has appointed him for.

In verse 2, we see the character a high priest must have in fulfilling His God-appointed role. Instead of being exasperated or frustrated with the ignorant and wayward ways of the people, he must be gentle, knowing firsthand the weakness that besets the human condition. In other words, a high priest must be forbearing, being personally mindful of human weakness and moved to be gentle in his disposition toward people as a result. And because "he himself is beset with weakness," it demands, as verse 3 indicates, that "he is obligated to offer sacrifice for his own sins just as he does for those of the people." In other words, a high priest's God-appointed role in his actions on behalf of men and women, in order to satisfy God's expectations of them in their relationship with Him, is to make a sacrifice for the people's sins. And because he himself sins, he needs to make a sacrifice for himself as well (a key contrast with Jesus, which we'll take up later).

And finally, and very importantly, verse 4 states, "And no one takes this honor for himself, but only when called by God, just as Aaron was." No one can claim the role of high priest for themselves. Only God's appointment to this calling makes a high priest's ministry legitimate.

So here's the summary of the job description: Fully human, able to satisfy the role, gentle and humble in this role, faithful in making every *necessary* sacrifice for sins on behalf of himself and the people, and serving in the role by God's appointment and none other. So how does Jesus stack up in light of the qualifications? Perhaps the better question is, "Who could possibly stack up in light of the qualifications?"

In verses 5–10, we learn that Jesus alone perfectly fulfills God's qualifications to act on humanity's behalf, beginning with His unique and everlasting *appointment* in verses 5–6. In verse 5, Jesus's appointment to His high priesthood came from the Father, and the author proves his point by quoting, for the second time in Hebrews, Psalm 2:7: "You are my Son; today I have *begotten* you." If you remember, we discussed this quote when he first introduced it back in 1:5 and how this statement in Psalm 2 was the Father's declaration of the Son's appointment to the role of the coming King. Here, it serves to emphasize His appointment as our high priest. But not after the order of Aaron and his descendants in accordance with the Mosaic law, but as "a priest forever, after the order of Melchizedek" (verse 6). This second quote in which Melchizedek is referred to comes from Psalm 110, a psalm that also affirms the Son's role as the coming King and so indicates that the Father has appointed the Son to serve as both *King and high priest* forever. No other figure in scripture could claim such a dual role except … Melchizedek! Melchizedek makes his appearance in Genesis 14:18 as king of Salem (Jerusalem) and priest of God Most High. He's a mysterious figure, and we're not going to solve the mystery in this book, nor do we need to. The text in Genesis simply indicates Melchizedek was both priest and king, and so he serves as a type foreshadowing Jesus's role as both priest and king. David uses Melchizedek this way in Psalm 110, and so the author quotes the psalm to support his case. Jesus meets God's qualification (appointment) to serve as high priest, but His order is unique and far superior to the order of the priesthood in the Mosaic law. The remaining qualifications to be high priest can be summed up as being fully human and able to fully satisfy the role in action and character. So how does Jesus stack up in light of these qualifications?

To begin with, we see His full humanity with the phrase "In the days of his flesh" (verse 7), and His character to serve as our high priest is affirmed in what follows in verses 7–8: "Jesus offered up prayers and supplications, with loud cries and tears, to him who was able to save him from death, and he was heard because of his reverence. Although he was a son, he learned obedience through what he suffered."

What's likely being referred to here is Jesus's prayer to the Father in Gethsemane the night before He was crucified. Here's Matthew's account of this time: "Then he said to them 'My soul is very sorrowful, even to death; remain here, and watch with me.' And going a little farther he fell on his face and prayed, saying, 'My Father, if it be possible, let this cup pass from me; nevertheless, not as I will, but as you will'" (Matthew 26:38–39). Note here, as we compare Hebrews and Matthew, that the Lord prayed fervently for deliverance from His suffering and death (just like we would), "and he was heard because of his reverence" (character). Note as well that His prayer was *not* answered according to His desires, but according to the Father's will (which He submitted to) and so "he learned obedience through what he suffered" (as the scriptures teach we do as well). Yet again, I love how F. F. Bruce sums up what's happening here: "The fact that the cup was not removed qualifies him all the more to sympathize with his people; when they are faced with the mystery and trial of unanswered prayer they know that *their high priest was tested in the same way* and did not seek a way of escape by supernatural means of a kind that they do not have at their disposal."[19]

And through His obedience to the Father's will to suffer on our behalf, Jesus, our high priest, became the perfect sacrifice for our sins, once for all, and so the author writes, "Being made perfect, he became the source of eternal salvation to all who *obey* him" (verse 9). No earthly high priest could make such a claim. Jesus's high priesthood, in comparison to any other, is superlatively unique, "being designated by God a high priest after the order of Melchizedek" (verse 10). Therefore, let us draw near (and stay), knowing that in Christ, help in time of need is always near.

Once more in 4:16, the text reads, "Let us then with confidence draw near to the throne of grace." I believe this is an appeal to us to come to the Father in prayer just as Jesus Himself modeled in His life such as in Gethsemane. And I believe this is an appeal to stay near. To live a life of prayer. To live in such a way that when we are tempted, prayer is our first recourse; and the confidence with which we are drawing near "to the throne of grace" is not confidence in ourselves, but rather, confidence in Christ who is the source of our salvation and so *is the source of power to live like we're saved*, to live like Him.

Celebrity chef, writer, and TV personality Anthony Bourdain said in a 2014 interview for *Men's Journal*, "Look, I understand that inside me there is a greedy, gluttonous, lazy, hippie—you know? I understand that … there's a guy inside me who wants to lay in bed, and smoke weed all day, and watch cartoons, and old movies. I could easily do that. My whole life is a series of stratagems to avoid, and outwit, that guy … I'm aware of my appetites, and *I don't let them take charge.*" Four years later, Anthony Bourdain committed suicide on June 8, 2018, at the age of sixty-one.[20] The great lie that Satan convinces us of is that we can control our sinful appetites. To the contrary, James teaches (1:14) that it is those very appetites that have the upper hand when he writes, "Each person is tempted when he is lured and enticed by his own desire."

Neglect Connections

In the heat of the moment of temptation, what do you draw near to, your own desires or the throne of grace? You can only walk in one place or the other! In 2 Corinthians 5:7, Paul writes, "We walk by faith, not by sight." This verse is often quoted but not often well understood. Real life in Christ—a "real" walk—is a life of faith that perseveres and grows. We know God calls us to obedience, and we know the faithful will hold fast to a faithful walk. But the faithful don't do this—in fact, can't do this—in their own strength and by their own means ("by sight"). To walk by faith is to walk *faithfully*, believing that the power of Jesus Christ's risen life imparts to us "mercy and … grace to help in time of need." This is the truth by which we experience our salvation in this life: our growing deliverance from sin's unbridled power over our lives.

Paul writes in 1 Corinthians 10:13, "No temptation has overtaken you that is not common to man. God is faithful, and he will not let you be tempted beyond your ability, but with the temptation *he will also provide* the way of escape, *that you may be able* to endure it." Read this verse carefully and understand it. Your ability to faithfully endure temptation is always from Him, always through the means He provides. And His help in time of need is always near. Is this part of your Christian walk? Is this part of your great salvation? If not, then you are probably neglecting your great salvation. Better said, you are probably neglecting Christ's supremacy over your life for your own good. If so, then draw near to Him and stay near, trusting in Him alone when that help is needed—and it's always needed.

9

Press On to Maturity!
(HEBREWS 5:11–6:12)

Punt! This is what my "inner coward" says as I consider taking up this next passage in Hebrews. It is a passage with both an extremely challenging message and an extremely difficult section to interpret in 6:4–8. Ironically, my desire to avoid the challenge of tackling this passage would make me the target of the author's critique of his readers. Hebrews 5:11–6:12, along with the rest of chapter 6, is a digression away from the topic the author wants to take up with his readers: the nature of Jesus's priesthood. He has just finished introducing this topic, and as we'll see, he's going to take it back up again in earnest and at length in chapters 7–10. But he pauses in 5:11–6:20 because he questions the spiritual maturity of his readers and their willingness to follow his train of thought. As the NLT puts it in 5:11, what he wants to write to them "is difficult to explain, especially since you are spiritually dull and don't seem to listen"; but he goes on to chastise them because at this time in their Christian walk, they should be at the point where they can follow his reasoning. In light of his concern about their spiritual maturity, we're going to see in this passage that the author has a strong desire for his readers to get out of their rut and press on to maturity; therefore, *what he writes here has an underlying pastoral purpose of motivating them to do this.*

But in the midst of this passage is Hebrews 6:4–8, a profoundly difficult section of text to handle. The passage, overall, has four distinct parts of which 6:4–8 is one part; therefore, what I'm going to do in this chapter is quickly address the three parts that focus on the author's desire for his readers to press on to maturity (which is his singular concern in this passage) but spend most of the time helping us understand how the warning in 6:4–8 is *fitting into his train of thought*. So let's begin with a relatively easy part of the text: how we should walk.

A Mature Walk with Christ Is Grounded in a Deep Understanding of God's Word

In Hebrews 5:11–14, the author wants to get into a deep theological discussion on the nature of Jesus's priesthood, but he's wrestling with the difficulty of the task "since you have become dull of hearing." This choice of words in verse 11 suggests his readers are suffering more from a problem of their will rather than of their intellectual capacity to follow him and that this is a state of being they have allowed themselves to fall into (and so can bring themselves out of it as well). In verses 12–14, he then chastises them, essentially telling them that by now, they ought to be teachers—but they're not. They ought to be skilled in handling the deeper matters of God's Word—but they're not. They ought to be mature in their understanding and handling of God's Word—but they're not! And then in the last part of verse 14, we see the consequences of spiritual immaturity, for the mature are "those who have their powers of discernment trained by constant practice to distinguish good from evil."

And here is a direct cause-and-effect spiritual truth: you cannot walk (live) rightly before God without a deep understanding of His Word tied to a life that is constantly practicing the principles and precepts that come from that deep understanding. *A danger of spiritual immaturity is in the kind of life that is lived as a result of it.* Paul makes this point in Ephesians 4:13–14, saying that our aim in our Christian life is full maturity in Christ "so that we may no longer be children, tossed to and fro by the waves and carried about by every wind of doctrine, by human cunning, by craftiness in deceitful schemes." Spiritual immaturity leads to a life that is susceptible to falling for anything. Conversely, grace leads us to grow out of our spiritual immaturity.

Spiritual Maturity Is the Movement, *by God's Grace*, to Deeper Theological Understanding

In Hebrews 5:12, the author indicates that his readers have not advanced beyond the basics, the "milk" of God's Word. But unlike Paul who had a similar problem with the Corinthians and told them, "I fed you with milk, not solid food, for you were not ready for it" (1 Corinthians 3:2), in 6:1, the author tells his readers, "Therefore let us leave the elementary doctrine of Christ and go on to maturity." The fact that he is pressing on to "solid food" rather than sticking with the "milk" indicates, once again, that his readers' shortcomings had more to do with their *will* to understand deeper things than with their *ability* to understand deeper things, and I think he gives us an indication of what deeper things entail by how he describes "the elementary doctrine of Christ" in verses 1–2: "Repentance from dead works ... faith toward God ... instruction about washings, the laying on of hands, the resurrection of the dead, and eternal judgment." In the interest of time, I won't unpack each of these things, so here's the summary. Each of these things addresses basic essentials of the Christian faith, which would have been understood as basic essentials of faith in God to a faithful Jew *but who find their fullest expression in Christ*. This helps explain why the author has gone to great pains to show the superiority of Christ over *the pillars of Judaism*: the ministry of angels, Moses and his message of the law given to him by angels, and the high priesthood under the Mosaic law that mediated the relationship between God and His people under the old covenant. As Paul teaches in Galatians 3:24, these things served as a "guardian" of the faith of God's people "until Christ came," but now that Christ has come, the author challenges his readers to take their foundation of the basics "and go on to maturity."

And it is with respect to this challenge to "go on to maturity" that he says in 6:3, "And this we will do *if God permits*." Spiritual maturity is the movement, *by God's grace*, to deeper theological understanding. It comes to pass in our lives if He permits it, and I think Jesus gives us a sense of the conditions God sets for Him to do this work in our lives when He says "Ask, and it will be given to you; seek, and you will find; knock, and it will be opened to you. For everyone who asks receives, and the one who seeks finds, and to the one who knocks it will be opened" (Matthew 7:7–8). God's grace is freely and fully available *to those willing to seek it*, once again, pointing to a spiritual problem of the will for the author's readers. They are sluggish, lacking the inclination of the will to "leave the elementary doctrine of Christ and go on to maturity." As we've already seen, there are dangers that accompany spiritual immaturity, and based on the flow of argument in this passage, I believe the author's intent in this next and very difficult section of the text is to warn his readers of *the great danger of the neglect of our salvation*, not of the loss of our salvation as many believe.

Beware of the Danger of Spiritual Immaturity

Hebrews 6:4–8 is profoundly difficult to understand and has been diversely interpreted, leading to a good bit of controversy in matters of faith and practice. If you're not accustomed to reading your Bible side by side with a book like this one, this would be a good time to adjust your custom as you'll need to pay careful attention to the text of Hebrews 6:1–8 as we move through it. I'm going to begin a study of this passage by first focusing on verses 4–6 in light of verses 1–3. We're about to walk through some of the many different interpretations of verses 4–6, but before we do, we need to keep in mind that whatever interpretation we come to over verses 4–6 (and verses 4–8 as a whole), these verses are *grammatically connected with, and subordinate to, verses 1–3*, and their purpose is to explain, in particular, what the significance is of the statement, "And this ["go on to maturity," verse 1] we will do if God permits" in verse 3. So let's begin with *the hypothetical argument*.

The basic sentence in verses 4–6 is "for it is impossible … to restore *them* again to *repentance*." Everything in verses 4–6 in between these two parts of the basic sentence explains who "them" is and everything after "repentance" in verse 6 explains why "it is impossible … to restore them again to repentance." The point emphasized in *the hypothetical argument* view is that what's being described here is an impossibility simply for the sake of argument. I don't endorse this view for several reasons:

1. What's the point? A hypothetical argument does nothing to explain, as verses 1 and 3 require, why we will *"go on to maturity … if God permits."*
2. Biblical writers are not prone to using hypothetical arguments.
3. Every other warning passage in the book of Hebrews is purposeful and concerned with the real spiritual condition of the readers. A second common interpretation of this passage is that the "person" in verses 4–6 is *not a "genuine"* Christian.

This is the view my favorite commentator on Hebrews, F. F. Bruce, takes; and I disagree with him. Bruce believes this passage is a continuation of the author's emphasis that genuine faith perseveres (which I agree with), but I disagree that this is the point the author is making here. Remember, his concern here is his readers' progress to spiritual maturity. Bruce and those who hold to this *not a "genuine" Christian* view believe the person described in verses 4–6 is one who does not persevere—that is, proves to not be a believer—but a key problem with this conclusion is that all the qualities described in verses 4–6 ("been enlightened," "shared in the Holy Spirit," etc.) are used elsewhere in Hebrews and the New Testament to unquestionably describe believers. The people described in these verses are clearly believers, and another clue from the text makes this point as well. In Hebrews 6:1, the author describes "repentance … and faith toward God" as foundational in our Christian faith, and it is! This is the first response of the genuine believer to the Gospel! Therefore, if the person described in verses 4–6 only "appears" to be Christian but truly isn't, then how can they be restored *"again* to repentance"? How can they do something *"again,"* which they've yet to truly do? So if this section of text truly describes a Christian, then what does this teach to a Christian? Another very common interpretation is that *a Christian can lose their salvation.*

Many argue *against* this view because of a theological conviction they read into this passage using texts outside the book of Hebrews. For example, consider Paul's assertion in Romans 8:38–39: "For I am sure that neither death nor life, nor angels nor rulers, nor things present nor things to come, nor powers, nor height nor depth, nor anything else in all creation, *will be able to separate us from the love of God in Christ Jesus our Lord."* Likewise, Jesus's assertion in John 10:27–29: "My sheep hear my voice, and I know them, and they follow me. I give them eternal life, and they will never perish, and *no one will snatch them out of my hand.* My Father, who has given them to me, is greater than all, and *no one is able to snatch them out of the Father's hand."* These are powerful statements of eternal security. Both passages make for a strong argument that losing the salvation God gives by His grace through our faith in Jesus Christ is impossible.

But reading theological views into a text to make it fit your view is a poor method of interpretation. Those who argue you can lose your salvation from this text make the point that the people described here "have fallen away" (verse 6) and are "near to being cursed, and its end is to be burned" (verse 8). Additionally, coming back to our main sentence, the reason "it is impossible … to restore them again to repentance" is that their falling away has led to them "crucifying once again the Son of God to their own harm and holding him up to contempt" (verse 6). This is a frightening statement to have applied to you regardless of how you take it, and the impossibility of repenting of this sin brings a reminder of the unpardonable sin of "blaspheming against the Holy Spirit" (Mark 3:29). All told, you can make a strong case that a Christian can lose their salvation from this section of the passage, but I believe you can make an even stronger case from this section, in light of the passage as a whole and the passage in Hebrews 6, which follows this one, that a Christian can *forfeit the blessing of spiritual maturity.*

First of all, let's remember the author is telling his readers in 6:1 and 6:3, "Therefore let us leave the elementary doctrine of Christ and *go on to maturity* … And *this* we will do *if God permits.*" As I've already mentioned, this teaches us that going on to maturity is a work of God's grace, but it also begs a question. What would keep God from permitting this? We've already talked about how the text of Hebrews reveals problems of willingness. The reading audience is "dull of hearing" (5:11), and as we'll see in the last point, they're "sluggish" (6:12). We've also discussed about how Jesus taught that God stands ready to give of His grace to us if we seek it—again, a matter of the will. But what if the will doesn't revive from its dullness and sluggishness? The keyword in most interpretations of this section of text is "fallen away" in verse 6, but what does this mean?

Earlier in Hebrews 3:12, in another warning passage, the author of Hebrews writes, "Take care, brothers, lest there be in any of you an evil, unbelieving heart, leading you to *fall away* from the living God." He leaves little doubt that he's dealing with "an evil, unbelieving heart" here, not an immature Christian, but the word translated "fall away" in 3:12 is a *different one* than the word he uses in 6:6. In Hebrews 3:12, the word used means to actively withdraw or forsake someone, but in 6:6, according to the Greek lexicon of the New Testament, the word translated "fallen away" means "to fail to follow through *on a commitment,*" and it's the only time this word is used in the New Testament. Additionally, Cleon Rogers, in his lexicon of the Greek New Testament, writes that this word, "Only suggests they are going astray or missing what Christ has provided." To sum up, the sense of this word translated as "fallen away" in 6:6 is more in line with *the problems of the will the author of Hebrews has already highlighted*; and on the basis of this sense, the warning makes sense. A believer will "go on to maturity … if God permits"; and the warning clearly indicates that a failure to "go on to maturity" at some point will leave you stuck in your spiritual rut, removed from the blessings God intends for the mature and subject to the consequences of a life tossed to and fro by the waves and carried about by every wind of doctrine, by human cunning, by craftiness in deceitful schemes" (Ephesians 4:14). That the warning here is to the consequences of forfeiting maturity fits even more with the passage as a whole since it is *maturity* that the author returns to in the last section of the text. But how does this interpretation fit with verse 8?

Here's where I ask you to press on to maturity with me into a deep theological argument like the author was urging his readers to. Verse 8 clearly is a warning to the people in question in verses 4–6: "But if it bears thorns and thistles, it is worthless and near to being cursed, and its end is to be burned." First of all, notice it is *"near* to being cursed, and its end is to be burned." Does this not sound similar to what Paul wrote in 1 Corinthians 3:15, saying, "If anyone's work is burned up, he will suffer loss, though he himself will be saved, *but only as through fire"* (and also in a passage addressing spiritual immaturity)? And now, here's where we get really deep: "Thorns and thistles." Sounds like the parable of the soils, right? In Luke 8:13, Jesus says, "And the ones on the rock are those who, when they hear the word, receive it with joy. But these have no root; they believe for a while, and in time of testing fall away." No root, no fruit, "and in time of testing *fall away."* "Fall away" here is the same word in the same sense used in Hebrews 3:12: "Take care, brothers, lest there be in any of you an evil, unbelieving heart, leading you to *fall away* from the living God." I believe this is a picture, both in Luke 8 and Hebrews 3, of people who have a form of faith that is proven to not be genuine; it does not persevere. But then Jesus shifts to the next type of person in Luke 8:14: "And as for what fell *among the thorns,* they are those who hear, but as they go on their way they are choked by the cares and riches and pleasures of life, and their fruit *does not mature."* There is fruit, and so there must be root. But there is no maturity in that fruit! Not a slam dunk, but a pretty strong case that the author has not left the topic of spiritual maturity to all of a sudden warn his readers they can lose their salvation. *The warning here is against spiritual immaturity;* the consequences are grave enough to merit a strong warning, but I do not believe the warning is that you can lose that which God gave as an irrevocable gift to the faithful.

Lastly, the strongest reason for ruling out that losing your salvation is being taught here is in our next passage, 6:13–20, for there are fewer passages that offer believers stronger assurance in their salvation than the very next one in the book (which would make no sense; if he just finished teaching, we can lose our salvation). So then, in light of the warning against spiritual immaturity, let's press on to maturity!

Continue to Imitate the Walk of Those Who, through Faith and Patience, Inherit the Promises

Now we come to the author's pastoral heart and concern. In verse 9, he writes, "Though we speak in this way, yet in your case, beloved, we feel sure of better things—things that belong to salvation." After giving the strongest warning thus far in the book, he calls them "beloved" for the first and only time in the book; and it's clear that whatever he intended to communicate in verses 4–8, it doesn't presently apply to them, but rather, as we'll see in verses 11–12, the concern is over their present state of spiritual maturity and how that may lead to very unfavorable long-term consequences.

Clearly, they have a reputation for good works, which is still their testimony as he writes, "For God is not unjust so as to overlook your work and the love that you have shown for his name in serving the saints, as you still do" (verse 10). Their walk has been, and presently is, pleasing to God, but this emphasis on their walk also reemphasizes the concern he raised back in 5:11–14: that a life that is immature in its understanding of God's Word is a life susceptible to the dangerous inability "to distinguish good from evil" (5:14) and live accordingly. Right living in the Christian life follows right understanding; therefore, if they remain stuck "on milk" (5:13) and never move to "solid food" (5:14), the danger that awaits them is the danger that faces those who walk in this world like children: "Tossed to and fro by the waves and carried about by every wind of doctrine, by human cunning, by craftiness in deceitful schemes" (Ephesians 4:14). It is the danger of a life that falls into the snares and the traps of the devil and will stay there "if God permits"!

So then, the author concludes this passage, writing, "And we desire each one of you to show the same earnestness to have the full assurance of hope until the end, so that you *may not be sluggish*, but imitators of those who through faith and patience inherit the promises" (verses 11–12). The word *sluggish* here is the same word translated as "dull" in the phrase "dull of hearing" in 5:11. Just as their lack of progress in their deep understanding of God's Word was a matter of the will, the author's concern is that this same lack of will may overtake how they live, that their walk would become "sluggish." Each of us should be a theologian in our own right. Each of us should be constantly about the hard work of carefully considering God's Word for the sake of forming right convictions about how we live our lives in thought, word, and deed. To be "those who have their powers of discernment trained by constant practice to distinguish good from evil" (5:14). And to press on to maturity, following the examples of the heroes of the faith "who through faith and patience inherit [God's irrevocable] promises" (6:12) of *so great a salvation*! To not *"neglect such a great salvation"* (2:3).

Neglect Connections

The *need* for spiritual maturity is not on the radar for many Christians and churches, and warnings against the dangers of spiritual immaturity don't prompt much *concern* from many Christians. But both the *need* and the *concern* should be at the heart of our Christian walk and the ministry of our churches. In a verse I quoted several times in this chapter, Paul warns of the danger of spiritual immaturity in Ephesians 4:14. Spiritual "children" are susceptible to tacking in any direction some new crafty and deceitful doctrine may take them. They're as helpless as a floating piece of debris on a stormy sea. But Christ isn't building a church just to leave it stuck in this immature state. As Paul teaches in Ephesians 4:11–16, Christ's aim is to bring the Father's children "to mature manhood, to the measure of the stature of the fullness of Christ" (verse 13), and *the path to maturity is also the remedy for immaturity*. Christ gives a local church the gifted leaders it needs, and when these leaders are faithful to "equip the saints for the work of ministry" (verse 12), the church is built up by the body *as it serves in ministry*. A great area of neglect of so great a salvation in a great many churches is the broad absence of service in ministry as church is a spectator sport for too many believers. And one spectator in a local church is one too many.

Paul's point in this Ephesians 4 passage is that the whole body should grow together to become more like Christ "in every way," but most especially in our "love" (verse 15). And we do this to the extent the Father wills for us when "the whole body, joined and held together by every joint with which it is equipped, when each part is working properly, makes the body grow so that it builds itself up in love" (verse 16). The whole body, each part, working properly. One spectator in a local church is one too many because even one spectator inhibits the growth of all "to the measure of the stature of the fullness of Christ."

10

Take Refuge in God's Unfailing Promise

(HEBREWS 6:13–20)

As I mentioned in the previous chapter, there's a connection between the text we just covered (Hebrews 5:11–6:12) and this chapter's passage. Both passages combine to detour us away from the author's desire to go into a lengthy teaching about Jesus's ministry as our great high priest. Thus far, the detour has entailed a warning to the reader about the dangers of spiritual immaturity that included the author's concern that his readers weren't willing and ready to dive into such a discussion. But at the end of the previous passage, as an exhortation to his readers, the author tells them, "We desire each one of you to show the same earnestness to have the *full assurance* of hope until the end, so that you may not be *sluggish*, but imitators of those who through *faith and patience* inherit the promises" (6:11–12). In other words, "full assurance" in the hope of our salvation doesn't come through being "sluggish" in our walk, but by imitating the "faith and patience" of those who inherit the very promises of God we believe. And at the very core of our assurance in the hope of our salvation is none other than God Himself. Our assurance in the promise of our salvation is rooted in something that cannot change: "The unchangeable character of his purpose" (verse 17). Therefore, we must take refuge in Him and His purposes.

I have shared with you what I believe to be a strong argument against taking Hebrews 6:4–8 as a passage that teaches you can lose your salvation, but I also shared with you that the fullness of the case I was making awaited the message we find in this passage, a passage that is hard to fathom if you believe the author has just finished teaching you can lose your salvation. I pray, instead, that you become even more convinced that losing your salvation is hard to fathom *in light of this passage*. To believe we can lose that which God promises to bring to pass says more about what we believe about God than it does of what we believe about the promise, and we begin to see the nature of God as primary over the promise in the example of the faithful life of Abraham.

God's Promise to Abraham Was Certain Because It Was Rooted in Who God Is

Verse 13 begins with "For when God made a promise to Abraham." The *for* in the beginning of the verse tells us we need to look back to see what this statement is referring to, and we see the reference in verses 11–12: "And we desire each one of you to show the same earnestness to have the full assurance of hope until the end, so that you may not be sluggish, *but imitators of those who through faith and patience inherit the promises*." For the sake of having "the full assurance of hope until the end" in the promises we stand to inherit, the author indicates there are many examples whose "faith and patience" we can imitate. In Hebrews chapter 11, we'll see a whole slew of examples, but here, the author narrows his readers' focus to perhaps the greatest human example of "faith and patience" apart from Christ: Abraham. So then, he takes us back to Abraham's example of patient faith in Genesis and how God gave Abraham the highest possible assurance that His promise was trustworthy.

The author writes in verses 13–14, "For when God made a promise to Abraham, since he had no one greater by whom to swear, he swore by himself, saying, 'Surely I will bless you and multiply you.'" The reference to God swearing by Himself comes from the account in Genesis 22 and God's call to Abraham to sacrifice Isaac. After Abraham was faithful not to withhold Isaac from God, he received God's deliverance of a substitute sacrifice for Isaac and the reiteration of a promise God had made to Abraham four times before: to bless and multiply him. But here's how the Lord reiterated His promise to Abraham in Genesis 22:16–17: "*By myself I have sworn*, declares the LORD, because you have done this and have not withheld your son, your only son, I will surely bless you, and I will surely multiply your offspring as the stars of heaven and as the sand that is on the seashore." We're going to see the author explain in much greater detail the significance of God swearing by Himself in verses 16–20, but for now, just consider the significance of the point in verse 13 that God "swore by himself" because "he had no one greater by whom to swear." God gave Abraham the highest possible assurance that His promise was trustworthy, and the patient faith of Abraham confirmed he took the Lord at His word.

Abraham's faith proved to be genuine, and he was rewarded with the promise in verse 15: "And thus Abraham, *having patiently waited*, obtained the promise." Note that Abraham's patience rather than his faith is emphasized here, but as we'll see in a moment, the basis for his patience was his astounding level of conviction that God's word could be trusted. How patient was Abraham? He was seventy-five years old when God promised him that He would multiply Abraham's offspring from his "very own son" (Genesis 12:1–4, 15:1–4). And although there were some missteps on the way in Abraham's faith, they were more a lack of understanding than a lack of trust in God's promise. By age ninety-nine, this promised son had still not arrived when God reiterated His promise to Abraham, making it clear to him that the son, Isaac, would come from his wife Sarah within the year, despite the fact that Sarah was barren and they were both well past childbearing years (Genesis 17:1–19, 18:9–14). And sure enough, at the ripe old age of one hundred, Abraham received the promised son through Sarah (Genesis 21:1–7). After twenty-five years in his old age, "Abraham, having patiently waited, obtained the promise." But the promise was not yet completely given.

Several years after the birth of Isaac, in Genesis 22:1–2, the scripture says, "God tested Abraham and said to him, 'Abraham!' And he said, 'Here I am.' He said, 'Take your son, your only son Isaac, whom you love, and go to the land of Moriah, and offer him there as a burnt offering on one of the mountains of which I shall tell you.'" How amazing was Abraham's patient faith?

As we know from the text in Genesis 22, Abraham heeded God's seemingly impossible *command* to sacrifice the very son he had waited decades for and the son through whom the *promise* of multiplying his descendants would come. How do you reconcile the *command* and the *promise*? You take God at His word and obey His commands! In Hebrews 11:17–19, the author gives us Abraham's faithful conclusion about His God: "By faith Abraham, when he was tested, offered up Isaac, and he who had received the promises was in the act of offering up his only son, of whom it was said, 'Through Isaac shall your offspring be named.' *He considered that God was able even to raise him from the dead*, from which, figuratively speaking, he did receive him back." Notice here that faith is coupled with the action that demonstrates the faith, and through this genuine faith, the fullness of the promise came to Abraham. God's reiteration of His promise to Abraham in Genesis 22:17–18 included not only the promise to multiply Abraham's descendants, but also the promise that "your offspring shall possess the gate of his enemies, and in your offspring shall all the nations of the earth be blessed, *because you have obeyed my voice.*" The promise of salvation to all the nations through the Messiah would come through Abraham, not because Abraham believed God, but because he believed *and* obeyed God! Therefore, James writes (2:21–23), "Was not Abraham our father justified by works when he offered up his son Isaac on the altar? You see that faith was active along with his works, and faith was completed by his works; *and the Scripture was fulfilled* that says, 'Abraham believed God, and it was counted to him as righteousness.'"

So then, as we've seen throughout the book of Hebrews, Abraham is a model of genuine faith because his faith persevered and *evidently so* because his trust in God was confirmed by his actions that reflected that trust. As James teaches, because of his faith, Abraham was credited with righteousness, but the nature of our salvation is progressive as Abraham demonstrates. The righteousness God credits to us is a righteousness He brings forth in us when our faith is genuine "for [we] are being transformed into the [image of Jesus Christ] from one degree of glory to another" (2 Corinthians 3:18). This is the *present* nature of salvation in the life of the believer.

God's Promise of Salvation to Believers Is Just as Unchangeable as His Promise to Abraham

God has a great desire to convince His children that our status as heirs of salvation is impossible to change. Coming back to the point that God "swore by himself" (verse 13) in making His promise to Abraham, the author writes in verse 16, "For people swear by something greater than themselves, and in all their disputes an oath is final for confirmation." He's making the point that on a human level, we make oaths or commitments by appealing to an authority greater than ourselves and we accept these human commitments as the most reliable and binding form of *human assurance.* Given that, he then builds on this point of common human experience to point to the nature of God's commitments, writing (verses 17–18), "So when God desired to *show more convincingly to the heirs of the promise the unchangeable character of his purpose,* he guaranteed it with an oath, so that by two unchangeable things, in which it is impossible for God to lie." If we trust in binding forms of human assurance, how much more should we trust in God's promise of salvation to us? Here's how much more! "It is impossible for God to lie." We believe that, right? Therefore, His promise must be true. But there's more!

He is unchangeable; therefore, His promise cannot change! We believe this, don't we? Therefore, the character of His purpose toward us, which He promises to bring to pass, so great a salvation that we stand to inherit (Hebrews 1:14, 2:3), must be unchangeable as well! But God's not finished in giving us His assurance! He "desired to show *more convincingly* to the heirs of the promise the unchangeable character of his purpose" to save us, so "he guaranteed it with an oath, so that by two *unchangeable things*"—God's promise and the oath He swore to confirm it (no greater authority in the universe)—we can have the greatest assurance possible that He will keep His promise to save us. Like Abraham, we may stumble from time to time in the "how" by which God is doing this, but like Abraham, we are called to hold fast to our hope in the "who" and the "what."

Our hope for the promise of salvation is anchored in our soul to the immovable presence of God. Because our status as heirs of salvation is impossible to change, the author writes in the second half of verse 18, "We who have fled for refuge might have strong encouragement to hold fast to the hope set before us." Refugees in worldly places of refuge suffer often because those places inevitably fail to deliver what they promise, but for us who have fled to the refuge God gives us through faith in Jesus Christ, the encouragement we have to hope in all that His refuge promises us is strong as we see in verse 18. How strong?

Look at the word *pictures* in verses 19–20! "Jesus has gone as a forerunner on our behalf" (verse 20) into the heavenly tabernacle and the Father's presence! Do you know what a forerunner does? He finishes the race, having paved the way for those who follow him, all the while drawing those who follow him in his wake! Our hope is rooted in the inevitability that Jesus Christ will draw us who follow him in his wake, and so "we have this [hope] as a sure and steadfast anchor of the soul" (verse 19). Our hope in Jesus Christ cannot slip. Whether the intent in the metaphor here is to convey that the anchor is lodged in heaven or in us, the point is that it is held "sure and steadfast" by the One who dwells there, for we know He dwells both in heaven—and in us. So then, all the while, we come to discover that He's the one holding fast to us!

Coming back to verse 17, the author indicates, "God desired to show more convincingly to the heirs of the promise the unchangeable character of his purpose." Brothers and sisters, are you "more convinced"? Is it possible to communicate any more powerfully and clearly that God's good purpose to save us through faith in Jesus Christ can be fully trusted? If you're convinced, then take hold of the anchor that won't let go.

Take Refuge in God's Unfailing Promise!

Abraham is an example for us to imitate because of his "faith and patience" (6:12). He was someone who endured, over a long period of time, great uncertainty because his circumstances often seemed to contradict God's promises. But at the heart of Abraham's "faith and patience" was hope, not as the world construes hope in an outcome that might or might not happen, but as genuine faith in God that construes hope. Genuine faith in God "is the assurance of things hoped for, the conviction of things not seen" (Hebrews 11:1), and this assurance and conviction are rooted in two things: an outcome and a person. Let me illustrate the outcome aspect of hope first.

Imagine you have two women of the same age, socioeconomic status, educational level, and temperament. You hire both and say to each, "You are part of an assembly line, and I want you to put part A into slot B and then hand what you have assembled to someone else. I want you to do that over and over for eight hours a day." Each woman operates in identical and equally monotonous settings, but with one difference between the two of them. You tell the first woman that at the end of the year, you will pay her thirty thousand dollars; and you tell the second woman that at the end of the year, you will pay her thirty million. After a couple of weeks, the first woman says, "Isn't this tedious? Isn't it driving you insane? Aren't you thinking about quitting?" while the second woman says, "No. This is perfectly acceptable. In fact, I whistle while I work." What leads to the difference between the two? It is their hope for the future.[21] But if I stop here, it is still hope as the world construes it with its "maybe" or "could be" or "might be." For all these women know, the person making the promises could be corrupt, or the conditions could radically change for this business to preclude them from keeping the promise. For such hope to move to the kind of hope the scriptures say we can have (and so live accordingly), we need a person who can guarantee the outcome, and such examples are not completely foreign to human experience no more than oaths sworn by higher authorities are foreign to our human experience.

Krista and Jeremy Bourasa decided to hold their wedding ceremony at the groom's fire station in St. Paul Park, Minnesota, knowing it was possible an alarm could disrupt things. They made it through their ceremony without a hitch, but while taking photos before the reception, an alarm sounded that required Jeremy to respond. Krista told her new husband to go ahead and fight the fire. "I've got the rest of my life with him," she told a Minneapolis TV station. "They needed him for that moment." Three hours later, Jeremy returned to the reception, and the bride and groom had their first dance.[22] During the ceremony, Jeremy most likely made vows to his soon-to-be bride. Do you think Krista had the "maybe" kind of hope that Jeremy would return, or did she have the "assurance and conviction" kind of hope? And if it was the latter, why is that? Because of the character of a husband she knew and loved.

Now, compare these human examples to the one we see in this Hebrews 6 passage. The promised outcome is our salvation! The person who made the promise is our God who swore by Himself because He could swear by none greater. He cannot lie, and He is unchangeable! Moreover, there are no circumstances in heaven, on earth, or in us that can alter "the unchangeable character of His purpose" or dislodge our hope in His saving purpose that binds our soul to Him like an anchor set and held in place by Him! You "who have fled [to Him] for refuge" are in the Father's hands if you are truly in Christ. None can snatch you from His refuge; therefore, "take refuge in God's unfailing promise!" with "the assurance of things hoped for, the conviction of things not seen."

Neglect Connections

One of the great and tragic ways Christians neglect their salvation is by not understanding the nature of our salvation and the author of our salvation. One way to look at this passage is through the assertion, "God does what He says He does." This is an important and unchanging aspect of the author of our salvation, yet I suspect most believers share the conviction of this assertion. But when it comes to the assurance of our salvation, Christians often find their assurance detached from strong examples like Abraham. By all accounts in Genesis, John, Romans, and James, Abraham is an example of God *imputing* someone with righteousness because of their belief and then progressively *imparting* His righteousness through a life of faithful obedience, all by His grace through faith. Many Christians embrace the imputed part but shun the imparted part of our salvation, perhaps sometimes because we fear the implication that our faith in Christ not only should change us but must change us if the Gospel of the author of our salvation is true. This isn't an assertion of works. It is the theology of *grace working* in the life of the believer, which is thoroughgoing in the scriptures.

In the world of theology shaped by social media, there are many gems to be found (speaking tongue in cheek). In a meme I recently encountered on Facebook, a site posted a D. L. Moody quote which read, "I'm glad we are saved by grace, not by good works. Because I don't want to sit in heaven and listen to everybody brag for eternity of how they got there." I didn't fact-check to see if this truly came from Moody because I was far less concerned about the source than I was about the reaction to the quote. There were several dozen comments of the "Amen!" and "Truth!" variety and nearly one thousand shares. I normally don't fish in the pond of comments when I see these things, but sometimes my tongue is immune to the pain when I'm biting it. So I chimed in my two cents with this: "True, but I suspect you will want to listen to how God's workmanship in Christ Jesus brought forth the good works in His people, which God prepared beforehand, that we should walk in them. This is what grace does to His glory."

Both the supposed Moody quote and my response are rooted in Ephesians 2:8–10, which begins, "For by grace you have been saved through faith. And this is not your own doing; it is the gift of God, not a result of works, so that no one may boast." We clearly won't brag about *our* works in eternity, but the passage concludes, "For we are his workmanship, *created in Christ Jesus for good works*, which God prepared beforehand, that *we should walk in them*." The same power that raised Christ from the dead is the same power that guarantees eternity with Him *and* that "we too might walk in newness of life" (Romans 6:4). A "walk in newness of life" now, just as much by grace through faith as our walk will be in eternity, and this is great and real assurance in the life of a believer when we see God doing in us what He says He does in us. Don't neglect so great a salvation by selling short what God *will do* (Philippians 2:12–13) in your life now.

11

See How Great He Is!

(HEBREWS 7:1–10)

In this passage, the author of the book of Hebrews returns to teaching his readers about Jesus's high priesthood through a mysterious figure in the Bible: Melchizedek. Warren Wiersbe once said, "If you can explain what God is doing in your ministry, then God is not really in it,"[23] and sometimes I feel the same way about the scriptures. I'm pretty sure I *can't* satisfactorily explain to you who Melchizedek is, but I think I can give you at least a sense of how the Lord is using him as an example in this passage. We are about to begin a long journey through the author's teaching about Jesus's priesthood, and along the way, we'll see in Hebrews 8:5 that he describes the ministry of the priests under the Old Testament law, saying, "They serve a copy and shadow of the heavenly things."

A shadow has a source in something greater than itself. In Hebrews 8:5, that something greater is heavenly things. In day-to-day life, shadows are typically cast by the sun, something far greater than the shadow. Yet on a beautiful moonlit night, the moon can cast a shadow as well, yet its ability to do so has something greater as its source: the sun. Still, the moon is greater than the shadow it casts as well and, in a sense, can be used to point us from the lesser thing—a shadow—to a greater thing, either the moon or the sun, which is greater still as the source of the moon's light. Melchizedek is like that intermediate "greater thing," which reveals the Old Testament priesthood to be but a shadow, and he does so ultimately for the purpose of pointing us not to himself, but to the One who is even greater still. And in pointing us to Jesus, our great high priest, we see Jesus as the substance from which the shadow takes its form. We see how great He is!

Whoever Melchizedek truly is, his greatness is intended to point us to the vast greatness of Jesus's high priesthood over the priesthood of the Mosaic law, just as vastly as the glory of the sun eclipses the very shadows it casts. And so after detouring from the topic by warning his readers against spiritual immaturity and encouraging them in the full assurance of God's promise of so great a salvation, the author comes back to his teaching target as he indicated in Hebrews 6:19–20: "We have this as a sure and steadfast anchor of the soul, a hope that enters into the inner place behind the curtain, where Jesus has gone as a forerunner on our behalf, having become a high priest forever after the order of Melchizedek." As the moon casts a shadow by the glory of the sun's light, so Melchizedek's priesthood points us in the direction away from the Old Testament priesthood and toward the greater glory of Jesus's priesthood because Melchizedek himself is also great. In this passage, we see his greatness in two ways: because his priesthood is superior to any priesthood perpetuated by mortal men and, as we'll consider first, through the nature of Melchizedek's priesthood.

Melchizedek Is Great because He Resembles the Son of God

At the end of verse 3, the author says this of Melchizedek: "*Resembling* the Son of God he continues a priest forever." As we'll see, he supports this assertion in an interesting way from a few verses in Genesis 14, but he could just as easily have made this assertion from Psalm 110:4 where, in prophesying about the future role of the Messiah, David writes, "The LORD has sworn and will not change his mind, You are a priest forever after the order of Melchizedek." But he's already used Psalm 110:4 back in chapter 5 to preview his use of Melchizedek in teaching his readers about the nature of Jesus's high priesthood, so now, as he begins his lengthy teaching on Jesus's ministry as our great high priest, he comes back to what we can learn about Melchizedek from his encounter with Abraham in Genesis 14 where we see that Abraham honored Melchizedek as his superior.

Keep in mind that the author's aim is to make the case, *at length*, that Jesus's priesthood is superior to any other and we can learn just how much so from Melchizedek's priesthood because Jesus has become "a priest forever *after* the order of Melchizedek." We begin to learn about Melchizedek's "order" through Abraham's response to him. In verses

1–2, we read, "For this Melchizedek, king of Salem, priest of the Most High God, met Abraham returning from the slaughter of the kings and blessed him, and to him Abraham apportioned a tenth part of everything." According to the Genesis narrative, "the slaughter of the kings" refers to an instance where several kings outside the land where Abraham dwelled entered the land and defeated the kingdoms of Sodom, Gomorrah, and their neighbors and carried off a large number of captives, including Lot, Abraham's nephew. In response to this attack, Abraham formed a force of his own, pursued these invading kings, overtook them near Damascus, and defeated them in a surprise nighttime attack. Abraham then recovered the captives and the plunder, and upon his return to the land, Melchizedek met and blessed Abraham, and Abraham gave him a tithe of the plunder.

In contrast to this encounter, Abraham was also met by the grateful king of Sodom who proposed that Abraham keep all the spoils of war. But unlike his interaction with Melchizedek, Abraham did not honor the king of Sodom but told him that he had sworn before the Lord, "I would not take a thread or a sandal strap or anything that is yours" (Genesis 14:23). Abraham honored Melchizedek as his superior by giving a tithe to one who was both a king and a priest and by receiving Melchizedek's blessing. And we know that receiving a blessing is Abraham's acknowledgment of Melchizedek's superiority, for the author teaches us in verse 7 that in this act of blessing, "it is beyond dispute that the inferior is blessed by the superior." As one who was both king and priest, Melchizedek was like Jesus, but his superiority to Abraham was rooted in more than these roles for Melchizedek resembled the *character* of the Son of God.

Simply put, in the second half of verse 2, the author writes, "He is first, by translation of his name, king of righteousness, and then he is also king of Salem, that is, king of peace." Although the account in Genesis doesn't state this, oftentimes in scripture, a person's name speaks of their character; and sure enough, as this verse indicates, Melchizedek literally translates to "king of righteousness." Additionally, he is king of the city of Salem (which means "peace" and is most likely Jerusalem before the time of Israel in the land). So then, Melchizedek resembles the likeness of the Son of God as a king of righteousness and peace. But the resemblance goes beyond his character for Melchizedek also resembled the *nature* of the Son of God.

Verse 3 reads, "He is without father or mother or genealogy, having neither beginning of days nor end of life, but resembling the Son of God he continues a priest forever." Interestingly, there's nothing in scripture that explicitly teaches what the text in Hebrews says here. It is rather an argument from silence in Genesis 14, in other words, based on what Genesis 14 doesn't say but also coupled with the Psalm 110:4 statement that the Messiah would be "a priest *forever* after the order of Melchizedek." Like the Son of God, then, the nature of Melchizedek's priesthood, mysteriously, is an everlasting one; and in verse 8, the author will make some additional comments about Melchizedek, which only adds to the mystery. But the point to be taken thus far is that *Melchizedek is no ordinary figure*, as indicated by the way one as great as Abraham interacted with him and by the way his nature and character resemble the Son of God. And with this understanding of Melchizedek's greatness, the author then gets to the heart of his train of thought by explaining the significance of Melchizedek's greatness.

Melchizedek Is Great because His Priesthood Is Superior to Any Priesthood Perpetuated through Descent by Mortal Men

Commands are relatively rare in the book of Hebrews. The last command we've encountered was way back in 3:13, and the only one in this passage is in verse 4 where the text reads, "See how great this man was to whom Abraham the patriarch gave a tenth of the spoils!" Interestingly, the ESV translates "See how great this man *was*" here, but there is no "to be" verb in the Greek text. The Greek literally reads, "And see this great one!" But in the way the sentence is constructed, a "to be" verb is typically implied, and so, the translators insert it. So then, the ESV inserts the past tense *was*, but if as verse 3 states that the mysterious Melchizedek has "neither beginning of days nor end of life," then Melchizedek still "is"! And so, the NRSV translates the beginning of verse 4 as "see how great he *is!*"

Another interesting aspect of the Greek text of verse 4 is that the word *patriarch* is pushed to the end of the sentence for emphasis, giving verse 4 a sense that goes something like this: "This man was so great that Abraham gave him a tenth of the spoils … and Abraham was *the* patriarch!" The father of the Jewish nation! And the fact that he gave Melchizedek a tenth is significant as we see in verses 5–6.

"And those descendants of Levi who receive the priestly office have a commandment in the law to take tithes from the people, that is, from their brothers, though these also are descended from Abraham. But this man who does not have his descent from them received tithes from Abraham and blessed him who had the promises." In other words, Abraham, the father of the Jewish nation, gave the same proportion to Melchizedek, which the law required Israelites to give to the Levites, who in turn gave a tenth of it to those of them who were appointed priests (Numbers 18:20–32). And both the priests (as descendants of Levi) and those who gave them the tithes all descended from Abraham, yet here, we see Abraham himself making the same level of payment to someone *outside* his own family. Why is this significant?

Follow this train of thought. Abraham is greater than his descendant Levi whose descendants *received* the tithe as priests. Abraham is also greater than the descendants of his other great-grandchildren (Levi's brothers) who *gave* their tithe to the priests. Yet Abraham *gave tithes* to Melchizedek and received a blessing from him; therefore Melchizedek's priesthood is both *distinct from* the priesthood appointed through the law and *greater than* this priesthood, which was appointed to the descendants of Levi. In fact, Levi himself also paid tithes to Melchizedek.

In verse 7, the author now plainly states the conclusion that one should come to in light of his command in verse 4 to "see how great this man was." He is greater than Abraham for "it is beyond dispute that the inferior is blessed by the superior" (verse 7). And in verse 8, the mystery around Melchizedek's greatness grows as the author compares the priesthood under the law with Melchizedek's priesthood, saying, "In the one case tithes are received by *mortal men*, but in the other case, by one of whom it is testified that he lives." The word translated "mortal men" here refers to those priests under the law and literally means "those destined to face death" whereas Melchizedek is described as "one of whom it is testified that he lives." In other words, Melchizedek's priesthood stands in contrast with any priesthood exercised by mortal men. *His priesthood can only be rightly compared to one who no longer faces the prospect of death* for Melchizedek "lives" (present tense). Or, once again as verse 3 indicates, he has "neither beginning of days nor end of life."

It's a fairly widespread view that Melchizedek is an angelic being, not just a figure in human history; but *whatever he truly is*, he stands above any order of priesthood exercised by mortal men, including the priesthood of the descendants of Levi. Verses 9–10, therefore, read, "One might even say that Levi himself, who receives tithes, paid tithes through Abraham, for he was still in the loins of his ancestor when Melchizedek met him." In an argument from the greater (Abraham) to the lesser (Levi), the author makes the point that Melchizedek's superiority to Abraham applies even more so to Levi. So then, the author's argument through his teaching on Melchizedek reaches its intended conclusion: the Old Testament Levitical priesthood is most evidently inferior to that of Melchizedek and therefore to that of anyone who belongs to Melchizedek's "order," particularly the Son of God to whom the Lord swore, "You are a priest forever *after the order of Melchizedek*" (Psalm 110:4). So then, look carefully at this Jesus.

See How Great He Is!

Yes, the author gave this excited command in verse 4 of this passage, and yes, he was referring to Melchizedek when he wrote it. But if you think his intention in doing so was to have his readers become enamored with Melchizedek's greatness, then you're missing the point. Melchizedek is a stepping stone in an argument leading his readers away from giving their faith and affection over to the provisions of the law and leading them toward fully giving their faith and affection over to the provisions of the Lord Jesus. As the great nineteenth-century British poet Alfred Lord Tennyson once wrote,

> Our little systems have their day;
> They have their day
> and cease to be;
> They are but
> broken lights of thee,
> And thou, O Lord,
> art more than they.

Remember that the author's great desire for his readers is to "leave the elementary doctrine of Christ and go on to maturity" (6:1). And in leaving elementary things, as we begin to see in this passage, he's not only appealing to his readers to move on to greater things but also to move on to the greatness of Christ. He wants them to see that elementary things are a foundation, but that the foundation is not to be their fixation. Christ must be their fixation as he will tell them later in 12:2 (NASB) to run this Christian life "fixing our eyes on Jesus, the author and perfecter of faith." Only Jesus can be "the author and perfecter of [our] faith," and as we grow in our faith, I believe the constant challenge to us from this passage is to "see how great He is!" In his children's series *The Chronicles of Narnia*, C. S. Lewis gives us a memorable picture of what this looks like.

One of the young heroines in the series is named Lucy, and Lucy meets a majestic lion named Aslan (a figure of Christ in the series) in the enchanted land of Narnia. After meeting Aslan, Lucy returns to her home, but then she and the other children make a return visit a year later. The children discover that everything has changed radically, and they quickly become lost. But after a series of dreadful events, Lucy finally spots Aslan in a forest clearing, rushes to him, throws her arms around his neck, and buries her face in his mane. Aslan then rolls over on his side so that Lucy falls, half sitting and half lying between his front paws. As Aslan bends forward toward Lucy, she gazes up into his amazing face, and he says to her, "Welcome, child."

Lucy then replies in wonder, "Aslan, you're bigger!"

Aslan explains to Lucy, saying, "That's because you're older, little one."

With a bit of confusion, Lucy replies, "Not because you are?"

To which Aslan replies, "I'm not. But each year you grow, you'll find me bigger."

And each year we grow, we grow all the more to see how great He is! He's not one of the shadows He casts, nor is He one of the lesser lights that reflect His glory. He is glorious like none other and should be the exclusive object of our attention just as He proclaims when He says, "I am the light of the world. Whoever follows me will not walk in darkness, but will have the light of life" (John 8:12).

Neglect Connections

I think if Barna did a survey of Christians on Jesus's ministry as our great high priest, the ignorance of this facet of Jesus's ministry would prove to be widespread. In Hebrews 2:17, we see the first mention of Jesus as our high priest. He came into this world and took on our humanity fully "so that he might become a merciful and faithful *high priest* in the service of God, to make *propitiation* for the sins of the people." It was in His role as our high priest that He made *propitiation* for our sins; that is, He satisfied God's wrath toward us because of our sins so that we would be delivered from His wrath. That's probably worth knowing well.

In Hebrews 4:14–16, we read that Jesus's work as our "great high priest" (verse 14) makes it possible for us to "with confidence draw near to the throne of grace, that we may *receive mercy* and *find grace* to help in time of need" (verse 16). How remarkable that we have peace and reconciliation with God through Jesus Christ so that we can draw near to His throne to find every provision we need to live every moment of every day for Him! That's probably worth knowing well.

In Hebrews 8:1–7, we learn that as our high priest, "Jesus is seated at the right hand of the throne of the Majesty in heaven" (verse 1). He has no need to make repeated offerings on our behalf. "Every high priest is appointed to offer gifts and sacrifices; thus it is necessary for this priest also to have something to offer" (verse 3), and He did, once for all, through His cross. So then the author writes, "Christ has obtained a ministry that is as much more excellent than the old as the covenant he mediates is better, since it is enacted on better promises" (verse 6). Better covenant, better promises, better high priest, so great a Savior, so great a salvation—which we must not neglect. That's probably worth knowing well.

12

Jesus Christ Brings a Better Hope!

(HEBREWS 7:11–19)

The late John Claypool, a pastor from Birmingham, Alabama, in an essay titled "The Future and Forgetting," wrote about a strong thunderstorm that came through the Kentucky farm where his forebears had lived for six generations. In the orchard, the wind blew over an old pear tree that had been there longer than anyone could remember. His grandfather was really aggrieved to lose the tree where he had climbed as a boy and whose fruit he had eaten all his life, and a neighbor came by and said, "I'm really sorry to see your pear tree blown down."

The grandfather said, "I'm sorry too. It was a real part of my past."

The neighbor said, "What are you going to do?"

The grandfather paused for a long moment and then said, "I'm going to pick the fruit and burn what's left."[24]

Many things in our lives that are no longer part of our lives served a purpose for a season, and there is a particular wisdom in what we do with them after they're gone that can benefit us. However, entrenching ourselves in the beneficial things in our life that have passed and gone does not renew the benefit of those things. Rather, it traps us in a false hope that those things can no longer satisfy.

In the book of Hebrews, and in this passage in particular, I believe the author deals with a similar problem among his readers. The old covenant priesthood established through the law of Moses mediated the relationship between God and His people Israel, and it served its purpose while it was in effect. But the hope it offered to God's people was not the fullness of what God had in store for them. As this passage shows us, a better hope needed to be introduced, and Jesus Christ brings that better hope! But for the author's readers to turn back to what God had done in the past for His people Israel through the priesthood "after the order of Aaron" would be like turning to those beneficial things in our life that have passed and gone. It would not renew the benefit of those things for them but rather would trap them in a lesser hope in things that cannot bring them to the perfection in their lives God desires for them. Going back to his concern about their spiritual maturity, this failure to discern the better promise and hope of Jesus's priesthood would leave them stagnated in a relationship with God that would not go on to *maturity—a form of perfection* He seeks to bring us to in this life, pointing to the fullness of the perfection He will bring us to in the life to come.

Perfection Is God's Aim for the Priesthood to His People

We see this in verse 11 as the author writes, "Now if perfection had been attainable through the Levitical priesthood (for under it the people received the law), what *further need* would there have been for another priest to arise after the order of Melchizedek, rather than one named after the order of Aaron?" Perfection in His faithful people is clearly His aim, and the need is for a priest who can bring this to pass in their lives—and it's a "further need." Just as clear is the implication that the priesthood "after the order of Aaron" could not attain perfection for the faithful. Something needed to change.

This aim of perfection necessitated a change of both law and priesthood. Looking again at verse 11 where it says, "Now if perfection had been attainable through the Levitical priesthood (for under it the people received the law)," we see that the law and the priesthood "after the order of Aaron" was a package deal, inextricably intertwined. As the NIV translates here, "The law given to the people established that priesthood." And so if this priesthood wasn't a capable means to God's ultimate end for His people and needed to be replaced, then the same must be said for the law. Therefore, the author writes in verse 12, "For when there is a change in the priesthood, there is necessarily a change in the law as well." And this change wasn't obscure; it was evident.

The Lord Jesus clearly represents this change. The author writes in verses 13–14, "For the one of whom these things are spoken belonged to another tribe, from which no one has ever served at the altar. For *it is evident* that our Lord was descended from Judah, and in connection with that tribe Moses said nothing about priests." Where the text reads, "For the one of whom these things are spoken," it's referring to the Lord Jesus as the change of means God brings: He is the "priest to arise after the order of Melchizedek" (verse 11). And it's clear that Jesus could not be "after the order of Aaron" because the priesthood given to Aaron was given under the law to the descendants of Levi whereas "it is evident that our Lord was descended from Judah, and in connection with that tribe Moses said nothing about priests." There was nothing given in the law that gave provision for a descendant of Judah to serve in the priesthood. As long as the Mosaic law remained in effect, only the Levites "served at the altar"; and by the authority of the law, Jesus, of the tribe of Judah, is automatically excluded from priesthood. In fact, the scriptures indicate in several instances that the old covenant priesthood was jealously guarded from any outside interference, including interference from the kings who were descended from David, who descended from Judah: the line of kings through whom God promised to bring the Messiah, the Christ, the Lord Jesus. This is why a new and different legal basis for Jesus's priesthood needed to be established: a priesthood "after the order of Melchizedek" who was also both priest and king.

Such a change in law—the authority commanded by God—gives Jesus the divine legal basis to serve as priest and king as well. Assuming again that the author's audience is a community of Jewish believers perhaps being drawn to turn once again to the old covenant law as a means of living out their relationship with God, the notion of a priesthood other than the Levitical priesthood would have been a concept out of a theological left field, especially if their level of spiritual maturity left them disinclined to dig deeper and consider the implications of Psalm 110:4 (the central text from which the author has been making his case since the beginning of chapter 5), that "The LORD has sworn and will not change his mind, 'You are a priest forever after the order of Melchizedek.'" This is a new and unchangeable command, and so a new and unchangeable law that came after the law was given to Moses, a new order and priesthood that will stand forever with the power to accomplish God's aim toward His people.

The Priesthood of Jesus Very Evidently Accomplishes God's Aim of Perfection

The author begins in verse 15, writing, "This becomes *even more evident*." And when he writes "this," he's referring to everything he's said up to this point in this passage. It is the entire argument he's made about the need for a change in the law so that a new order of priesthood could take the place of "the order of Aaron," and if it was going to replace "the order of Aaron," then it needed to entail more than just the difference between descent from Judah versus descent from Levi. To bring God's aim of perfection to pass in the lives of His people, there needed to be a monumental change in the *nature* of the priesthood, and one way to understand the change is to understand it as a change from weakness to power. The priesthood of Jesus very evidently accomplishes God's aim of perfection by the power of an indestructible life.

Verses 15–16 read, "This becomes even more evident when another priest arises in the likeness of Melchizedek, who has become a priest, not on the basis of a legal requirement concerning bodily descent, but by the power of an indestructible life." When the author writes, "On the basis of a legal requirement concerning bodily descent," he's referring to the law's provision that the priesthood "after the order of Aaron" is maintained through the physical descent of people who suffer from the weakness of mortal limitations. No priest of Aaron's line could have been described as "a priest forever" for the simple reason that each one of them died in their due time. But our great high priest is immortal. Having died once for all and risen from the dead, he ministers on His people's behalf in the power of the very life God alone possesses, which can never be destroyed. And because of this "indestructible life," the scripture testifies about Him: "You are a priest forever, after the order of Melchizedek" (verse 17, Psalm 110:4). The priesthood of Jesus very evidently accomplishes God's aim of perfection through the power of His indestructible life and so changes the basis for our hope from what is weak and powerless to one who is mighty indeed. Therefore, Jesus accomplishes God's aim of perfection through the introduction of "a better hope."

Verse 18 and the first half of verse 19 reads, "For on the one hand, a former commandment is set aside because of its *weakness and uselessness* (for the law made nothing perfect)." The author is comparing the effectiveness of the law and its priesthood in bringing about perfection with the effectiveness of Jesus's high priesthood, and the comparison isn't flattering. The law is weak and useless when it comes to perfecting a believer, which begs the question about the law's purpose. That's an extensive topic, but Paul gives us several straightforward explanations for the law's purpose, such as in Romans 3:20 when he writes, "Through the law comes *knowledge of sin*." And later in Hebrews 10:1–3, we see the role of the priesthood of Aaron's order in bringing this awareness of sin as well when he writes, "The law … can never, by the same sacrifices that are continually offered every year, make perfect those who draw near. Otherwise, would they not have ceased to be offered, since the worshipers, having once been cleansed, would no longer have any consciousness of sins? But in these sacrifices, *there is a reminder of sins every year*."

Under the old covenant, drawing near brought the constant reminder of sin. And as a constant reminder of sin, Paul sheds further light on the law's purpose in Galatians 3:23–24 when he writes, "We were held captive under the law, imprisoned until the coming faith would be revealed. So then, *the law was our guardian* until Christ came." In essence, in bringing a constant reminder of sin to the faithful among God's people Israel, the law guarded them by keeping in the forefront of their minds the need for a better solution to the problem of their sin than just a constant reminder. They needed a "better hope" for "those who draw near." And so, the author completes the comparison to the law and its priesthood, writing in the second half of verse 19, "But on the other hand, a better hope is introduced, through which we draw near to God." And we can draw near to God in a way not possible through the old covenant because we have a great high priest who is seated at the right hand of the Father. We can, as the author taught back in 4:16, "with confidence draw near to the throne of grace, that we may receive mercy and find grace to help in time of need." And this "grace to help in time of need" is a present hope we have through the ministry of our great high priest, the Lord Jesus Christ, and the power of His indestructible life He is imparting to us!

Jesus Christ Brings a Better Hope

And He does so, not only for the future but also now! The scriptures teach that the very power of God dwells in us by the presence of His Holy Spirit, and it is an effective power because of the life of Jesus Christ. It is the effective power of God's work in us now that gives us hope for things to come. As Paul teaches in Romans 5:5 (NASB), this is a hope that "does not disappoint, because the love of God has been poured out within our hearts through the Holy Spirit who was given to us." Through Christ, we draw near to God in a way that makes Him as real as any relationship we have. "Oh, taste and see that the

LORD is good! Blessed is the man who takes refuge in him!" (Psalm 34:8). In His refuge, He becomes as real to us as what we perceive with our senses! And I am firmly convinced that unless He is this real to us, our hope in Him can be as fleeting as the next thing we hear, which tells us we can't "taste and see" Him or that there's something better to "taste and see." I think this is part of the major flaw in the modern American church's approach to youth ministry.

Instead of treating our youth who know the Lord as disciples and are a meaningful part of the body, we treat them like adolescents (an American creation by the way) who need to be entertained more than they need to see the Lord working in and through them like any one of His disciples. We deny them the kind of life in the church that makes Him real to us! And when they don't discover the hope in Christ, which "does not disappoint," what's left for them to discover is the hope the world offers.

Max Tegmark, an MIT professor and cofounder of the Future of Life Institute, looks forward to what he calls Life 3.0. Here's how he outlines his three stages of human development: Life 1.0 is our biological origins. In Life 2.0, humanity develops culture and early technology. But our hope lies in Life 3.0: the merging of the human body with artificial intelligence; with the potential for almost unimaginable power. Tegmark writes,

> The human race is in need of an upgrade. Yet despite the most powerful technologies we have today, all life forms we know of remain fundamentally limited by their biological hardware. None can live for a million years, memorize all of Wikipedia, understand all known science, or enjoy spaceflight without a spacecraft. None can transform our largely lifeless cosmos into a diverse biosphere that will flourish for billions or trillions of years, enabling our universe to finally fulfill its potential and wake up fully. All this requires life to undergo a final upgrade to Life 3.0, which can design not only its software but also its hardware. In other words, Life 3.0 is the master of its own destiny, finally fully free from its evolutionary shackles.[25]

Friends, this is all the rage in the industry of hope in our day, and as the progress of science and technology approaches the point of bringing it to pass, this kind of upgrade for the human race becomes all the more plausible. But even if it could deliver on this promise, there remains a problem.

As former Ivy League professor of philosophy Alston Chase once wrote back in the latter part of the twentieth century, "Every age has its illusions. History is merely a portrait of the past that reflects the myths of the present … Those born early in this (20th) century were sustained by a misguided sense of progress. They confused technological improvements, of which there were many, with cultural advancement, of which there was little."[26] But the Lord best grasped the implications of a hope rooted in living forever without the solution to our greatest problem: our sin nature.

In Genesis 3:22–24, Moses writes,

> Then the Lord God said, "Behold, the man has become like one of us in knowing good and evil. Now, lest he reach out his hand and take also of the tree of life and eat, *and live forever*—" therefore the Lord God sent him out from the garden of Eden … He drove out the man, and at the east of the garden of Eden he placed the cherubim and a flaming sword that turned every way to guard the way to the tree of life.

A life forever trapped in the bonds of our sin nature ultimately becomes hell, even if it is a forever life as an artificial intelligence–enhanced cyborg "finally fully free from its evolutionary shackles." Any upgrade short of what Jesus Christ promises offers no greater hope than hell itself. Real hope: the "better hope" that "does not disappoint" is the hope in the "upgrade" Jesus Christ offers, Jesus Christ and none other.

Not the hope of modern technology, nor the hope that can be gained through the Mosaic law and its priesthood, nor any other thing. As Peter teaches in 1 Peter 1, our hope in Christ is a "living hope." Peter writes, "Blessed be the God and Father of our Lord Jesus Christ! According to his great mercy, he has caused us to be born again to a living hope through the resurrection of Jesus Christ from the dead, to an inheritance that is imperishable, undefiled, and unfading, kept in heaven for you, who by God's power are being guarded through faith for a salvation ready to be revealed in the last time" (1 Peter 1:3–5). This is the real "Life 3.0," experienced now and "ready to be revealed in the last time." This is the only hope with the power to deliver perfection. This is the better hope. This is our best hope. Through Christ and Christ alone.

Neglect Connections

In this passage, the author draws our attention to the force of attraction the old covenant brought into the lives of his readers. It was a familiar way of relating to God for them, and we love familiar. For example, it's hard to move. It's hard to leave "familiar" and relocate to a new home, neighborhood, schools, friends, jobs—a new church. As a military family, Lucia and I learned over time to trust the Lord with our many moves and especially to trust Him in leading us to a new church family home. And along the way, one thing we learned was to never look for our previous church. We learned not to hold a church the Lord was leading us *to* under the expectation that it must be like the church the Lord was leading us *from*. Within the bounds of "the faith that was once for all delivered to the saints" (Jude 3), there is a fair diversity of faith and practice in a local church. But there are traditions of faith and practice that don't fall within the bounds of "the faith that was once for all delivered to the saints"; many I have ministered to over the course of my life came out of such traditions, and they're typically comfortable traditions.

You may be a daughter or son of Jacob wrestling with the truth of Jesus's claim to be your Messiah. You sense the power of His claim and that His claim does offer "a better hope … through which we draw near to God" (Hebrews 7:19), and yet there's fear in the change and in the cost such change represents when the author of that "better hope" also says, "If the world hates you, know that it has hated me before it hated you. If you were of the world, the world would love you as its own; but because you are not of the world, but I chose you out of the world, therefore the world hates you" (John 15:18–19).

Change and a price to pay for the change make for a daunting step, and this holds true for any tradition you step out of that makes strong claims upon its adherents. Perhaps you come from a tradition that claims salvation is through the church rather than Christ. Or perhaps the tradition is a system of rules and such through which salvation is gained and kept. Regardless, the common experience of each is that they're familiar, rooted in longstanding tradition, typically rooted in things *you can do*, and bound by a sense of coercion (subtle or overt) that sends the message of a price to be paid should you turn from it. If this is you, then Jesus's offer to you isn't a comfortable offer. His offer comes with a cost, but it's a price that pales in comparison to "a better hope." To exchange "a better hope" for the comfort of a tradition that doesn't lead you to Christ alone by faith alone through grace alone is another form of neglecting a great salvation.

13

Be Saved to the Uttermost!

(HEBREWS 7:20–28)

Back in 2018, Richard Edelman, president and CEO of Edelman PR Company, made an interesting observation about the nature of "trust" in our culture, saying, "The United States is enduring an unprecedented crisis of trust. This is the first time that a massive drop in trust has not been linked to a pressing economic issue or catastrophe … In fact, it's the ultimate irony that it's happening at a time of prosperity, with the stock market and employment rates in the US at record highs."[27] Trust is an incredibly important dimension of our Christian life because it is ultimately proven by the actions we take in relation to the one or thing we trust. A crisis of trust in our culture is one thing, but a crisis of trust in our faith is another thing altogether, and the crisis is ultimately revealed in our actions. Do we believe in the promises of God, and if so, do our actions confirm our trust?

"Be saved to the uttermost" is taken from Hebrews 7:25, where the author promises us that Jesus can do that very thing for "those who draw near to God through him." Would you describe your life today as one that draws near to God through Jesus Christ and stays there? This passage essentially makes an impassioned case for us to do so in order to experience the kind of life in Christ that is saved "to the uttermost," and it makes the case on the basis of a guarantee from none other than Jesus and why His guarantee is trustworthy.

Jesus Is the Guarantor of a Better Covenant

The word *covenant* is mentioned for the first time in Hebrews in this passage as a preview for the approach the author is going to take in chapters 8–10. In chapters 8–10, he's going to make the case that Jesus's ministry as our high priest is superior to the ministry of the priests under the old covenant because, as he writes in Hebrews 8:6, "Christ has obtained a ministry that is as much more excellent than the old as the covenant he mediates is better, since it is enacted on better promises." Therefore, a way to take this passage is that it is *a preview* of why the promises under the new covenant are better. To begin with, because Jesus is the "guarantor" of this "better covenant" (verse 22).

The word *guarantor* was used for a person who would provide for the bond, collateral, or some other form of guarantee that a promise would be fulfilled. The more valuable the bond or collateral provided, the greater the likelihood that the "guarantor" would follow through on the promise, a principle that still holds true today. And in this instance, the thing of value that Jesus, the "guarantor," gave to secure what was promised in this "better covenant" was Himself. So then, if the reason the new covenant Jesus guarantees is better is because of Jesus (!), then one would expect the author to now focus on Jesus and the reasons why Jesus is the guarantor of a better covenant. And He is. First, because the Lord swore an oath to give Him an everlasting priesthood.

If you remember from the last half of Hebrews chapter 6, the message of the text there was an overwhelming confirmation of God's commitment to keep His promise to bring to pass the great salvation we have in Jesus Christ. God desired to give us the greatest possible assurance in our salvation, so much so that "when God desired to show more convincingly to the heirs of the promise the unchangeable character of his purpose, he guaranteed it with an oath" (Hebrews 6:17). There is no greater way to assure us that God will keep His promise than by swearing by Himself to do so. With that review from chapter 6 in mind, look at verses 20–22. "And it was not without an oath. For those who formerly became priests were made such without an oath, but this one was made a priest *with an oath* by the one who said to him: 'The Lord has sworn and will not change his mind, "You are a priest forever."'" This makes Jesus the guarantor of a better covenant."

So then, we see two reasons why Jesus is "the guarantor of a better covenant." One, because the old covenant priests did not become priests through the unchangeable oath of God (which indicates the limitations of that priesthood), and two, because the Lord's unchangeable oath made Jesus's priesthood everlasting, one with no end. But just the fact that the Lord has made Jesus's priesthood everlasting doesn't get to the full detail as to why the covenant he guarantees is better. There are some essential blessings that come with an everlasting priesthood, which the author now elaborates on.

As "a priest forever," Jesus is the guarantor of a better covenant because His intercession for us as our high priest *never ceases*. In verses 23–24, the author reiterates the inferiority of the old covenant priesthood because their mortality limited their priesthood, whereas Jesus (remember 7:16) "has become a priest, not on the basis of a legal requirement concerning bodily descent, but by the power of an indestructible life." Therefore, as verse 24 states in comparison to the old covenant priests, "he holds his priesthood permanently, because he continues forever." Still, what is the benefit for us of Jesus being "a priest forever"?

The benefit is this. "Consequently, he is able to save to the uttermost those who draw near to God through him, since he always lives to make intercession for them" (verse 25). Remember all the way back in 4:14, the author writes, "Since then we have a great high priest who has passed through the heavens," alluding to the fact that Jesus has returned to the Father's right hand. But as 6:19–20 indicates, He did so as "a hope that enters into the inner place behind the curtain, where Jesus has gone as a forerunner on our behalf, having become a high priest forever." In other words, the road Jesus *necessarily* took as our "high priest forever" was through the cross where His blood was shed for us within the true holy of holies in heaven as a perfect sacrifice "once for all" (verse 27). And here is why Jesus's ministry as our great high priest is so incredibly significant to us.

By His death and resurrection, we are saved by grace through faith in Jesus Christ. But it is as our great high priest, always making intercession for us, that Jesus is bringing our salvation to pass, leading us to the finished work the Father has sworn by Himself to make of us. In other words, Jesus's ongoing ministry of intercession for us guarantees the promises of the new covenant. In other words, Jesus is *still* our "guarantor." Without His ongoing ministry as our great high priest, the process of our salvation would be incomplete. But with His ongoing ministry, "he is able to save to the uttermost!" As we've seen in Hebrews, we can draw near to God with the assurance of constant and immediate access, and we know that He sympathizes with our weakness and supplies the mercy and grace to help us in time of need. And we know that in times of temptation, He can deliver us, and when we fail, He can restore us as He demonstrated with Peter in Luke 22 and John 21. And perhaps most powerfully, Paul teaches that because of the intercessory ministry of our great high priest, "who shall bring any charge against God's elect? It is God who justifies. Who is to condemn? Christ Jesus is the one who died—more than that, who was

Are We Neglecting a Great Salvation?

raised—who is at the right hand of God, *who indeed is interceding for us*" (Romans 8:33–34). I pray now that we have a clearer sense of what's on the line over the matter of priesthood.

Unlike Jesus, the priests of the old covenant could not even begin to presume that they could "save to the uttermost those who draw near to God through" their ministry. As F. F. Bruce writes concerning the comparison made between the two priesthoods in this passage, "As long as the old order endured, a new priest was always at hand to step into the place of his predecessor, but people might feel that because of certain personal qualities which he possessed over and above the sacredness of his office, the late priest was a more effective intercessor with God than his successor could ever be. No such misgivings could be entertained with regard to the high priesthood of Christ, however. He would never have to hand it over to someone less well qualified."[28] His priesthood is everlasting, His intercession for us is unceasing, and as we'll see in this last point, Jesus is the guarantor of a better covenant because His qualifications are matchless; His intercession for us as our high priest is perfect.

The author affirms Jesus's perfection in His qualifications in three ways. First, because *His character is perfect*. Verse 26 reads, "For it was indeed fitting that we should have such a high priest, holy, innocent, unstained, separated from sinners, and exalted above the heavens." Simply put, the new priesthood is better because the new priest is Jesus. This is a description of a man who is both perfectly human and humanly perfect, a sinless man who perfectly bears the perfect character and nature of God. As mentioned earlier, Hebrews 8:6 says of Jesus, "The covenant he mediates is better," but Jesus is no ordinary mediator who comes between two parties with the hope of bringing them to agreement. He is *the* unique mediator between God and humanity because he combines Godhood and humanity perfectly in his own person. In other words, by virtue of who He is, Jesus brings agreement between God and humanity in Himself!

And because He is who He is, His intercession for us as our high priest is perfect because *His sacrifice is eternally effective*. Verse 27 reads, "He has no need, like those high priests, to offer sacrifices daily, first for his own sins and then for those of the people, since he did this once for all when he offered up himself." Our sinless Savior "has no need … to offer sacrifices daily" either for Himself because it was unnecessary or for us because His single sacrifice of Himself was all that was needed, "once for all." And who are the "all" Jesus died "once for"? All who have placed or will yet place their faith and trust in Him as Savior unto the end of human history and back to the beginning as well! His sacrifice is eternally effective! It is not bound by time as He is "the Lamb who was slain from the creation of the world" (Revelation 13:8 NIV). Therefore, as Hebrews 11 indicates, the likes of Abel, Enoch, Noah, Abraham, Moses, Rahab, David, and many more, "though commended through their faith, did not receive what was promised, since God had provided something better for us, *that apart from us they should not be made perfect*" (Hebrews 11:39–40).

Finally, Jesus's intercession for us as our high priest is perfect because *He is the perfect Son of the Father who appointed Him.* Perfect character, perfect sacrifice, perfect Son! Verse 28 reads, "For the law appoints men in their weakness as high priests, but the word of the oath, which came later than the law, appoints a Son who has been made perfect forever." This passage begins with the force of the guarantee that comes through the Lord's oath to appoint Jesus "a priest forever" (verse 21), and like an emphatic bookend, it concludes with a reference to the same oath. Again, referring to the oath in Psalm 110:4 by God's inspiration through David, the author makes the self-evident point that this oath "came later than the law" and so was destined to supersede the law. But notice the subtle difference between verse 21, where the oath resulted in Jesus's appointment as "*a priest* forever," and verse 28, where the oath results in the appointment of "*a Son* who has *been made perfect* forever." Verse 26 teaches us "*it was indeed fitting* that we should have such a high priest," reminding us of 2:10 when the author writes, "For *it was fitting* that he, for whom and by whom all things exist, in bringing many sons to glory, should make the founder of their salvation *perfect through suffering.*" But it was not just the suffering that made our Savior perfect, but the fact that "although he was a son, he *learned obedience through what he suffered.* And *being made perfect*, he became the source of eternal salvation to all who obey him, being designated by God a high priest after the order of Melchizedek" (5:8–10).

Remember we discussed the nature of Jesus's perfection when we discussed these earlier references. It doesn't refer to flaws Jesus had that needed to be corrected. It refers to *the work of obedience* to the Father's will Jesus needed to accomplish in the face of suffering—particularly His sacrificial death on the cross on our behalf—in order to finish the work He was sent to do. And so, not unlike Abraham, with whom *the Father swore by Himself* to keep His promise to Abraham when, in obedience to the Father's will in the face of suffering, *he did not withhold his son*, his only son Isaac. So again, *the Father swore by Himself* to appoint His one and only Son "a priest forever" when *He did not withhold Himself* for our sakes and for our salvation. And this makes Him "the guarantor of a better covenant" because He makes Himself the bond, the collateral, the security that the promise would be kept. And the more valuable the bond or collateral provided, the greater the likelihood that the "guarantor" would follow through on the promise. And how great that likelihood is when the value of the security for the promise of so great a salvation is infinite. Therefore, once again, embrace the promise with all the assurance we have in our "guarantor" Savior.

Be Saved to the Uttermost!

One of the struggles I face as a parent is in the way my wife and I represent a source of great help in time of need for our kids, help that can bring great blessing to them. It was true when they were very young, and I've come to discover that this truth about our relationship doesn't change when they're adults. It's just the nature of the help and blessing that changes over time. Some of that help comes through a form of grace that acts on our kids' behalf whether they ask for it or not. But much of it, especially as they get older, is there for the asking and not always taken advantage of.

As I've mentioned many times, it's significant that the author dedicates more time to the topic of Jesus's high priesthood *than any other topic in the book*. I pray in this reading that you've come to learn even more why. Our salvation is a lifelong work in progress pointing toward a future resurrection, but if there is no ministry of Jesus Christ as our great high priest, then there is no bold access to the throne of grace, no sympathy with our weakness, no mercy and grace to help us in time of need, no deliverance from temptation, no restoration when we fail, no rebuff of condemning accusations against us, no source of eternal salvation! Jesus saves us to the uttermost! He is on the job now and always ready to bring about salvation in us now.

Neglect Connections

He is all the help we need, but if we don't know enough to seek it or don't desire to do so, then pressing on to maturity, as we've already seen, runs the risk of the grace of God being removed from the equation for "this we will do *if God permits*" (6:3). But "he is able to save to the uttermost those who draw near to God through him," a declaration of His ability in which we play a part with the implication we can limit His work in us to something short of "the uttermost." The burden is upon us to draw near continuously, but the blessing is the abundant life in Christ, which *we can choose to neglect* by failing to "draw near to God through him." Ultimately, I believe the degree to which we do so reflects the degree to which we truly trust Him.

Our nation is in a crisis of trust despite unprecedented prosperity because *circumstances don't produce trust, relationships do!* Jesus Christ has set us free but does not set a heavy hand upon us to seek Him. During the days of the civil war before America's slaves were freed, a Northerner went to a slave auction and purchased a young slave girl.

As they walked away from the auction, the man turned to the girl and told her, "You're free."

With amazement, she responded, "You mean, I'm free to do whatever I want?"

"Yes," he said.

"And to say whatever I want to say?"

"Yes, anything."

"And to be whatever I want to be?"

"Yep."

"And even go wherever I want to go?"

"Yes," he answered with a smile. "You're free to go wherever you'd like."

She looked at him intently and replied, "Then I will go with you."[29] Her answers indicate the breadth of choices freedom affords us. This little girl wisely chose to cling to the person who won her freedom. We should do likewise.

14

The "Best" Is Always "Better"

(HEBREWS 8:1–13)

One of the things I loved about preaching through Hebrews was that it is nonstop Jesus! In nearly every paragraph of the book, the author takes up some new angle about Jesus that's meant to impress upon us a deeper sense of His greatness and majesty. As we've come to discover, his method for doing this is comparison, and in every comparison, Jesus proves to be incomparable with any other object of faith or any other course a person might presume to take to find God and live in the right relationship with Him. And the word that the author loves to use to sum up these comparisons is *better*. In Hebrews 1:4 (NASB), Jesus is "much *better* than the angels." In Hebrews 7:19, Jesus introduces "a *better* hope." In 7:22, Jesus is "the guarantor of a *better* covenant." In 8:6 (NASB), "He is also the mediator of a *better* covenant, which has been enacted on *better* promises." In 9:23, Jesus's sacrifice of Himself is described as "*better*." In 10:34, the eternal inheritance Jesus promises is described as "a *better* possession and an abiding one." In 11:35, the great women of faith were praised for fixing their hope on the promise of Jesus the Messiah "so that they might obtain a *better* resurrection." And in 12:24 where the author will return to Jesus's role as our great high priest, we learn that we come in worship "to Jesus, the mediator of a new covenant, and to the sprinkled blood that speaks a *better* word than the blood of Abel."

In every possible way then, it seems our Lord Jesus and what He brings into our lives is "better," but that shouldn't surprise us because the best is always better! And again, when Jesus is shown in Hebrews to be "better" by comparison, He's not marginally better or somewhat better, but mind-bogglingly "no comparison" better! And this theme of mind-bogglingly "no comparison" better continues in chapter 8 and is still focused on the superiority of Jesus's ministry as a high priest. Chapter 8 is previewed in 7:26 where the author writes of Jesus, "It was indeed fitting that we should have such a high priest, holy, innocent, unstained, separated from sinners, and exalted above the heavens," a statement that focused on Jesus's nature and character, but concluded with His exalted position.

Jesus's Priesthood Is Better

This passage begins to further make the case that Jesus's priesthood is better because of His exalted position. And from that exalted position, we first see that Jesus's priesthood is better because His sanctuary is indestructible. "Now the point in what we are saying is this: we have such a high priest, one who is seated at the right hand of the throne of the Majesty in heaven, a minister in the holy places, in the true tent that the Lord set up, not man" (Hebrews 8:1–2). Unlike the high priest after Aaron's earthly order, Jesus ministers "in the true tent" set up by the Lord in the holy places of heaven, not in some earthly sanctuary fashioned by men's hands, which, as we'll see in verse 5, is only "a copy and shadow of the heavenly things." As F. F. Bruce describes the contrast, the sanctuary Christ ministers in as our great high priest is "the only one which is not an imitation of something better than itself, the only one whose durability comes anywhere near to matching the eternity of the living and true God whose dwelling-place it is."[30] And from the incomparable sanctuary from which Christ ministers, we see that Jesus's priesthood is better because His offering is incomparable.

Verse 3 reads, "For every high priest is appointed to offer gifts and sacrifices; thus it is necessary for this priest also to have something to offer." On one level, this verse is making the simple point that Jesus must have something to offer if He is truly a high priest. But a closer look reveals something special about the nature of Jesus's offering. Where the text reads, "For every high priest is appointed to offer gifts and sacrifices," the act of offering is in the present tense, indicating the act of offering is continuously repeated as the priesthood after Aaron's order had to do. But where the text reads, "Thus it is necessary for *this* priest also to have something to offer," the phrase "this priest" refers to Jesus, and the Greek text here uses a form of the past tense to describe the act of offering, indicating the offering was made once in the past and is now a completed action. The NIV shows this more clearly where it translates, "And so it *was* necessary for this one also to have something to offer." Moving to verses 4–5, the text reads, "Now if *he were on earth*, he would not be a priest at all, since there are priests who offer gifts according to the law. They serve a copy and shadow of the heavenly things. For when Moses was about to erect the tent, he was instructed by God, saying, 'See that you make everything according to the pattern that was shown you on the mountain.'"

Once again, this verse makes a simple point we've already seen in chapter 7: according to the law, Jesus can't be a priest "on earth" because the law appointed the priesthood to descendants of Levi whereas Jesus is a descendant of Judah. But once again, a closer look reveals a more substantive point. Jesus isn't on earth in a tent erected by Moses or some other man. He doesn't minister on our behalf in a "shadow of the heavenly things," which, like a shadow, is fleeting and lacks the substance of the real thing. Jesus is in heaven in the indestructible sanctuary fashioned by the hand of God. In essence, verses 4–5 give us yet another almost absurd comparison as they, in fact, emphasize the vastly greater dignity and worth of Jesus's perfect sacrifice offered once for all, which makes forever possible His ongoing ministry of mediating our relationship with our heavenly Father. He is better indeed! And it keeps getting better!

Jesus's Ministry Is Better

His ministry is better because He mediates a better covenant enacted on better promises just as verse 6 indicates: "But as it is, Christ has obtained a ministry that is as much more excellent than the old as the covenant he mediates is better, since it is enacted on *better promises.*" There are two terms worth considering in verse 6 before we continue: *covenant* and *mediates.* A covenant is a binding agreement entered into between two parties prescribing the terms of the relationship between the parties. When God enters covenant relationship with people, He is the one who prescribes the terms and takes the initiative in calling people into the relationship. Humanity, therefore, is called to pursue a relationship with God *on His terms.* A mediator in the case of such a relationship is someone who comes between the two parties to facilitate the relationship.

So then, Jesus Christ, as our great high priest, mediates our new covenant relationship with God; and in Jesus, we have the most effective mediator possible in our relationship with God as He fully represents both sides of the covenant. As the Son of God who is fully God, He represents God to us; and as our "brother" (2:11) who is also fully human, He represents us to God. In other words, Jesus's mediation of our relationship with God is as perfect as His perfect nature—one person who is both fully God and sinless man—as He mediates a better covenant "enacted on better promises." And once again, the author shows us how the new covenant is better than the old by comparison for the old covenant was as flawed as human nature.

We see this in verses 7–9:

> For if that first covenant had been faultless, there would have been no occasion to look for a second. For he finds fault *with them* when he says: "Behold, the days are coming, declares the Lord, when I will establish a new covenant with the house of Israel and with the house of Judah, not like the covenant that I made with their fathers on the day when I took them by the hand to bring them out of the land of Egypt. For they did not continue in my covenant, and so I showed no concern for them, declares the Lord."

A key point to take away from these verses is that *the flaw in the old covenant wasn't the law, the terms God prescribed* as He called His people Israel into covenant relationship with Him. The fault was with His people Israel "for they did not continue in [His] covenant." This lines up with what Paul teaches about the law in Romans 7:12 as he writes, "So the law is holy, and the commandment is holy and righteous and good" but then points to himself as the source of the problem in keeping the law when he says "For I have the desire to do what is right, but not the ability to carry it out" (Romans 7:18). The promise of the old covenant law was life—if you could keep the law. And so Paul wrote in Romans 7:10, "The very commandment that *promised life* proved to be death to me." And because the old covenant was flawed in this way, the Lord promised His people Israel that a new covenant was forthcoming: a better covenant "enacted on better promises." And these promises are better because of the one upon whom they are dependent.

The new covenant is as perfect as "I Am" promising "I will." Look with me at verses 10–12 and focus on the phrase "I will."

> For this is the covenant that *I will* make with the house of Israel after those days, declares the Lord: *I will* put my laws into their minds, and write them on

their hearts, and *I will* be their God, and they shall be my people. And they shall not teach, each one his neighbor and each one his brother, saying, "Know the Lord," for they shall all know me, from the least of them to the greatest. For *I will* be merciful toward their iniquities, and *I will* remember their sins no more.

So what will the Lord do? What are His terms for Himself in this new covenant? To begin with, He will impart to our minds and our hearts His laws. This isn't just imparting supernatural powers of memory. It is the supernatural power of *knowing and doing*, not unlike as Ezekiel writes in 11:19–20: "And I will give them one heart, and a new spirit I will put within them. I will remove the heart of stone from their flesh and give them a heart of flesh, *that they may walk in my statutes and keep my rules and obey them.* And they shall be my people, and I will be their God." This is the language of new creations with divine ability and so the better promise to be able to continue in His covenant relationship. And because He says "I will," notice that *"they shall* be my people … *they shall* all know me," not in some superficial way where His existence is acknowledged, but in an intimate and personal way. And the relationship in this new covenant can no longer be made hostile by our sins, for His mercy will cover them and so He shall cast any remembrance of them forever away from Himself. The old covenant came with promises but nothing like these! These are better promises. These are the best promises!

There Is Amazing Grace in These Promises

There is amazing grace particularly to God's people Israel. Remember the spiritual problem the author is addressing: spiritual immaturity and the lack of inclination to press on to maturity. His readers seem to have failed to grasp that Jesus Christ and His ministry are essential to their Christian walk to press on to maturity and that Jesus Christ and His ministry are *exclusively effective* in bringing to pass so great a salvation in their lives. The inference to be made in the prolonged comparison between Jesus and the pillars of Judaism under the old covenant (with Jesus proving to be irrefutably better at every turn) is that his readers *haven't yet come to this conclusion on their own* to their own present detriment and future danger. And so with a lingering fascination in their lives with the old covenant as a suitable supplement or alternative to Jesus Christ and the new and better covenant He mediates, the author writes to his readers in verse 13, "In speaking of a new covenant, he makes the first one obsolete. And what is becoming obsolete and growing old is ready to vanish away."

A new covenant was part of God's plan for Israel; therefore, the obsolescence of the old covenant was part of His plan as well. In industry, planned obsolescence is the purposeful implementation of strategies designed to get customers to buy another very similar product by making the older one useless, undesirable, or nonfunctional within a set period of time. For example, in the early twentieth century, major lightbulb manufacturers colluded to purposefully reduce a lightbulb's lifetime to one thousand hours by the mid-twentieth century even though engineers were capable of designing bulbs that were much longer lasting. This kind of planned obsolescence sought to compel people to move from one product to another, but it did so with the selfish motive of what was best for the bottom line of a manufacturing sector.

But in God's version of planned obsolescence, His selfless grace is His motive and His purpose in the law was to move His people to something better—to the best. As Paul writes in Galatians 3:19, "Why, then, was the law given? It was given alongside the promise to show people their sins. But the law was *designed to last only until* the coming of the child who was promised" (NLT). In an upside-down kind of analogy, just as an inferior lightbulb was intended to move people to purchase a new one, so too an old covenant destined to become flawed because of our sin nature was put in place for a time to reveal the sins of His people and point them to their need for their Messiah. In Hebrews, we see God's grace toward His people Israel as its inspired author bears God's impassioned message to them to embrace the great high priest of His new covenant with them for the "old is ready to vanish away." And as Gentiles who have come to Christ, we must always be humbly reminded that there is amazing grace for Gentiles through God's new covenant promises to Israel.

Neglect Connections

There remains a prevailing prejudice toward Jews among the predominantly Gentile church in America, a mindset that seems to despise them for being so stiff-necked and missing the obvious in Jesus, the Messiah. If that inclination arises within you, keep in mind God's word to His people Israel in Exodus 19:5: "If you will indeed obey my voice and keep my covenant, *you shall be my treasured possession among all peoples*, for all the earth is mine."

Just as we can't fully fathom just how much "better" Christ truly is in every way, so too I don't think we can fully fathom how great the Father's love is for Israel and how great His desire is for them to be able to continue in His covenant. Remember the passage we've just covered. Quoting from God's promise of a new covenant in Jeremiah 31, the author writes, "Behold, the days are coming, declares the Lord, when I will establish a new covenant *with the house of Israel and with the house of Judah*" (8:8). Notice Gentiles are not in this promise! It is directed exclusively toward those whom God desires to be His "treasured possession among all peoples." As Gentiles, we only find our way into the new covenant promises through God's grace toward Israel as Paul teaches in Romans 11:15 when he writes, speaking of Israel, "For if their rejection means the reconciliation of the world, what will their acceptance mean but life from the dead?"

By God's grace, Israel's rejection (for a time) opens the door for reconciliation with God to the world. Paul then goes on to write to Gentiles in Romans 11:17–20:

> But if some of the branches were broken off, and *you*, although *a wild olive shoot, were grafted in* among the others and now share in the nourishing root of the olive tree, *do not be arrogant toward the branches*. If you are, remember it is not you who support the root, but the root that supports you. Then you will say, "Branches were broken off so that I might be grafted in." That is true. They were broken off because of their unbelief, but you stand fast through faith. So *do not become proud, but fear.*

We Gentiles are wild branches grafted into God's new covenant promises to Israel by His grace. We have everything that is better through Christ because of God's grace and loving intention toward His people Israel, a fact that ought to move us to humility and fear, knowing that God acted in judgment against the unbelieving among His people Israel so that a faithful remnant would be preserved as His "treasured possession among all peoples." So then, Paul concludes in Romans 11:21–22 (and sounding very much like the author of Hebrews by the way), "For if God did not spare the natural branches, neither will he spare you. Note then the kindness and the severity of God: severity toward those who have fallen, but God's kindness to you, *provided you continue in his kindness.* Otherwise you too will be cut off." As we have seen in a point so often made in the book of Hebrews, genuine faith finishes the race. The scriptures are remarkably consistent on this point, yet a growing life in Christ cannot grow side by side with a disdain for the Jewish people, through whom God has mysteriously and wonderfully used to make such a great salvation possible.

15

Lessons from the Shadows

(HEBREWS 9:1–10)

If you're not a pilot at some professional level, then you've probably never heard of a Link Trainer. Link Trainers are designed to be a minimal replica of an aircraft cockpit. Most military aircraft today still use Link Trainers for the purpose of familiarizing aircrew members with the location of flight controls, switches, gauges, dials and displays, and the basic movements of the flight controls as well as many switches and knobs. In a minimal way, they're like the real thing, and they do offer some help in transitioning aircrew members to the real thing. But when you throw switches in a Link Trainer, power doesn't come online, lights don't illuminate, jet engines don't rev up with all their associated noises, and the flight controls don't cause rudders, ailerons, and flaps to move. And although you can imagine yourself rolling down the runway to take off or rolling inverted at high speed a few hundred feet above the ground while in the Link Trainer, the experience is so far removed from the real thing that it almost isn't worth comparing. A Link Trainer can create the expectation for the real thing, but it can't possibly satisfy the expectations of the real thing. And no pilot who longs to fly would ever be content with never moving beyond the copy to the real thing.

In the previous chapter, we learned that the priests of the old covenant ministering in the tabernacle or temple of the old covenant served "a copy and shadow of the heavenly things." Similarly, in the section of Hebrews that we'll cover in the next chapter, the author teaches that the earthly places where these priests ministered were "holy places made with hands, which are copies of the true things" (9:24). So then, as a Link Trainer can serve to teach a pilot, to some level, about the nature of the real thing, so too can "a copy and shadow of the heavenly things" teach us about those heavenly things. In other words, we can learn lessons from the shadows.

In this passage, we get a brief description of the shadows: the earthly places God ordained for His people to worship Him and regulations for that worship. But when we're done with this passage, you're probably going to feel like the message is incomplete and rightfully so because the passage creates an expectation that there is something better than the shadow. It sets the stage for the rest of chapter 9 where we see just how much better "the true things" are than the "copy and shadow" for "the true things" "save those who are eagerly waiting for" Jesus Christ (9:28). But as His people who are, I hope, eagerly waiting for the Lord Jesus's return, we can learn lessons from the shadows while we wait, beginning with the "earthly place of holiness" where the old covenant priests ministered.

The Tabernacle

Verse 1 reads, "Now even the first covenant had regulations for worship and an earthly place of holiness." Already, you can sense that a comparison is once again brewing. We saw this in Hebrews chapter 8 with its emphasis on how much better the new covenant was in comparison with the old, and the beginning of chapter 9 is essentially the preamble to another comparison. In verse 1, we get a preview of the comparison; it will focus on the *regulations* for worship (really for the priesthood) and the *places* of worship, and in verses 2–5, the author begins with the places. Once more, as a good summation as to why he's focusing on a place, R. T. France writes in his commentary, "The tabernacle set up by Moses on God's instructions was intended as a 'copy and shadow' of the true heavenly sanctuary (8:5). It follows, therefore, that a study of the 'copy' can be expected to yield by analogy a better understanding of the heavenly ministry of our great high priest."[31]

In verses 2–5, the author walks us through a brief description of the tabernacle, concluding in verse 5 by writing, "Of these things we cannot now speak in detail." You get the sense that he would love to speak of these things in detail, but he's given us enough to make his point; I think his point is that the tabernacle and its furnishings were beautiful! The larger section of the inner tent has a beautiful name: "The Holy Place." Yet the smaller section has an even more beautiful name, "the Most Holy Place," where God promised that His presence would dwell. And within "the Most Holy Place," the beauty and worth of the furnishings is emphasized with "the golden altar of incense and the ark of the covenant covered on all sides with gold, in which was a golden urn holding the manna," along with artifacts of the old covenant precious to the people of Israel: "Aaron's staff that budded, and the tablets of the covenant." And in the crowning moment of his description, the author writes in verse 5, "Above it [the ark] were the cherubim of glory overshadowing the mercy seat." This is the specific spot where God promised Moses in Exodus 25:22, "There I will meet with you, and from above the mercy seat, from between the two cherubim that are on the ark of the testimony, I will speak with you about all that I will give you in commandment for the people of Israel."

So what lessons from the shadows do we learn about this "earthly place of holiness"? That it was holy, beautiful, precious, and blessed by the glorious presence of God. And if that's true of the copy—the shadow—then how much more so the "true things" in heaven must be holy, beautiful, precious, and blessed by the glorious presence of God. In other words, we should have great anticipation right about now for the even better side of this comparison. We get this through a study of the places and things, and as we move to verses 6–7, we see this as well in a study of the people and their ministry.

The Regulations for Worship

The regulations for worship in the tabernacle were likewise a shadow cast by a heavenly ministry. As I mentioned earlier, these are actually the regulations for the ministry of the priests within the tabernacle, which the author describes in verses 6–7, writing, "These preparations having thus been made, the priests go regularly into the first section, performing their ritual duties, but into the second only the high priest goes, and he but once a year, and not without taking blood, which he offers for himself and for the unintentional sins of the people." We've already considered the regularity and nature of these "ritual duties," but one point inferred here is that the priests had the privilege of ministering in this "earthly place of holiness."

For example, in Luke 1:8–9, we see Zechariah, a priest and the father of John the Baptist, serving in "the holy place" to burn incense. Most scholars estimate that the large number of priests (about eighteen thousand) who ministered in the temple made it likely that this opportunity for Zechariah may have been the only opportunity he had to minister in this way in his lifetime. This privilege for a priest, therefore, would have been perhaps the most significant moment of his life. But the description of the duties performed in "the first section" are very general whereas the ministry in "the second" (referring to "the Most Holy Place" in verse 3) is described in more detail, and it too is a limited opportunity for "only the high priest goes, and he but once a year."

But in a shift to the solemn aspect of the "regulations for worship," we learn the high priest entered "the Most Holy Place" but "not without taking blood, which he offers for himself and for the unintentional sins of the people." Upon one man, and relatively infrequently, rested the responsibility to mediate the old covenant relationship between God and His people, and not without the shedding of blood. Not without a necessary death on the people's behalf and, in the case of the old covenant, on the high priest's behalf as well. And if that's true of the copy, the shadow, then how much more so the "true things" in heaven must be effective in mediating our relationship with God and dealing with the problem of our sins? Once more, knowing that the copy is pointing us to something similar, yet better by far, we should once again have great anticipation at this point for the even better side of this comparison. And in verses 8–10, we catch a glimpse of the nature of the comparison and the purpose of this shadow of heavenly things.

The Shadows Point Us to the Time of Reformation

In verse 8 and the first part of verse 9, the author reveals a significant point about the requirements for the high priest's ministry he has just described in verse 7. "By this the Holy Spirit indicates that the way into *the holy places* is not yet opened as long as the first section is still standing (which is symbolic for the present age)." So then, the Holy Spirit reveals that the ministry of the high priest has a somewhat negative connotation: "That the way into the holy places is not yet opened" and he's referring to "the holy places," not "an earthly place of holiness" as in verse 1. We see the reference in 9:11–12, which reads, "But when Christ appeared as a high priest of the good things that have come, then through the greater and more perfect tent (not made with hands, that is, not of this creation), he entered once for all into *the holy places*." In other words, the earthly tabernacle or temple, as a shadow of heavenly things, could only show us that a way needed to be opened ("disclosed," NIV and NASB) to enable entry "into the holy places" in heaven where "the greater and more perfect tent (not made with hands, that is, not of this creation)" is located. The tabernacle or temple and the ministry of the priests within it served as an illustration while the ministry of the old covenant priesthood was in effect as the NIV shows us, that the way "into the holy places" in heaven "had not yet been disclosed as long as the first tabernacle was still functioning. This is an illustration for the present time" (8–9).

So then, in a more positive sense, the Holy Spirit also reveals through these details that a day would come when "the way into the holy places" would be "disclosed." No longer would access into the presence of God be made possible for only one person alone under the most stringent and limited conditions. The day would come when the way would be open for all God's people to enter in "with confidence" (4:16) because our great high priest has now entered the heavenly sanctuary on our behalf as our "forerunner" (6:19–20), drawing us in His wake "to the throne of grace" (4:16). This is "the time of reformation" referred to in verse 10, or as the NIV translates, "the time of the new order." And this is a new order of priesthood: the great high priesthood of our Lord Jesus who has been appointed by the Father as "a priest forever, after the order of Melchizedek" (5:6). And until Christ came, making the necessary arrangements for us to be able to draw near to God through Him, and so to be changed by Him, the priesthood of the old covenant could only give what a shadow could offer and not the substance of the real thing for "according to this arrangement, gifts and sacrifices are offered that cannot perfect the conscience of the worshiper, but deal only with food and drink and various washings, regulations for the body imposed until the time of reformation" (verses 9–10).

The old covenant operated through provisions for the flesh; the new order of the new covenant promises what the old cannot—to "perfect the conscience of the worshipper." A contrast Paul points out in 2 Corinthians 4:16 when he writes "Though our outer self is wasting away, our inner self is being renewed day by day," and similarly, as Jesus teaches in John 6:63 when He says, "It is the Spirit who gives life; the flesh is no help at all." F. F. Bruce sums up this passage, writing, "Now we see what our author wishes to teach his readers. The really effective barrier to a man or woman's free access to God is an inward and not a material one; it exists in the conscience. It is only when the conscience is purified that one is set free to approach God without reservation and offer him acceptable service and worship."[32]

And this is where this passage leaves us: there is a lesson to be learned from the shadows, but with only a partial picture of what that lesson is! "A copy and shadow of the heavenly things" gives us an expectation of "heavenly things" but can't possibly satisfy those expectations. And how great are those expectations in comparison with the "copy and shadow"? I don't think human language and experience can give us anywhere near the fullness of the sense of how great and wonderful the difference will ultimately be.

Neglect Connections

There are several sections within the scriptures that lead most believers to glaze over as they read them. Genealogies for starters! I also find reading through the lengthy passages describing the construction of the tabernacle, the production of all the instruments of worship that go into the tabernacle, and all the regulations for worship to be, at times, tedious. And then I start to feel like the dinosaur character Rex in the first *Toy Story* movie who, after shunning Woody, only to realize at the end that Woody was actually trying to help Buzz, says, "Great! Now I have guilt!" All kidding aside, what challenges me even more is thinking about what the treasures of the Gospel Hebrews reveals to us from those "tedious" sections of the Old Testament together with Luke's description of Jesus's conversation on a walk to Emmaus: "And beginning with Moses and all the Prophets, he interpreted to them in all the Scriptures the things concerning himself" (Luke 24:27).

I have grown to make it a point in my ministry as a pastor to force myself to preach and teach more often out of the Old Testament, and it has proven to be very rewarding. It's hard work, but it's worth it. In a recent study of Zechariah, which I led with one of our men's groups, one of the men shared an epiphany during one of the sessions, saying, "I used to think the Old Testament was nothing more than a collection of stories." By studying Zechariah in the community of a men's study, he has come to see that the Old Testament is so much more than that! I suspect that a general ignorance of the Old Testament is widespread within the church, and that general ignorance is essentially another way of neglecting a great salvation—but it ought not to be.

16

Good Things Have Come!

(HEBREWS 9:11–28)

Proverbs 18:22 says, "He who finds a wife finds a good thing and obtains favor from the LORD." Back in 2019, my wife Lucia and I witnessed this "good thing" come to pass in our son's life. Waiting for that wedding day comes with a great deal of anticipation, and although life together in dating or engagement is good, for those who seek to be wed in ways faithful to what the Lord calls us to, the relationship before the wedding pales in comparison to the goodness of the relationship after the wedding and the Lord's favor that comes with it. When that wedding day and married life has come, without doubt, you can say, "Good things have come!"

In Hebrews 9:1–10, we learned how the nature of the old covenant relationship with God was merely a copy and shadow of the good things that would come to God's people when Jesus Christ would reveal the way to a close relationship with God, in His presence in the holy places in heaven where He dwells. Yet as we saw, even the places and ministry of the old covenant were holy, beautiful, precious, and blessed by the presence of God. And if that was true of the copy and shadow, how much more must it be true for the real thing that Jesus Christ has brought into our lives! "Good things … have come" (verse 11) to us through Jesus Christ, and yet good things are coming! It all starts the moment we place our faith and trust in Jesus Christ, and it never ends.

Only Jesus Brings Redemption for Us Now and Always

And this redemption brings deliverance *from* something and *for* something. Beginning with the "from," Jesus's perfect sacrifice exclusively secures our eternal deliverance from the power and presence of sin. In verse 14, the text reads that Jesus "offered himself without blemish to God." There was no flaw in Him as He offered Himself for our sakes upon the cross. And so now He is "a high priest of the good things that have come," and what are these "good things"? Whereas the high priest of the old covenant repeatedly sacrificed animals in an earthly sanctuary, which, as we saw in 9:8, served to teach the people that the way into the holy places in heaven had not yet been revealed, Jesus entered "once for all into the holy places … by means of his own blood, thus securing an eternal redemption," a perfect sacrifice that needed to only be offered once and can only be offered once and secures "an eternal redemption" for all who turn to Jesus. This redemption is our eternal deliverance from the enslaving power of sin and all its consequences, and again, notice that this is "the good things that have come." In this life, we begin to experience the new covenant blessing of deliverance from the power and presence of sin, foreshadowing the complete deliverance we will receive in eternity. As our high priest, Jesus and none other brings us this redemption now and always. And as we experience these "good things that have come" now, our redemption from sin's power delivers us for faithful service to God.

In verses 13–14, we read, "For if the blood of goats and bulls, and the sprinkling of defiled persons with the ashes of a heifer, sanctify for the purification of the flesh, how much more will the blood of Christ, who through the eternal Spirit offered himself without blemish to God, *purify our conscience from dead works to serve* the living God." The old covenant sacrifices had no power to deal with the sinful impurities of our inner person: our heart, mind, soul, and will. They could remind one of the ever-present stains of sin within us and point us to the need for a real solution to our sin problem, but only Jesus Christ "through the eternal [Holy] Spirit [can] purify our conscience from dead works to serve the living God." And this too is part of our redemption, "the good things that have come." In Christ, and by the Holy Spirit, we are His works in progress. We are no longer helplessly bound to the dead works of our sinful nature. And not only that, we will also someday be without blemish like Him for Jesus Himself will ultimately "present the church to himself in splendor, without spot or wrinkle or any such thing, that she might be holy and without blemish" as Paul writes in Ephesians 5:27. And until that day, we get the great honor and privilege of being "God's fellow workers" (1 Corinthians 3:9) as we serve

Him in bringing to pass His kingdom purposes in this world. This is the blessing, both now and always, of "the good things that have come" in our new covenant relationship with God through our faith in Jesus Christ, a blessing that came at a great price.

Jesus's death Was Necessary for Our New Covenant Relationship with God To Be Possible

This is the point the author makes in verses 15–22, and he does it in a very interesting but also complicated way. Up to this point, he's focused on the new covenant blessings of redemption: a term that uses the imagery of a slave freed from bondage by paying a ransom price. But he's already indicated that this redemption is eternal, so now he's going to shift to the eternal nature of these redemption blessings as an "eternal inheritance." We've already seen the author refer to our salvation as our inheritance and how Jesus is "the heir of all things" (1:2). And if you recall chapters 1 and 2, we made the connection with the rest of the scriptures that we are joint heirs with Jesus as "the heir of all things" and that "all things" means—all things! A new heaven, a new earth, a new universe, made forever new and forever good by Jesus Christ who "upholds the universe by the word of his power" (1:3). This is the "promised eternal inheritance" of the new covenant, but like any inheritance, a covenant that promises an inheritance can only take effect after a death.

And here's where the author's line of reasoning to make the case that Jesus's death was necessary gets interesting—and hard to follow—so I'll go slowly in the hope we can follow his line of reasoning together! Covenants are typically not used as a legal mechanism to distribute an inheritance. A will is used for this, and in the Greek, the word for "will" and "covenant" is identical, the context determines the meaning intended. What the author does in verses 15–22 is use "covenant" and "will" as a play on words to make the point that the blessings of the new covenant—an eternal redemption that results in an eternal inheritance—can only come through the death of the one who leaves the inheritance to others, just like a will. This is essentially the point in verses 16–17, which reads, "For where a will is involved, the death of the one who made it must be established. For a will takes effect only at death, since *it is not in force as long as the one who made it is alive.*" He then goes on to say in verse 18, "Therefore, not even the first covenant was inaugurated without blood," and then summarizes in verses 19–22 how prolific the bloody deaths of animals were under the old covenant. But as the reader of the text, it has to beg the question,

"What kind of inheritance could slaughtered calves and goats leave us?" Clearly nothing but the constant reminder of sin and death. Jesus's death was necessary for our new covenant relationship with God to be possible because a will (a covenant) that promises an inheritance from God can only take effect if our sins are forgiven, "and without the shedding of blood there is no forgiveness of sins" (verse 22).

So then, for us to receive an eternal inheritance of "all things" with Jesus, we needed the death of the one who leaves the inheritance to others (a necessity for a *will*) while leaving the heirs forgiven by His shed blood on the cross (a necessity for the new *covenant*). Now, come back to verse 15, which reads, "Therefore he is the mediator of a new covenant, so that those who are called may receive the promised eternal inheritance, since a death has occurred that redeems them from the transgressions committed under the first covenant." We can "receive the promised eternal inheritance" because of the covenant relationship we have with God because Christ's death has redeemed us from our transgressions against God's law.

We rebel against God's laws by nature, offenses that merit His condemnation, not the blessing of His eternal inheritance. We need to be saved *from* our condemnation to be saved *for* our inheritance as John teaches in John 3:17–18, saying, "For God did not send his Son into the world to condemn the world, but in order that the world might be saved through him. Whoever believes in him is not condemned, but whoever does not believe is condemned already, because he has not believed in the name of the only Son of God." And the only way anyone escapes a just condemnation is with a pardon, with forgiveness. Once more, "and without the shedding of blood there is no forgiveness of sins." We can only enjoy the eternity God promises us if we are in the right covenant relationship with Him. Our sin makes this impossible apart from the blood of Jesus Christ, shed once for all, which brings forgiveness of sins to all who believe He died, and necessarily so, to save us. But He's not done saving us!

Jesus Will Return "to Save Those Who Are Eagerly Waiting for Him"

Verses 23–28 read,

> Thus, it was necessary for the copies of the heavenly things to be purified with these rites, but the heavenly things themselves with better sacrifices

than these. For Christ has entered, not into holy places made with hands, which are copies of the true things, but into heaven itself, now to appear in the presence of God on our behalf. Nor was it to offer himself repeatedly, as the high priest enters the holy places every year with blood not his own, for then he would have had to suffer repeatedly since the foundation of the world. But as it is, he has appeared once for all at the end of the ages to put away sin by the sacrifice of himself. And just as it is appointed for man to die once, and after that comes judgment, so Christ, having been offered once to bear the sins of many, *will appear a second time, not to deal with sin but to save those who are eagerly waiting for him.*

This section of text seems to tie up many loose threads. The true heavenly things are much better than the earthly copies that point to them. The better sacrifice of Jesus Christ that gives us bold access into the heavenly places is much better than its earthly counterpart through the Jewish high priest. And His sacrifice was once for all, as the author points out both the impossibility and absurdity that Jesus should have to mimic the endless repetition of the earthly sacrifices "for then he would have had to suffer repeatedly since the foundation of the world. But as it is, he has appeared once for all at the end of the ages to put away sin by the sacrifice of himself" (26). He ties these threads together, but then concludes his train of thought in this passage, similar to his play on words with "covenant" and "will," only this time, with a play on the reality of death and judgment.

Verse 27 is very well known and reads, "And just as it is appointed for man to die once, and after that comes judgment." Human beings are appointed to die once, not repeatedly. And once we have experienced death, the judgment of God over us inevitably follows it. There are no opportunities after we breathe our last to reverse the judgment God will render against us based on what we do in this life. But the phrase "just as it is" indicates he's using our death and subsequent judgment as an analogy to Christ's experience, for he writes in verse 28, "So Christ, having been offered once to bear the sins of many, will appear a second time, not to deal with sin but to save those who are eagerly waiting for him." Jesus Christ, who is both fully God and fully human—like us in every way, yet without sin—also died once, and He too became the object of God's judgment ... for our sins and not His own. So then, He has already dealt with sin. Therefore, He has already dealt with the judgment that awaits us after death because of our sin.

It's appointed for us to die once and suffer judgment. Jesus died once and suffered our judgment for us. For those who place their faith and trust in Jesus to have done this for them, Jesus changes your eternal equation! And for those who believe in Him to do so, good things have come, and our great hope is that good things are coming for Jesus "will appear a second time, not to deal with sin but to save those who are eagerly waiting for him." And when the author says He's coming to save us, He's referring to the fact that Jesus has secured our eternal redemption by His better sacrifice, and He will come bearing the promised eternal inheritance to all who believe. Good things have come; good things are coming. But are you "eagerly waiting for him"?

Neglect Connections

What does this even look like in our lives? I read a story once of a little boy who packed his Spider-Man pajamas into his backpack and waited in his upstairs bedroom for Jesus's return. That's charming and would bring a big smile to my face if that were my son. But does eagerly waiting for Jesus mean putting everything else on hold and waiting for His return?

In the 2015 Boston marathon, long after the sun had set, the official clock turned off, and the crowds had all but gone home, thirty-nine-year-old Venezuelan Maickel Melamed crossed the finish line around 4:00 a.m., twenty hours after the race began. What made Maickel's race significant is that he suffers from a disease similar to muscular dystrophy, which meant he didn't so much run the race as walk it. As he reflected on his accomplishment, Maickel stated, "In any marathon, you have to know why you're doing it. Because in the last mile, the marathon will ask you."[33]

In the last mile, the marathon will ask you! How about your last mile? What will it ask you? In Matthew 24:44, Jesus told His followers, "Therefore you also must be ready, for the Son of Man is coming at an hour you do not expect." We don't know when our last mile will come; we need to run like we're ready to finish! Jesus then goes on to say in 24:45–46, "Who then is the faithful and wise servant, whom his master has set over his household, to give them their food at the proper time? Blessed is that servant whom his master will find so doing when he comes." How do you eagerly wait for Jesus? Know why you're running! It's to always serve Him and to be found doing so when He returns! As the text for this chapter teaches, we are the blessed recipients of Jesus's ministry "as a high priest of the good things that have come" because His work of redemption on our behalf purifies "our conscience from dead works to serve the living God." We should eagerly wait for Christ by serving Him faithfully until He returns or calls us home.

In a remarkable parallel between Jesus's teaching here in Matthew 24 and the text in Hebrews, the author teaches in verse 15 that this life where we are called to serve God leads to "the promised eternal inheritance." Notice how Jesus essentially teaches the same thing in Matthew 24:47 when He says, "Truly, I say to you, he will set him over all his possessions." Are you "eagerly waiting for him"? Perhaps the best way to answer that question is with another question. Are you faithfully serving Him? Are you "the faithful and wise servant" serving your Lord Jesus in His household? Good things have come; good things are coming to those who do.

17

The Case for Christ? Case Closed!
(HEBREWS 10:1–18)

In his book *The Case for Christ*, author Lee Strobel reflected on his attitude toward Jesus Christ in his earliest investigations into who Jesus was. Strobel was a skeptic when it came to Christ and recalled of himself that "as far as I was concerned, the case was closed. There was enough proof for me to rest easy with the conclusion that the divinity of Jesus was nothing more than the fanciful invention of superstitious people."[34] As many of you may know, Strobel eventually changed his tune and embraced Jesus Christ fully after he had further considered the facts of the matter. Very similarly, as we've seen in our long journey through Hebrews, the author has been making a case for Christ since the very first verses of the book to an audience with a deficient view of Jesus.

Remember, he came out with theological guns blazing, writing that God "appointed [Jesus] the heir of all things, through whom also he created the world" (1:2) and that "He is the radiance of the glory of God and the exact imprint of his nature, and he upholds the universe by the word of his power" (1:3). That is one remarkable and matchless résumé, but then he concluded 1:3 in a way that might have struck us odd at the time. Alluding to Psalm 110, he wrote, "After making purification for sins, he sat down at the right hand of the Majesty on high." In this allusion, we see the direction his case for Christ was going to take as Psalm 110 would be the central text he would use from the scriptures, teaching about Jesus's everlasting ministry as our great high priest and why that makes Him superior to any competitor his readers might be entertaining as the means to enter into and live out their relationship with God. It has been a long road that now brings us to chapter 10, but in Hebrews 10:1–18, the journey for making this case for Christ comes to an end.

The author now introduces little that is new, but rather focuses on tying the main threads of his argument together as if to say, "The case for Christ? Case closed!" He has relied heavily on comparing Jesus to many heavy hitters in the pantheon of old covenant Judaism, seeking to dissuade Jewish believers from lapsing into relying upon that pantheon to live out their relationship with God. In closing his case, the author emphatically closes the door on that pantheon and equally emphatically revisits why Jesus Christ and Him alone is the sole source for the life God promises us now and forever. And among the pantheon of Judaism, there is no heavier hitter—no greater pillar—than the old covenant law given by God to His people Israel through angels and by His servant Moses.

It Is Impossible for the Sacrifices Commanded by the Law to Take Away Sins

This point is not new in the case the author has been making. He's already made it implicitly, so what he does here is summarize the points he's already made but then clearly states the implication. And here's how he gets there. "The good things to come" (verse 1) as we learned of in the previous chapter are the blessings, both now and in eternity, of new covenant relationship with God through Jesus Christ, a relationship that accomplishes, both now and in eternity, God's aim in us to "make perfect those who draw near" (verse 1). As a shadow of these things, the law and its ritual sacrifices cannot possibly do what the real thing does. It can only point to the real thing. The fact that the law is ineffective in bringing about the whole-person kind of change God does in our lives is made by a logical point in verses 1–2 when he writes, concerning the law that "it can *never*, by the same sacrifices that are continually offered every year, make perfect those who draw near. Otherwise, would they not have ceased to be offered, since the worshipers, having once been cleansed, would no longer have any consciousness of sins?" In other words, if the law produced *perfection* (spiritual maturity in this life, sinless perfection through resurrection), then wouldn't the endlessly repeated sacrifices have stopped at some point? And then in a subtle, yet powerful statement, he writes in verse 3, "But in these sacrifices there is a reminder of sins every year."

Why is this powerful? Remember that in Hebrews 8–10, the Old Testament text the author is building his case for Christ on is God's promise of a new covenant in Jeremiah 31, and remember that part of what God does for us in His new covenant is this: "For I will be merciful toward their iniquities, and I will remember their sins no more" (8:12). There is perhaps no greater contrast the author draws than the contrast between the old covenant law that brings "a reminder of sins every year" and a new covenant relationship where, because of Christ, God "will remember [our] sins no more"! And so, with his case for Christ up to this point in the book more than adequately summarized, the author boldly states what he's been alluding to for some time: "For it is impossible for the blood of bulls and goats to take away sins" (verse 4). There needs to be a "better sacrifice," but remember, in Christ, God gave us more than "better"; He gave us the "best"!

The Sacrifice "of Jesus Christ Once for All" Makes Us Holy

Once again, as we've so often seen in Hebrews, the author makes this point through a contrast between Jesus's sacrifice and the sacrifices commanded by the law. This is not new; he's used contrast and comparison repeatedly to make his case. What is new is *who he appeals to* in order to make his point that the sacrifices commanded by the law did not satisfy God's will for us.

Verses 5–6 read, "Consequently, when *Christ* came into the world, *he* said, 'Sacrifices and offerings you have not desired, but a body have you prepared for me; in burnt offerings and sin offerings you have taken no pleasure.'" This is fascinating! He's quoting here from the Greek translation of Psalm 40:6, a psalm of David. And by the inspiration of the Spirit, the author reveals that with these words of David, he foretold the very words of Christ at a miraculous and mysterious moment in history: when He came from heaven to take on our human form and nature! And so Jesus Himself, in the time of His incarnation, declared the inadequacy of the old covenant sacrifices and offerings. They did not please God nor satisfy His desire or will. What does satisfy the Father's will is hinted at by what Christ said when he came into the world to become like one of us: "A body have you prepared for me" (verse 5).

The sacrifice of Jesus Christ, and none other, established God's will to make us holy. Continuing His quotation of Psalm 40 and his attribution of its words to Jesus, the author writes in verse 7, "Then I said, 'Behold, I have come to do your will, O God, as it is written of me in the scroll of the book.'" So much can be said of Christ's words to the Father here when He says, "I have come to do your will, O God, as it is written of me in the scroll of the book," but the closest New Testament parallel to these words is perhaps Paul's summary of the Gospel in 1 Corinthians 15:3–4 when he writes, "For I delivered to you as of first importance what I also received: that Christ died for our sins in accordance with the Scriptures, that he was buried, that he was raised on the third day in accordance with the Scriptures." The will of God Christ came to do "as it is written of me in the scroll of the book," or as Paul says "in accordance with the Scriptures" was to offer His body, which was prepared for Him—to die for our sins. But it entailed more than dying upon a cross for us, for Jesus said in John 6:38, "For *I have come* down from heaven, not to do my own will but the will of him who sent me." In other words, Jesus's entire life was a willing act of perfect obedience to the Father's will, which is why His sacrifice on our behalf, unlike the sacrifices of the law, is once for all and perfect.

So then the author writes in verses 8-10, "When he said above, 'You have neither desired nor taken pleasure in sacrifices and offerings and burnt offerings and sin offerings' (these are offered according to the law), then he added, 'Behold, I have come to do your will.' *He does away with the first in order to establish the second.* And by that will we have been sanctified through the offering of the body of Jesus Christ once for all." The will of the Father through the perfect life and perfect sacrifice of His one and only Son Jesus was to do away with the law, to nullify it, no longer in effect. There's a new order, a new covenant, a new and great high priest who, through the power of His perfect life and sacrifice, makes us forever holy in God's sight ("we have been sanctified … once for all") because God imparts to us the holiness of His son Jesus when we place our faith in trust in Him as our Savior. The author's case for Christ as our Lord, our Savior, and our coming King, all of which we come to know (and to know Him more) through His ministry as our great high priest, is nearly closed. But there's one more point to revisit before He does.

Jesus Christ, Our Great High Priest, Saves Us Fully

The author makes this point from two perspectives as he draws his case for Christ to a close. One perspective is the reality of the perfecting work God is doing in us now through Jesus Christ, and a second perspective is one last dig at why the old covenant law can't bring both the "now and forever" aspect of this glorious reality in us to pass. Let's consider the "now" part of our reality in Christ first.

His saving work is ongoing. Verse 14 reads, "For by a single offering he has perfected for all time those who are being sanctified." One of the tensions in scripture that describes our Christian life is the tension of "already, not yet." Our hope in Christ is rooted in God's will from eternity past. If an infinite and sovereign God has determined, from eternity past, to save those who will turn to Him by faith, then there has never been a time from the perspective of a God who is not bound by time when His promises to us in Christ have been incomplete or unrealized. But when we who are mortal and exist in time receive these promises, *we receive what is certain while it is in progress.* And you see this tension in verse 14. "He has perfected" reflects what has been done and is true of us now and "for all time." It is unchangeable if we are Christ's. But it is true for us "who are being sanctified." The present tense ongoing work of God in us is on a trajectory to sinless perfection through our resurrection. But as verse 14 also indicates, His saving work is as good as done.

The author has made this point in verse 14, but he surrounds it with, once again, a subtle and powerful dig at the shortcomings of the old covenant law that he has spent nearly ten chapters seeking to dissuade his readers from turning back to. And how does he do that? He turns once more to the greatness of our great high priest, especially in light of the contrast between Christ and the copy and shadow of the real thing. In verse 11, we see once more the endless repetition of ineffective sacrifices by priests who "[stand] daily." They can never sit down because their work never accomplishes God's aim in the life of His people. All their work can do is remind them that their work is ultimately ineffective! "But when Christ had offered for all time a single sacrifice for sins, he *sat down* at the right hand of God" (verse 12). You see, when your high priest actually accomplishes God's will by His sacrifice, He sits down!

Once again alluding to Psalm 110, He sits down as one who is "a priest forever after the order of Melchizedek" (Psalm 110:4). And as our high priest forever, "he is the mediator of a new covenant, so that those who are called may receive the promised eternal inheritance" (9:15). And as the mediator of the new covenant who will make our "promised eternal inheritance" a reality, Jesus's ministry brings what we see in verse 13 and verses 16–17. Jesus brings the promise of ultimate victory over the enemies of God, the new life we have as new creations of God whose hearts and minds are truly being transformed by His law and the everlasting forgiveness for our sins. Only one high priest can be this and do this for us. There are no competitors. He is better! He is the best! Any other object we seek to make central in our walk with God, be it angels, or the law given through the angels, or a great figure like Moses who "was faithful in all God's house as a servant" (3:5), not only can't compare with Christ but doesn't even merit comparison or even consideration "for Jesus has been counted worthy of more glory than Moses—as much more glory as the builder of a house has more honor than the house itself" (3:3). Speaking to believers, as I believe the author is doing, the case He makes for Christ is essential and vital for us to embrace.

Neglect Connections

Is He your great high priest? Before you dismiss this as a secondary or inconsequential part of Jesus's ministry, consider that it was an important enough question for the author to devote much of the first ten chapters of this book addressing. Do you look to Him as "the radiance of the glory of God and the exact imprint of his nature … [who] upholds the universe by the word of his power?" (1:3). Who else can be that? Do we see Him as the one who was "crowned with glory and honor because of the suffering of death, so that by the grace of God he might taste death for everyone"? (2:9). Do we believe He is the one who destroyed "the power of death, that is, the devil, and [delivered] all those who through fear of death were subject to lifelong slavery"? (2:14–15). Do we believe that "Christ is faithful over God's house as a son. And we are his house, if indeed we hold fast our confidence and our boasting in our hope" (3:6) and that "we have come to share in Christ, if indeed we hold our original confidence firm to the end"? (3:14). Do we believe that "since then we have a great high priest who has passed through the heavens, Jesus, the Son of God, let us hold fast our confession. For we do not have a high priest who is unable to sympathize with our weaknesses, but one who in every respect has been tempted as we are, yet without sin?" (4:14–15). If you say yes to these things, "let us then with confidence draw near to the throne of grace, that we may receive mercy and find grace to help in time of need."

Is your great high priest, Jesus Christ, in your life in this way? Is He truly always near and able to always help you and in any circumstance? And as such, is He the greatest influence in your life? Is it your delight to do His will? Just as the wind and waves obey Him, can you say that your life is moved by Him in every way? May it be said of each of us who know Jesus Christ as our Lord and Savior that we know Him as our great high priest as well. May it be said of each of us that "we have this as a sure and steadfast anchor of the soul, a hope that enters into the inner place behind the curtain, where Jesus has gone as a forerunner on our behalf, having become a high priest forever after the order of Melchizedek" (6:19–20). May we be unshakably rooted in Him, that there is no further need to make a case for Christ to us for He has overtaken our lives, body, heart, mind soul, strength, and spirit. May it be that all that we are is given to Him, surrendered to Him, and dependent upon Him. Case closed!

18

How Now Should We Live?

(HEBREWS 10:19–31)

The author has concluded his case for Jesus Christ to his readers in 10:18. Now, the book of Hebrews takes a turn, focusing from now to the end of the book on the kind of life we should live as Christians based on all that we have learned about who Jesus is and all He has done, is doing, and will do to save us. In other words, we've been given what I would call an impassioned theology of Jesus Christ up to 10:18 by a divinely inspired writer with a pastor's heart for his spiritually wayward readers. Now he's going to, with equal passion and heart, spur his readers on to live a faithful life in Christ.

So "how now should we live?" Not surprisingly, we'll see that we should live in a manner pleasing to God, but thankfully, we have all the means we need to live this way through faith in Jesus Christ. We *can* live this life; and because of Christ, our great high priest, we should be confident that we can live this life, that we can "with confidence draw near to the throne of grace, that we may receive mercy and find grace to help in time of need" (4:16). All the help of heaven is available to us to live this life, but as the author's seemingly wayward readers may have given him cause for concern, we can choose a life of sin over Christ. But this is a choice God will not sit idly by and watch, which leads the author to warn his readers for a fourth time, this time about the fearful consequences of such a choice. To choose a life of sin over Christ is, among other things, profoundly foolish because we have the best choice available to us in Christ.

In Christ, We Have All We Need to Confidently Live in a Manner Pleasing to God

Faith is confidence in who Jesus Christ is and His mighty power. In verses 22–25, the author encourages his readers to live a life of faith, hope, and love and to do so with confidence in who Jesus is and what He has done for them. At this point in his message to them, both who Jesus is and what He has done for them is not a mystery. He has spent the better part of the first ten chapters teaching them these very things in his case for Christ, and now he's going to very strongly exhort His readers to live the life Christ has won for them. But coming back to the point that he has a pastor's heart for his readers, he starts this "how now should we live" part of his message in verse 19, saying, "Therefore, *brothers*." He then continues through verse 20, saying, "Since we have confidence to enter the holy places by the blood of Jesus, by the new and living way that he opened for us through the curtain, that is, through his flesh." And we should have confidence to come into God's presence through the way Jesus has made possible by His perfect sacrifice because Jesus Himself teaches us this very same thing confidently in John 14:6 when he says, "I am the way, and the truth, and the life. No one comes to the Father except through me." He is the living way to the Father, and at the Father's right hand, Jesus ceaselessly ministers as our great high priest as the author has so thoroughly demonstrated to us. "And since we have a great priest over the house of God" (verse 21), we can draw near to God by faith.

Verse 22 reads, "Let us draw near with a true heart in *full assurance of faith*, with our hearts sprinkled clean from an evil conscience and our bodies washed with pure water." The Greek lexicon of the New Testament defines the word translated "full assurance" here as "a state of complete certainty."[35] This is faith that sells out completely to God, taking Him at His word without reservation or hesitation. We come to the Father through Jesus Christ with complete certainty because of Jesus Christ, and because of Jesus Christ, we can come to the Father as new creations through the promise of His new covenant to cleanse and transform our inner persons while "our bodies [are] washed with pure water."

This last part of verse 22 most likely refers to our baptism, which is Christ's first command to the believer and Peter ties together how baptism is an outward act that is a response to God through this inward transformation God has done in us. Peter writes in 1 Peter 3:21 (NLT), "And that water is a picture of *baptism*, which *now saves you*, not by removing dirt from your body, but as *a response to God from a clean conscience. It is effective because of the resurrection of Jesus Christ*." (*Saves* is present tense, the act is the response of the saved, and the power to work out our salvation in the act is Jesus's resurrection). This is a picture of a life that can draw near to God because we have unwavering faith in Him; and by His power, He is saving us, He is making us faithful, and our conscience confirms this as we come into His presence. And through faith working in us now in this way, we can have unwavering confidence in God's promises to us for eternity.

We can live with certain hope in God's promise of eternal salvation. Verse 23 reads, "Let us hold fast the *confession of our hope* without wavering, for he who promised is faithful." Very simply put, the author has portrayed our hope throughout the book as certain and focused on our eternal inheritance, and he simply reminds his readers here of a point he has made repeatedly: "He who promised is faithful." To lose hope in God's promises to us for eternity is to call God into question. But with a faith that holds fast to our hope because of who He is and what He's done (and is doing), wavering is out of the question. And so when our lives are rooted in faith in His work in us now and certain hope in His promise of finishing that work for eternity, we can serve one another with "love and good works" (verse 24).

This is the author's third exhortation to his readers based on the confidence they should have in Christ. He says in verse 24, "And let us consider how to stir up one another to love and good works." "Love and good works" are complementary terms. They both essentially are good things we do to meet the needs of others, and what makes them "good" is that they conform to the truth of what God's Word calls us to do, a point John teaches us in 1 John 3:18 when he writes, "Little children, let us not love in word or talk but in deed and in truth." The works of love are selfless. Not seeking our own interest, these works are done solely for the sake of what is good for another as God defines what is good. But because the influence of our old nature lingers throughout our Christian life, we can be very disinclined "to love and good works."

We need one another to stir one another up to live this life of love God calls us to, and the word translated "stir up" here is used only one other time in the New Testament. It's used in its negative sense to describe the "sharp disagreement" Paul and Barnabas had in Acts 15:39. It's used here positively but still carries the force and passion as it's used in Acts 15. In fact, a valid translation of verse 24 is "and let us consider how to *provoke* one another to love and good deeds" (NRSV). As one commentator notes, in using this word here, "It certainly shows that the author expected the 'encouragement' (verse 25) to be bracing and even confrontational rather than merely comforting."

Life in the church is not a spectator sport; it is a full-contact sport! We are invested and impassioned stewards of one another's Christian walk. Being a vital and active part of a faithful church is essential to your Christian walk, so much so that the author begins to transition into the warning part of this passage when he writes in verse 25, "Not neglecting to meet together, as is the habit of some, but encouraging one another, and all the more as you see the Day drawing near." Our Christian life is lived on the pillars of faith, hope, and love; and the context in which it is experienced and lived is within the church. It is through our faith in Christ that God is saving us—transforming our character and nature. It is our hope for eternity that helps us stand fast in our faith and motivates us as well ("all the more as you see the Day drawing near"). And it is our life of love learned and practiced within the church and so within the world as well that proves our love for God is genuine just as Jesus indicated when He taught, "If you love me, you will keep my commandments" (John 14:15, love God, one another, neighbor). Neglecting to be part of the church as it gathers together, and "all the more as you see the Day drawing near" is a bad habit that brings spiritual danger and denies the body the blessing of what God can do through you to "stir up" your brothers and sisters to a faithful life of loving Him by loving others. And it is to the danger of this neglect that the author now turns to by way of a strong warning.

To Choose a Life of Sin over a Faithful Life in Christ Brings Fear of Judgment

A life of willful sin brings a judgment to be feared upon those in covenant relationship with God. My bottom line up front here, folks, is that I believe verses 26–31 are a warning to believers, and the judgment here is not an eternal one. In other words, this passage does not teach that a believer can lose their salvation very similar to the case I made with the warning passage back in Hebrews 6:4–8. If this passage teaches we can lose our salvation, then the book of Hebrews is incoherent because the assurances given throughout the book to those with genuine faith in Jesus Christ are numerous and absolute. But let me make a brief case that the author is talking to believers here.

Remember, he starts the passage in verse 19 by calling his readers "brothers," and notice in verse 26 he writes, "For if *we* go on sinning deliberately." He then writes in verse 29 of the one who goes "on sinning deliberately," that this action profanes "the blood of the covenant by which he was *sanctified*," which must refer to a believer. And lastly, in verse 30, he quotes from Deuteronomy 32:36, saying, "The Lord will judge *his people*." He's clearly addressing believers in this warning passage, but what is the danger to "we [who] go on sinning deliberately after receiving the knowledge of the truth"?

The answer to this question is in the rest of verse 26 and 27 where he writes, "There no longer remains a sacrifice for sins, but a fearful expectation of judgment, and a fury of fire that will consume the adversaries." In a truth I'll flesh out in more depth in a moment, the scripture teaches that God renders judgment rather than forgiveness to His people when they persist in a life of intentional sin, hence "there no longer remains a sacrifice for sins." Notice he doesn't describe the persistent deliberate sin in verse 26, but he's probably referring to any persistent sin in our life *and* the sin in verse 25 of "neglecting to meet together, as is the habit of some" because the *for* at the beginning of verse 26 is explanatory. In other words, verse 26 and following is clearly meant to explain the implications of "neglecting to meet together" and may explain, as well, the implications of the failure to live in the ways verses 22–25 call us to.

So then, persistent willful sin in the life of those in covenant relationship with God risks the danger of judgment, but the author is very careful throughout the book to indicate when something is eternal that he does *not* do here. Many people go to the phrase "fury of fire" in verse 27 and interpret that as the fire of hell or the lake of fire, but in the Greek text, the phrase literally is "fiery zeal," which the NKJV accurately reflects with its rendering "fiery indignation." The fact of the matter is that when God's people deliberately sin against Him, even under the New Covenant, He does not ignore it. And as Hebrews 12:6 teaches, "The Lord disciplines the one he loves and chastises every son whom he receives" to restore His children to a right walk, and this discipline may come to any extreme the Lord chooses for us in this life, including bringing about our death if He wills. I believe this is what happened to Ananias and Sapphira in Acts 5, "And great fear came upon the whole church" (Acts 5:11), as a result. Perhaps less familiar is Paul's warning to a disobedient Corinthian church who were profaning the Lord's Supper by their persistently sinful attitudes and actions as a community. Paul writes in 1 Corinthians 11:27–31:

> Whoever, therefore, eats the bread or drinks the cup of the Lord in an *unworthy manner will be guilty concerning the body and blood of the Lord.* Let a person examine himself, then, and so eat of the bread and drink of the cup. For anyone who eats and drinks without discerning the body eats and drinks *judgment* on himself. *That is why many of you are weak and ill, and some have died.* But if we judged ourselves truly, we would not *be judged.*

It is very possible for believers, because of their sin, to reap judgment from God upon their lives now, including the judgment of sickness and death. This, I believe, is what the author is referring to when he writes, "A fearful expectation of judgment," which itself is a judgment since a life of "fearful expectation" is clearly devoid of the blessing of a life marked by faith, hope, and love. This is the lesson of a Christian who chooses a life of "sinning deliberately after receiving the knowledge of the truth."

This is also another lesson from the shadows. Remember, the author refers to all the aspects of the old covenant as a copy and shadow of the real thing, which Christ brings into our lives, and we saw from 9:1–10 that we can learn lessons from these shadows. One such lesson that carries over into the new covenant is the consequence of deliberate sin or, as the Old Testament describes it, sinning with a high hand. So to reinforce the assertion he makes in verses 26–27, the author goes back to the shadows in verses 28–31, writing,

> Anyone who has set aside the law of Moses dies without mercy on the evidence of two or three witnesses. How much worse punishment, do you think, will be deserved by the one who has trampled underfoot the Son of God, and has profaned *the blood* of the covenant by which he was sanctified, and has outraged the Spirit of grace? For we know him who said, "Vengeance is mine; I will repay." And again, "The Lord will judge his people." It is a fearful thing to fall into the hands of the living God.

Let's unpack this section of text beginning with verse 28. According to the law of Moses, the testimony of two or three witnesses could bring a death sentence. These were not eternal judgments, but judgments experienced in this life and a death verdict could be just as easily rendered for picking up sticks on the Sabbath day as rendered for idolatry and murder (God cares about obedience). The law could be merciless on matters of sins great and small, but none of these sins are as great as setting aside the life Jesus Christ died to win for you. And so the author uses vivid language to describe what such a sin entails: "One who has trampled underfoot the Son of God, and has profaned *the blood* of the covenant by which he was sanctified, and has outraged the Spirit of grace?" Notice again though that this is the sin of one who has been sanctified by Jesus's blood, which, as we know from 10:14 (preceding passage), can't suggest a loss of salvation and eternal judgment: "For by a single offering he has perfected *for all time* those who are being sanctified." Nonetheless, persisting in a life of deliberate sin or even any act of deliberate sin is a cause for "fearful expectation" because it reflects an attitude toward Christ that regards His death and shed blood as a common thing, an attitude God will not ignore when He finds it in His people. As verse 30 teaches, He reserves the right to take vengeance as He wills, and He will judge His people as He wills. "It is a fearful thing to fall into the hands of the living God." How fearful? Ask David.

Neglect Connections

The church today is immersed in a superficial and sappy theology about the nature of our salvation, touting our eternal security in Christ (which we have) as a form of deliverance from present consequences of our sin. "Once saved, always saved," and I agree. But that road of "always saved" is walked with "the living God" (verse 31) who cares about the course of life He has won for us by the blood of His one and only Son. We greatly neglect our great salvation when we fail to understand what the scripture plainly and thoroughly teaches about our life in Christ now, God's demands for holiness, and how He may choose to handle His children above all for His name's sake.

In 2 Samuel 24:1, the scripture reads, "The anger of the LORD was kindled against Israel, and he incited David against them, saying, 'Go, number Israel and Judah.'" The Lord was angry with His people Israel, and as the context of 2 Samuel 24 suggests, David had a determined and persistent issue with pride, most likely over the size of his kingdom. This was evident to David's army commander Joab who said to him, "May the LORD your God add to the people a hundred times as many as they are, while the eyes of my lord the king still see it, *but why does my lord the king delight in this thing?*" (2 Samuel 24:3). "But the king's word prevailed against Joab and the commanders of the army. So, Joab and the commanders of the army went out from the presence of the king to number the people of Israel" (2 Samuel 24:4).

It took Joab and his army nearly ten months to accomplish the task, and Joab reported back to David the greatness of his kingdom. "But David's heart struck him after he had numbered the people. And David said to the LORD, 'I have sinned greatly in what I have done. But now, O LORD, please take away the iniquity of your servant, for I have done very foolishly'" (2 Samuel 24:10). But even though David was repentant, his sin came at a great price. The Lord gave David three choices of judgment, none of which were pleasant. And so David responded to the Lord, "I am in great distress. *Let us fall into the hand of the*

LORD, for his mercy is great; but let me not fall into the hand of man. So, the LORD sent a pestilence on Israel from the morning until the appointed time. And there died of the people from Dan to Beersheba 70,000 men" (2 Samuel 24:14–15). This is David falling "into the hands of the living God" (verse 31), not some wicked and lost soul, a man after God's own heart as Paul refers to David in Acts. "It is a fearful thing to fall into the hands of the living God." How now should we live?

19

"Endure to the End and Be Saved!"

(HEBREWS 10:32–39)

Toward the end of my air force career, I had the opportunity to serve under General Mike Holmes as his deputy commander of the air wing at Bagram Air Base in Afghanistan. Airmen deployed to serve in the wing typically came to serve for deployments ranging from six months to a year; and when they arrived for duty, General Holmes greeted them with his motto "Start right, finish strong," which served as a memorable framework for a two-part message he gave them to express his expectations. To "start right" meant to get off on the right foot, doing the mission according to established tactics, techniques, and procedures under the proven assumption that this sets a standard that tends to continue through the deployment. To "finish strong" is an exhortation to combat the tendency over time to become lax or complacent in the mission. General Holmes demanded that his airmen maintain the same zeal for doing the mission right all the way to the end so that the commendation "well done" could be justifiably given rather than the shame of failure due to negligence. The "well done" is a great and lasting reward. The shame of negligence is a lasting consequence that outweighs any comforts or pleasures failing to "finish strong" may have brought.

In this final passage from chapter 10, the author reminds his readers of how they started right! But sensing that their walk may be lacking the zeal for following Christ faithfully to the finish, he reminds them in verse 36 that "you have need of endurance, so that when you have done the will of God you may receive what is promised." You have need to finish the way you started, for as Jesus teaches in Matthew 10:22, "the one who endures to the end will be saved."

I have heard the Christian life described as "upside-down living." What this statement means is that a life of faith leads us to think and feel and do in ways completely opposite to the way the world views things. For example, as we'll see in this passage, how can suffering be cause for joy? Or how does present loss lead to eternal gain? And why does eternity even matter in a life of here-and-now?

We Joyfully Endure to the End because Our Hope Is for Eternity

But this endurance does presume there was a beginning, something that characterized one's past and is worth meaningfully recollecting. I've mentioned before that commands are very rare in Hebrews, but in verse 32, the author commands his readers to remember how they started right, saying, "But *recall* the former days when, after you were enlightened, you endured a hard struggle with sufferings." These "former days … after [they] were enlightened" points back to the time in their past soon after they came to faith in Jesus, and the command to "recall" is really a command to restore their walk back to the pattern they faithfully followed at that time, the pattern of enduring "a hard struggle with sufferings."

The word translated "hard struggle" here was a word used for wrestling matches. In wrestling, you're in constant contact with your opponent. You don't relax or let down your guard; you endure the match, and you suffer from it because your opponent is trying to overcome you! And if you're not experiencing the personal consequences of the match, then you're obviously no longer in the contest! Wrestlers suffer from what their opponent inflicts upon them: fatigue, burns from the mat, pulled or strained muscles, etc. In verses 33–34, the author expounds upon what his readers suffered in their "contest." They were "sometimes being publicly exposed to reproach and affliction, and sometimes being partners with those so treated. For you had compassion on those in prison, and you joyfully accepted the plundering of your property." I don't think the author is describing injustice suffered here unrelated to their faith in Christ but because of their faith in Christ.

This is the "reproach and affliction" Jesus taught was to be expected in this world when we faithfully follow Him. As He says in John 15:20–21, "Remember the word that I said to you: 'A servant is not greater than his master.' If they persecuted me, they will also persecute you … But all these things they will do to you on account of my name, because they do not know him who sent me." And notice here that the author reminds his readers that they not only suffered in this way, but even when they were not the direct object of the persecution, they stood shoulder to shoulder with their brothers and sisters who were suffering.

This is remarkable because he then reminds them of the price they paid for joining their brethren in the line of fire rather than playing it safe when he writes, "For you had compassion on those in prison, and you joyfully accepted the plundering of your property." Again, this is likely referring to those imprisoned because of their faith in Christ, and we come to better understand the courage displayed in showing such prisoners "compassion" when we understand the dynamic of prisons and being a prisoner in this culture and time.

Prisoners in the ancient world depended on the active help of friends and family for the necessities of life, not just for moral support. Without this kind of "compassion," prisoners would ultimately succumb to death, but coming to a prison to render such aid was also an act of open identification with those in prison who were there because of their faith in Christ. This put visitors at great risk of the same punishment or some other kind of trial like "the plundering of your property." Yet notice they "joyfully accepted" this trial. Why? "Since you knew that you yourselves *had a better possession and an abiding one.*"

We endure to the end because our hope is for eternity, because the treasures of this world and life are worthless compared to the matchless riches of eternity, and we believe this! This mindset of enduring loss now because of the matchless riches of eternity is vitally important in the author's exhortation for living to his readers. He'll come back to it in 11:24–26, writing, "By faith Moses, when he was grown up, refused to be called the son of Pharaoh's daughter, *choosing rather to be mistreated with the people of God* than to enjoy the fleeting pleasures of sin. *He considered the reproach of Christ greater* wealth than the treasures of Egypt, *for he was looking to the reward.*" But again, we're not called merely to endure the trials of persecution, but to do so joyfully. Why?

I want to dig into this fully at the end of this chapter, but here's a preview to the answer to the question "why joyfully?" with Jesus's teaching in Luke 6:22–23: *"Blessed are you when people hate you and when they exclude you and revile you and spurn your name as evil, on account of the Son of Man! Rejoice in that day, and leap for joy,* for behold, your reward is great in heaven." In one sense, this joyful acceptance of persecution speaks to our confidence because it occurs in a Christian life overtaken with confidence in God's promise: His determination to give us an eternal inheritance.

We Endure to the End Because Our Confidence Is in God's Will

A great and constant question in the church is, "What is God's will for my life?" We often address that question over concerns of specifics in our lives, such as, "Should I take this job?" or "Should I go to this college?" or "Should I marry this girl?" or "Should I stay married to this guy?" etc. To that last one, some ladies may have been seeking truth through an old church bulletin that once carried this announcement: "Ladies, don't forget the rummage sale. It's a chance to get rid of those things not worth keeping around the house. Bring your husbands." All kidding aside though, the question "What is God's will for my life?" is often asked out of concern over details that would likely, by God's grace, take care of themselves if we simply sought to answer this question by doing what the scripture calls us to do.

God's will for our lives is to surrender it to Him now to receive His eternal reward. I think this is the plain point made in verses 35–36, which read, "Therefore do not throw away your confidence, which has a great reward. For you have need of endurance, so that when you have done the will of God you may receive what is promised." As we've seen throughout Hebrews, their confidence is in Christ, and it's not a vain confidence. Their walk started right—with confidence—because as 4:16 teaches us, "Let us then with confidence draw near to the throne of grace, that we may receive mercy and find grace to help in time of need." In those times of need in the face of persecution, these believers can "recall" (verse 32) that Jesus was their "grace to help," and His promise to always be there for them (and us) is just as sure as His promise of "a great reward." So mindful of their *right start* in Christ, he urges them to *finish strong* in Christ: "You have need of endurance, so that when you have done the will of God you may receive what is promised."

That phrase "when you have done the will of God" speaks to the believer finishing her or his race well and faithfully. God's will for our lives is to surrender it to Him now by living as Jesus's disciple, as one who obeys all He has commanded, knowing He is with you to the end of the age (Matthew 28:20) to bring you "grace to help in time of need" in every circumstance. In essence, this is a life of an enduring trust in His Word over trust in your circumstances because the one who is always with you is greater than your circumstances. A life so surrendered to God will be confident at Christ's return.

As we've seen the author do a few times in the book, he quotes from the Greek translation of the Old Testament in verses 37–38, from Habakkuk 2:3–4 as well as possibly from Isaiah 26:20. Both Old Testament passages have the same context: God's promise to

His people that He will ultimately come and act in judgment against their adversaries and that they must patiently endure trial for a time until He does. Interestingly, the Greek text of Habakkuk 2:3–4 makes an interpretive twist of the Hebrew text that God's means of deliverance will be "the coming one," the Messiah.

Verses 37–38 read, "For, 'Yet a little while, and the coming one will come and will not delay; but my righteous one shall live by faith, and if he shrinks back, my soul has no pleasure in him.'" Christ is coming, and where God demands vengeance against those who bring "reproach and affliction" upon us and plunder our property because we follow Jesus, our Lord and coming King, the Lion of Judah, will bring that vengeance perfectly. And no person of this world, though they might even take your life, can take the reward Christ will bring to His "righteous one" who has lived "by faith." And when Christ comes, the one who has endured to the end will look upon His Lord with confidence. "And he will be upheld, for the Lord is able to make him stand," as Paul teaches in Romans 14:4.

They say the proof is in the pudding and the day of Christ's return will be the test that proves faith as genuine or not. I believe that's the point in the statement, "If he shrinks back, my soul has no pleasure in him." It's a statement of a future reaction to "the coming one" when He comes, and it is a reaction that leads to God's everlasting judgment rather than reward as we see in verse 39, for the author continues encouraging his readers like a loving pastor when he writes, "But *we are not of those who shrink back* and are destroyed, but of those who have faith and preserve their souls" ("those who shrink back … are *destroyed*," indicating a lasting destruction). But this is not who they are! They are "those who have faith and preserve their souls," and this is not a faith that comes from the storehouses of our own power. Remember, as Peter teaches in 1 Peter 1:5, it is the faith of those who "by God's power are being guarded through faith for a salvation ready to be revealed in the last time." Endurance in our life of faith to the end must be our unquestioned commitment because it is the life God promises to produce in us. But we walk in the obedience of faith, not in our own confidence to endure, but in the confidence that the Lord Jesus is able to make us endure.

Neglect Connections

There is a necessary narrow application from this passage for us as twenty-first-century American Christians. The author writes in 11:1, "Faith is the assurance of things hoped for." We all want assurance of our salvation, and we see that "faith" brings this assurance, but how does this practically work in our Christian lives?

As we've seen in Hebrews, and as we see throughout the Bible, faith is not merely belief. Remember, James teaches that "even the demons believe—and shudder!" (James 2:19). Faith is an investment in our lives to study and know God's Word and then seek, by God's grace and the power of His Holy Spirit, to live a life of obedience to God's Word, even if our obedience comes at the cost of our well-being, freedom, or even our lives. We trust Him, as demonstrated by our faithful attitudes and actions, even in the face of trial and persecution knowing that *faithfulness brings us God's best both now and in eternity*. And in return, we gain assurance of our salvation because God proves Himself faithful in real and vivid and irrefutable ways in our lives through His "grace to help in time of need" (4:16). So then, we endure affliction together (church is a team contact sport) and we "joyfully [accept] the plundering of [our] property" when it is the price to pay for following Jesus Christ. But wait, this isn't a time for joy; this is a time for calling our lawyer to defend our inalienable rights!

This is an American theology, but it's not a very biblical one. Remember, Jesus teaches us that suffering for His name's sake is a blessing when he says, "Blessed are you when people hate you and when they exclude you and revile you and spurn your name as evil, on account of the Son of Man! Rejoice in that day, and leap for joy" (Luke 6:22–23). It's a blessing and a cause for joy, but why?

In Acts 5, the apostles were arrested by the Jewish supreme council for teaching and preaching about Jesus; and in Acts 5:40–41, Luke writes that when the council called in the apostles, "They beat them and charged them not to speak in the name of Jesus, and let them go. Then they left the presence of the council, *rejoicing* that *they were counted worthy to suffer dishonor for the name*." Why is enduring persecution faithfully a blessing and joy? Because the persecution is God's clearest and most powerful way of telling you He has counted you worthy! Why are we worthy? Because we are never more Christlike than when we endure suffering for doing the will of God. In 1 Peter 4:13–14, Peter teaches, "But rejoice insofar as you share Christ's sufferings, that you may also rejoice and be glad when his glory is revealed. If you are insulted for the name of Christ, you are blessed, because the Spirit of glory and of God rests upon you." Much could be said of these verses, but notice again that enduring persecution for Christ's sake is counted as a blessing and cause for joy. Why? Because it affirms to us that "the Spirit of glory and of God rests upon you."

Brothers and sisters, we should desire to endure faithfully to the end, especially in the midst of persecution and tribulations suffered for Christ's sake, because God's great purpose in bringing us into those times (and He does) is not so we can demand our rights to be forever kept from those moments, but so that God can give us the blessed assurance that we are His both now and forever through His mighty work in us in those times. This is why these times are cause for joy, and as Americans, I believe our faith is stunted because *we have stronger cultural convictions than we do biblical convictions* in this area and we passionately trade the blessings of God for the blessings of a worldly form of deliverance as a result.

The blessings of God and His work in us in these times are matchless riches: a point Paul makes in Romans 5:2–5 that I will leave you with in the hope my point here is not lost or resisted or angrily rejected.

> Through him we have also obtained access by faith into this grace in which we stand, and we rejoice in hope of the glory of God. Not only that, but *we rejoice in our sufferings*, knowing that *suffering produces endurance*, and *endurance produces character*, and *character produces hope*, and hope does not put us to shame, because God's love has been poured into our hearts through the Holy Spirit who has been given to us.

No pain, no gain. Don't trade the character and hope Christ gives you when you joyfully endure such times. Endure to the end and be saved!

20

A Great Cloud of Witnesses Part 1
(HEBREWS 11:1–7)

O r as the author will describe the likes of these examples in 12:1, we have "a great cloud of witnesses!" This passage is simple to sum up. In verses 1–3, the author gives us the key for how we should read and understand the examples of faith in chapter 11, and then he proceeds to illustrate for us in a powerful way what a life of faith in God looks like through these examples. Now a heads-up: we're not going to get to all the examples just yet. In fact, we're going to take three more chapters to learn from all of them. So with a long but wonderful road ahead of us, let's begin with the main takeaway each of these examples gives to us.

A Life of Faith Takes God at His Word, Lives Accordingly, and Experiences His Commendation

Since verses 1–3 give us the framework by which we should read and understand these examples in chapter 11, let's take a few minutes to unpack what they say. I'll be taking the verses a bit out of order to do so, beginning with verse 3 where we learn that faith exalts the testimony of God over the testimony of the visible order, for it is "by faith we understand that the universe was created by the word of God, so that what is seen was not made out of things that are visible." Genesis 1:3 reads, "And God said, 'Let there be light,' and there was light." In this first step of creation, and each step that followed, we learn that the visible creation we live in came fully into being through the invisible reality of the God whom we trust in. *There is no way to work your way backward through the evidence from the visible creation to find God apart from faith in God.*

As verse 3 teaches, it is "by faith we understand" this creation to be God's handiwork and that what we see can't be adequately explained by "what is seen." It is true as Paul teaches in Romans 1:20 that we are all without excuse because God's "invisible attributes, namely, his eternal power and divine nature, have been clearly perceived, ever since the creation of the world, in the things that have been made"; but remember, Paul is just beginning to make his case in these verses that we "all have sinned and fall short of the glory of God" (Romans 3:23). Knowing that he is making a case that we are all sinners, Paul goes on to teach what our sin nature, apart from faith in God, inevitably does with the testimony of creation. Even though we know the creation points to God, we "[exchange this] truth about God for a lie and [worship] and [serve] the creature rather than the Creator" (Romans 1:25). The world looks at creation as a self-contained visible reality because our sin nature wants to see it this way. It is only "by faith" in the testimony of God's Word over every other source that we come to understand God's invisible reality as both the power and source that explains and sustains the visible world. So if the invisible reality of God is what truly governs the nature of creation, then this is true for us as well. Therefore, faith embraces the testimony of God's word as supreme over what is seen and lives accordingly.

The author writes in verse 1, "Now faith is the assurance of things hoped for, the conviction of things not seen." When you see the words *assurance* and *conviction*, you could conclude that the author is teaching here that you just need to be certain, that if you just believe really hard, you'll have faith. But these words have a richer meaning than this that the CSB brings out in its translation: "Now faith is the *reality* of what is hoped for, the *proof* of what is not seen." Just as we saw in verse 3, faith truly believes in the power and promises of the invisible reality of God according to His Word and not in some vain or irrational way. As Paul commands believers in Romans 12:2 (NASB), "Be transformed by the renewing of your mind, so that you may *prove* what the will of God is." A life lived in obedience to God's Word becomes the living proof of the invisible God and embraces the promises of His Word as true even while they are still something to be "hoped for." And as Paul teaches in Romans 5:5 (NASB), this "hope does not disappoint."

Through this life of faith, the invisible reality of God is experienced. The author writes in verses 1–2, "Now faith is the assurance of things hoped for, the conviction of things not seen. For by it the people of old received their commendation." The word *commendation* literally means to bear witness or testimony to something; and in the sense that it's used here, it means the commendation of God's favor, that in His eyes, the saints of old received a good testimony from Him for their faith, as evidenced to us by the fact that we still have their testimony in the scriptures! Simply put, if we believe according to God's Word that the invisible reality of His power and promises are true, so much so that we reckon it to be true and order our lives accordingly, even if our circumstances completely contradict what His Word promises, then we will receive God's commendation. By His great grace working in and through our obedience, He will prove His power in us to be real and His promises to us to be true in His time and according to His will (which is for our best). In other words, He will prove to us *and in us* that His invisible reality we're called to embrace by faith is very real and very true. The likes of Noah, Abraham, and Stephen all experienced this and proved what God says of His faithful people: "My righteous one shall live by faith" (10:38). But these three aren't the only examples we have.

A Great "Cloud of Witnesses" Teach Us How to Live This Life of Faith: Abel

And the "cloud" begins with the example of Abel. The author writes in verse 4, "By faith Abel offered to God a more acceptable sacrifice than Cain, through which he was commended as righteous, God commending him by accepting his gifts. And through his faith, though he died, he still speaks." This is the author's brief description of Abel's faith, but how does it apply to us? Using the framework from verses 1 to 3, we need to first ask the question, "In what way did Abel's life demonstrate he embraced the testimony of God as supreme?"

In Genesis 4:3–5, Moses writes, "In the course of time Cain brought to the LORD an offering of the fruit of the ground, and Abel also brought of the firstborn of his flock and of their fat portions. And the LORD had regard for Abel and his offering, but for Cain and his offering he had no regard." With the limited details we have from the Genesis account and the comparison between Cain and Abel, Abel brought more than "*an offering.*" He brought the first of his flock and their best portions. We don't have the details of this in the Genesis account to explain why Abel brought a better offering, but one can infer that

Abel had a relationship with God through which God taught Abel what was pleasing to Him. In a principle seen throughout the scriptures, God teaches us that all we have is His and that a life of faith trusts Him by giving our best back to Him *first* and trusting in Him for whatever comes from that. It makes no worldly sense to do this, but in the invisible reality of God, it makes perfect sense to do this if you trust in His reality. And through these works of faith, Abel experienced God's commendation.

As we see in Genesis 4, "The LORD had regard for Abel and his offering." Abel received a favorable testimony from God, but notice what this brought into Abel's life. He was the first victim of persecution and murder for his faith. He was the first martyr. But Genesis 4:10 goes on to show that God chastised Cain, telling him, "The voice of your brother's blood is crying to me from the ground," in essence, teaching that God will vindicate His faithful people through the promise of eternity for them and judgment against their enemies, not unlike what we see in Revelation 6:10–11, where the faithful, who will be slain during the tribulation, cry out *from their place in heaven* (where I believe Abel is as well), "'O Sovereign Lord, holy and true, how long before you will judge and avenge our blood on those who dwell on the earth?' Then they were each given a white robe and told to rest a little longer."

Remember, the author has just told his readers, "You have need of endurance, so that when you have done the will of God you may receive what is promised" (10:36); and he will tell them in 12:3–4, "Consider him who endured from sinners such hostility against himself, so that you may not grow weary or fainthearted. In your struggle against sin you have not yet resisted to the point of shedding your blood," to the point of "shedding your blood" like Abel and Stephen did, for example. And with his command to them to "consider him who endured from sinners such hostility against himself," the implication is that Christ will be a *faithful high priest* to the faithful to strengthen them in the times when their faith will cost them their lives, if we trust in His invisible reality over our worldly reality.

So to sum up, here's Abel's example to us of what our life of faith should look like: always offer to God what is best and first and trust Him with the results, and should the results be hostility from sinners, even to the point of death, then trust in Him to sustain you by His power as you heed His command to endure in such times. That's Abel; now let's see what we learn from the example of Enoch.

A Great "Cloud of Witnesses" Teach Us How to Live This Life of Faith: Enoch

In verses 5–6, we read, "By faith Enoch was taken up so that he should not see death, and he was not found, because God had taken him. Now before he was taken, he was commended as having pleased God. And without faith it is impossible to please him, for whoever would draw near to God *must believe that he exists and that he rewards those who seek him.*" So then, once more, in what way did Enoch's life demonstrate he embraced the testimony of God as supreme?

The clue here is that Enoch "was commended as having pleased God," but what kind of life pleases God? In the brief account of Enoch's life in Genesis 5, Moses tells us twice that Enoch "walked with God." The only other individual in all of the scriptures who is commended in this way is Noah (once). Nineteenth-century Scottish theologian Marcus Dods gives a great description of what it means to walk with God as Enoch did.

> Enoch walked with God because he was His friend and liked His company, because he was going in the same direction as God, and had no desire for anything but what lay in God's path. We walk with God when He is in all our thoughts; not because we consciously think of Him at all times, but because He is naturally suggested to us by all we think of; as when any person or plan or idea has become important to us, no matter what we think of, our thought is always found recurring to this favorite object, *so with the godly man everything has a connection with God and must be ruled by that connection.*[36] (my emphasis)

Enoch walked with God because it was his delight to do so, joyfully submitting to the rule of God's will over his life, which we know is expressed to us today in His Word. We get this sense of passion in Enoch's walk with God when the author uses Enoch's example to make the point that faith must believe that God "rewards those who seek him." The NIV translates this phrase as "rewards those who *earnestly* seek him," drawing out that the word for "seek" here has a more intense meaning than the word normally used for "seek" in the New Testament. And keep in mind that Genesis 5:22 indicates Enoch walked with God in this earnest way for three hundred years! And in living a life pleasing to God, Enoch experienced God's commendation.

And in no ordinary way! "By faith Enoch was taken up so that he should not see death, and he was not found, because God had taken him" (verse 5). He was commended by God for his life before he was taken up, but Enoch was blessed with being delivered from the death that is the terrible consequence of our sin. At a time when the world was hurtling toward the great wickedness and worldwide judgment of Noah's day, Enoch received what God promises to the faithful of all ages through the timeless power of Christ's life, death, and resurrection: deliverance from the finality of death and restoration to eternal life with God!

So then, let's sum up the application of Enoch's example to us. The life of faith we're called to is a moment-by-moment, day-by-day, year-by-year, joyful, and earnest pursuit of a life in submission to God's will. It's a heart-and-soul walk that makes us realize that in seeking and walking with God, we experience the life He gives: the life of incomparable worth and consuming joy. And like Enoch, we too will be delivered from the finality of death through this life of faith, including the great hope we all have of being delivered like Enoch—to not experience physical death—for Paul teaches that those who are alive when Christ returns "will be caught up together with them in the clouds to meet the Lord in the air, and so we will always be with the Lord" (1 Thessalonians 4:17). This is quite a cloud of witnesses so far, but we have one more witness to consider for now: the example of Noah.

A Great "Cloud of Witnesses" Teaches Us How to Live This Life of Faith: Noah

"By faith Noah, being warned by God concerning events as yet unseen, in reverent fear constructed an ark for the saving of his household. By this he condemned the world and became an heir of the righteousness that comes by faith" (verse 7). So then, in what way did Noah's life demonstrate he embraced the testimony of God as supreme? Genesis 6:9 indicates that Noah, like Enoch, "walked with God"; but with Noah, we get a much more vivid and detailed picture of what this looks like. The word of God came directly to Noah "concerning events as yet unseen," in other words, still in the future. And Noah clearly demonstrated by His obedience in the great undertaking of building the ark that he took God's word more seriously than the evidence of his eyes, and like Enoch, He persisted in his walk with God and did so for what was probably a great length of time (and likely through a great deal of ridicule) in building the ark despite the evidence of his eyes *giving no support to God's warning.* Noah was unwavering in his trust in the unseen reality of God despite his circumstances, and note that he did so with "reverent fear." His closeness with

God as one who "walked with God" did not diminish Noah's healthy respect for the fact that "our God is a consuming fire," as the author teaches in 12:29. Mindful of this "reverent fear" that Noah had for God, Noah experienced God's commendation.

The works of Noah's faith "condemned the world" just as much as they made him "an heir of the righteousness that comes by faith." That's a difficult point to get our minds around, but I believe the scriptures teach in several places that God will use the faithfulness of the faithful to judge the faithlessness of the faithless. For example, in Luke 11:32, Jesus brings a charge against a Jewish crowd He earlier described as an "evil generation," saying, "The men of Nineveh will rise up at the judgment with this generation and condemn it, for they repented at the preaching of Jonah, and behold, something greater than Jonah is here." But in addition to knowing He will be commended in this way in the judgment, Noah experienced God's commendation in that God brought the promised reality of a worldwide judgment through the flood to pass that validated Noah's work of faith: the work of building the ark. And by this work of Noah, God saved Noah and his household. And because of his faith, Noah too is an heir of the eternity God promises to the righteous by their faith, a righteousness God reckoned to Noah by faith, but also a righteousness God brought to pass in Noah's life through his faith and the works that proved his faith to be genuine because, remember, "faith is the reality of what is hoped for, the proof of what is not seen" (11:1 CSB).

So then, one last time for now, our takeaway from Noah's life of faith is this: Be unwavering in your trust in the unseen reality of God despite your circumstances for He is faithful to confirm your trust, and as you walk with Him, don't lose sight of the fact that a close walk with God sustains a "reverent fear" of God. And like Noah, always know that no set of present or future circumstances, including God's wrath being brought upon the entire world, will keep you from inheriting God's promises for eternity to His faithful people.

Neglect Connections

Hebrews 11 teaches believers what genuine faith looks like—the kind of faith that saves us—and the examples challenge us greatly because we have watered down faith to nothing more than agreement with an idea. The examples of Abel, Enoch, and Noah challenge us in particular ways, so I'll leave us for now with the challenge of their examples by way of questions for us to ponder in introspection. Do you always offer to God what is best and first and trust Him with the results? Do you believe your high priest will be faithful to give you the "mercy and find grace to help in time of need" (4:16) when you face hostility from sinners, or is your first response in such moments to look elsewhere for your help? Is your life of faith in Christ a moment-by-moment, day-by-day, year-by-year, joyful, and earnest pursuit of a life in submission to His will? If so, do you experience the life of incomparable worth and consuming joy Christ gives to us now? And do you trust our great high priest to deliver us from the finality of death by the promise and power of His resurrection? In light of this promise of resurrection, are you unwavering in your trust in the unseen reality of God despite your circumstances, knowing that no set of present or future circumstances, including God's wrath being brought upon the entire world, will keep you from inheriting God's promises for eternity? Lastly, does your close walk with God sustain a "reverent fear" of God?

21

A Great Cloud of Witnesses Part 2

(HEBREWS 11:8–22)

Many of us, I'm sure, have friends we dearly love who have moved away to settle in places we've never been before. Imagine that you really want to go visit these friends whom you know well and long to be with again. So armed with directions they've given you, you head out into the unknown. When you finally get in the vicinity of their home, you remember them telling you to trust their directions because things will become confusing as you near their house, that you're going to think you're going north when you're really going south. The landmarks and signs will seem to convince you that you've made a wrong turn or gone too far. So as you drive and drive and drive, you feel the pressure mount. Your spouse and your kids say, "This can't be the way. You're getting us lost!" Then you have that conversation with yourself, asking, "Should I keep driving and look foolish, or stop and call my friends and feel foolish when they tell me 'you're on the right track' or 'turn around and go back to the point where you didn't feel lost and try again'?" If you think about it, the way you answer this question has a lot to do with what you believe about the person who gave you directions!

As we continue with this next round of examples of faith from Hebrews 11, a central theme in the life of the central example of faith in this passage, Abraham, is trusting in God's directions, not because they make sense on a human level, but because the destination He promises He's leading us to is wonderful beyond compare and beyond our wildest imaginations: "The city that has foundations, whose designer and builder is God" (verse 10), "a better country, that is, a heavenly one" (verse 16). In Abraham's journey, God's directions often make no worldly sense. But through the example of Abraham's journey, it's as if the Lord is telling us to trust him. We are never foolish for following His lead. He knows exactly where He's leading us to. Live your life as if He has already brought you to your destination, whether you see it in this life or not! So let's continue this journey through a "great cloud of witnesses" with the patriarchs, but primarily focusing on Abraham and Sarah.

A Great "Cloud of Witnesses" Teach Us How to Live This Life of Faith: Abraham and Sarah

Verses 8–11 read,

> By faith Abraham obeyed when he was called to go out to a place that he was to receive as an inheritance. And he went out, not knowing where he was going. By faith he went to live in the land of promise, as in a foreign land, living in tents with Isaac and Jacob, heirs with him of the same promise. For he was looking forward to the city that has foundations, whose designer and builder is God. By faith Sarah herself received power to conceive, even when she was past the age, since she considered him faithful who had promised.

Remember the framework from 11:1–3 for understanding the examples in Hebrews 11. They took God at His word, lived accordingly, and were commended for it (God favorably affirmed their faith to them in some demonstrable way). So then, in what way did Abraham and Sarah's life demonstrate they embraced the testimony of God in this way?

Let's look at Abraham first. Right away in verse 8, we see, "Abraham obeyed when he was called," and this calling was from God as we know from Genesis 12. There's no indication here or in Genesis 12 that Abraham hesitated in the slightest to heed God's direction: "And he went out, not knowing where he was going!" This is remarkable given Abraham's age (seventy-five, Genesis 12:4) and what Abraham was leaving, for the Lord tells Abraham in Genesis 12:1, "Go from your country and your kindred and your father's house." In other words, leave everything that brings you security, comfort, and stability. We see in verses 8–9 that the author summarizes one of God's promises to Abraham: that the place God was bringing Abraham to was a land He promised Abraham, along with his son Isaac and grandson Jacob. It was a land they would receive as an inheritance. But notice their circumstances. They're each heir of the land according to God's promise, but they're living in tents! Look carefully at this promise God made to them as recorded in Genesis 17:8: "And I will give to you and to your offspring after you the land of your sojournings, all the land of Canaan, for *an everlasting possession*, and I will be their God."

The land is not just an inheritance; it's an everlasting inheritance for Abraham, Isaac, and Jacob. They will dwell there forever in right relationship with God, but for now, it's "the land of your sojournings"! A time will come when it's their inheritance forever, but in this life, they're going to "live in the land of promise, as in a foreign land" (verse 9). And Abraham took God at His word and lived accordingly. Why? Because to Abraham, God's promised future was just as real as his present unsatisfactory circumstances, "for he was looking forward to the city that has foundations, whose designer and builder is God" (verse 10); the city that we know from Revelation 21 is the New Jerusalem with its twelve foundations that will come down from heaven to the new earth as God's dwelling place among His people for eternity.

Sarah's example shows the same pattern in that, despite being barren and well past childbearing years, she trusted in God's promise of a son "since she considered him faithful who had promised" (verse 11). Now those of us familiar with Sarah's story know that Sarah was more skeptical than faithful when God initially promised her a son, but in the sum of her life in the matter of Isaac's conception and birth, as one commentator puts it, "Even Sarah's ("Sarah herself," ESV, verse 11) acceptance of a promise that at first she seemed to hear with indifference is to the mind of the author of Hebrews a venture into the unseen world, which faith makes real."[37] Abraham and Sarah took God at His word, lived accordingly, and so Abraham and Sarah experienced God's commendation.

When Sarah heard God's promise that she would conceive and give birth to a son in Genesis 18, the story clearly reveals Sarah's doubts and frustration with life as well as her fear in knowing her thoughts and attitudes were known to God. In Genesis 18:14, the Lord responded to Sarah's reaction to His promise, saying, "Is anything too hard for the Lord? At the appointed time I will return to you, about this time next year, and Sarah shall have a son." God promised Abraham the land as an everlasting inheritance to him and his descendants; therefore, despite the seeming impossibility of having descendants, Abraham and Sarah experienced God's favorable affirmation of their faith in a very demonstrable way: He did the impossible! "Therefore, from one man, and him as good as dead, were born descendants as many as the stars of heaven and as many as the innumerable grains of sand by the seashore" (verse 12). This is an amazing example of Abraham and Sarah's obedient faith and God's real affirmation of their faith, but let's look at one more example from Abraham's life in verses 17–22: the example of Abraham in a time of testing.

Verses 17–22 are a powerful segue to what we've just covered. The backdrop is Genesis 22, and the account there is a vivid and significant example from Abraham's life, showing us how Abraham's life demonstrated his embrace of the testimony of God as supreme. Abraham and Sarah have received Isaac, the promised descendant through whom God's eternal promises to Abraham would come to pass, but in Genesis 22, God commands Abraham to sacrifice Isaac. And once again, Abraham obeys God without any indication from the text that he was hesitant to do so even though the command to take the life of the son through whom God's promises must be realized made absolutely no sense! But as we see in verse 17, Abraham's faith, as God is inclined to do with His people, was being put to the test. From our perspective, I think most (all?) of us would be thinking, *Lord, these directions can't be right! We must be lost! I think we need to turn around and try this again!* From God's perspective, it is "Abraham, do you trust me? Do you believe I know where I'm leading you and Isaac to?" What was Abraham to do?

In Genesis 22:5, after a three-day journey to the place where God commanded Isaac to be sacrificed, Abraham said to the young men who accompanied him, "Stay here with the donkey. *I and the boy will* go over there and worship and *come again to you.*" As you may know, God kept Abraham from taking the boy's life at the moment he "was in the act of offering up his only son" (verse 17), but Abraham's faith had already won the battle. Faith demands that God's commands must be obeyed, yet faith demands that one take God's promises as unbreakable; in fact, they are to be taken as that which is as good as done! How do you reconcile the apparent horrible contradiction between this command and the promise? Obey the command and trust in the promise: "He considered that God was able even to raise him from the dead" (verse 19), so much so that he told his young men, "I and the boy will … come again to you." This is amazing faith, and consistent with what we've seen thus far in chapter 11, Abraham experienced God's commendation; in the case of Isaac, this happened quickly!

Coming back to verse 19, the author writes, "He considered that God was able even to raise him from the dead, from which, figuratively speaking, he did receive him back."

Figuratively speaking, God gave Isaac back to Abraham as one alive from the dead for Isaac must have been as good as dead from Abraham's perspective. God's favorable affirmation of Abraham's faith was immediate, but it was also lasting. In Genesis 22:16–18, the Lord immediately tells Abraham,

> By myself I have sworn, declares the Lord, because you have done this and have not withheld your son, your only son, I will surely bless you, and I will surely multiply your offspring as the stars of heaven and as the sand that is on the seashore. And your offspring shall possess the gate of his enemies, and in your offspring shall all the nations of the earth be blessed, because you have obeyed my voice.

God's promise of future blessing to Abraham was because of his *obedience in faith*, and it is a remarkable promise of a remarkable future for Abraham and his descendants. I think this is why we get the somewhat cursory mention of Isaac, Jacob, and Joseph: three successive generations of descendants following Abraham of whom most of the last twenty-seven chapters of the book of Genesis is dedicated to. Much could be said of them, but here in verses 20–22, what seems to matter to the author is that they were like Abraham: they lived in the present (not perfectly) in light of God's promises for the future as examples we must learn from.

The "Takeaway" from the Examples of Faith in This Passage

If you remember from the previous chapter, I gave you my sense of the takeaway after we covered each example, but I don't do that here. The reason for this is because I believe the author gives us his takeaway from these examples pretty explicitly in verses 13–16, where he writes,

> These all died in faith, not having received the things promised, but having seen them and greeted them from afar, and having acknowledged that they were strangers and exiles on the earth. For people who speak thus make it clear that they are seeking a homeland. If they had been thinking of that land from which they had gone out, they would have had opportunity to

return. But as it is, they desire a better country, that is, a heavenly one. Therefore, God is not ashamed to be called their God, for he has prepared for them a city.

When he writes "These all died in faith" at the beginning of verse 13, he's referring to Abraham, Sarah, Isaac, and Jacob; but his thought here certainly applies to all who die "in faith" like Joseph in verse 22 who, *at the end of his life,* made mention of the exodus of the Israelites and gave directions concerning his bones." Joseph knew his people would come under slavery in Egypt but that God promised He would deliver them from slavery and back into the land of promise. He directed them that when this came to pass (centuries after he would die), his bones were to be buried in the land of promise. Verse 21 refers to Jacob blessing Joseph's two sons according to God's sovereign direction for the future of His people, and Jacob too does so "by faith ... when dying."

So then, takeaway no. 1 from the examples in this passage is to hold fast to a life of faith to your dying breath. In fact, I think a life that takes God at His word and lives accordingly up to our last breath is perhaps the most powerful testimony we can give. Ninie Hammon, a journalist in Louisville, Kentucky, wrote an article back in 2005 about a youth pastor whom she came to know of because she covered the story of his horrific death in 1988 when a drunk driver crashed into a bus carrying a church youth group, killing twenty-four children and three adults. Witnesses who survived the crash told of Chuck Kytta, the youth minister of the church who was seated in the front of the bus behind the driver. When the gas tank exploded a heartbeat after the collision, he was instantly encircled in flames. When Chuck saw the flames around him, witnesses said he looked up, lifted his hands, and cried out, "Jesus, I'm coming home!" Some of the kids said he was smiling. As a result of Chuck's life of faith, taking God at His promise and living accordingly up to his last breath, Ninie Hammon would come to Christ. She says, "Chuck Kytta planted a seed in me that took root in my heart. One day, I will see Chuck in heaven. I'll tell him how the manner of his death pointed me toward eternal life."[38]

A second takeaway from these verses is that we're called to have an unambiguous commitment to live in light of God's promises for the future beyond this life on this earth. "These [who] died in faith" knew of God's promises and knew this life would not see them come to pass, and so they "acknowledged that they were strangers and exiles on the earth." Therefore, as the text indicates, a life of faith looks forward to what God has in store. It seeks "a homeland." It desires "a better country—that is, a heavenly one"—and seeks no "opportunity to return" to "that land from which they had gone out." Is it your intention to die "in faith" like these?

Neglect Connections

Applying the life of faith from these examples to our life as Christ's followers in His church, consider Jesus's words in Luke 9:62: "No one who puts his hand to the plow and looks back *is fit* for the kingdom of God." Recollecting God's work in the past life of your church is a wonderful thing to spur you on to thankfulness and to remind you of the confidence we should have in His faithfulness, but kingdom work plows ahead, not backward! The work we're charged with as Christ's church is kingdom work. Like Abraham, this is the work of faith that obeys when we're called; and as "strangers and exiles on the earth," our labors in Christ are to see fields ahead of us that are white for harvest, to share the Gospel and its great promise of an eternal inheritance that moves lost people to "desire a better country, that is, a heavenly one." And when such light attachment to this world and deep attachment to His kingdom overtakes our desires in a life of faith, then we receive the great commendation from God that verse 16 teaches: "Therefore, God is not ashamed to be called their God, for he has prepared for them a city."

I once heard it said of the Christian life that the two greatest testimonies of the Gospel we can offer is in how we live and how we die. I have been blessed to witness brothers and sisters die "in faith." They die with peace as their companion in their departure and joy and longing as their passion for their destination. But I've also witnessed Christians die as practical atheists, terrified over what they're facing and pushing their plow along an erratic course as they head to the finish looking back. But if we truly take God at His word, regarding Him and His promises as eternally steadfast in any and every circumstance and living accordingly, then we ought to die accordingly. We are "strangers and exiles on the earth" (verse 13). We should "make it clear that [we] are seeking a homeland" (verse 14). We should "desire a better country—that is, a heavenly one"—for our God "has prepared for [us] a city" (verse 16).

> Then I saw a new heaven and a new earth, for the first heaven and the first earth had passed away, and the sea was no more. And I saw the holy city, new Jerusalem, coming down out of heaven from God, prepared as a bride

adorned for her husband. And I heard a loud voice from the throne saying, "Behold, the dwelling place of God is with man. He will dwell with them, and they will be his people, and God himself will be with them as their God. He will wipe away every tear from their eyes, and death shall be no more, neither shall there be mourning, nor crying, nor pain anymore, for the former things have passed away." And he who was seated on the throne said, "Behold, I am making all things new." (Revelation 21:1–5)

22

A Great Cloud of Witnesses Part 3

(HEBREWS 11:23–31)

We now move into our third chapter from Hebrews 11, and as we've studied this chapter, I hope you've noticed that the author has picked examples that move us chronologically through redemption history. He begins with examples from before the flood, then moves into examples from the time of the patriarchs, and now moves into the time of Moses and the Exodus. In Romans 15:4, Paul writes, "For whatever was written in former days was written for our instruction, that through endurance and through the encouragement of the Scriptures we might have hope," and so I think the author gives us these examples to encourage us to follow them in our own walk. But I also think he makes this progression through time to convey to his readers that *they* can pick up this progression and walk in this way as well and so be an example to others as well, that they can become a part of "a great cloud of witnesses."

And so can we if we follow their example, which throughout Hebrews 11 is this: a life of faith takes God at His word, lives accordingly, and experiences His commendation. We've seen this pattern of faith demonstrated in the saints of old before the flood and by the great patriarchs like Abraham, and now we'll see this pattern again in the likes of Moses and others who faithfully followed God in the time of the Exodus and the conquest of the Promised Land.

A Great "Cloud of Witnesses" Teaches Us How to Live This Life of Faith: Moses's Parents

In verse 23, we read, "By faith Moses, when he was born, was hidden for three months by his parents, because they saw that the child was beautiful, and they were not afraid of the king's edict." So then, in what way did the life of Moses's parents demonstrate they embraced the testimony of God as supreme? Well, we see that they hid Moses for three months because "the child was beautiful," but what parent doesn't think their child is beautiful? But in what way was Moses beautiful? Stephen, in his message on Moses's life and ministry in Acts 7, gives us some insight when he says, "At this time Moses was born; and he was beautiful in God's sight" (Acts 7:20). So once again, I think we can infer a relationship between Moses's parents and the Lord and their understanding of God's particular regard for Moses that led them to defy an active decree of Pharaoh that "every son that is born to the Hebrews you shall cast into the Nile, but you shall let every daughter live" (Exodus 1:22). Clearly defying the decree of one of the most powerful rulers on earth came with risks, but Moses's parents "were not afraid of the king's edict." They acted, instead, according to God's desire and plan for Moses. And in so doing, Moses's parents experienced God's commendation.

Ironically, they received this through actions somewhat consistent with Pharaoh's wicked desire to cast every Hebrew son into the Nile. In Exodus 2:3–10, we learn that a time came when Moses could no longer be hidden, so Moses's mother put him in a waterproofed basket and cast him on the Nile! Moses's sister followed the basket, which ultimately came to Pharaoh's daughter that led to an encounter with Moses's sister, which led to Pharaoh's daughter directing the sister to take the child back to his mother so the child could be nursed! Wow! And "when the child grew older, she brought him to Pharaoh's daughter, and he became her son" (Exodus 2:10). God affirmed the faith of Moses's parents by delivering their son from death, bringing him back into their home, and seeing him returned to Pharaoh's household in preparation for his great ministry of deliverance for His people Israel!

So then, what is the "takeaway" from this example of faith? Don't let worldly powers drive you to a fear that quenches your faith; and when you act in faith, never underestimate the great and mighty things God may do through your actions. He calls us to be faithful in *the possible* (safely cast your child on the Nile) so that He can do *the impossible* (raise up a man through whom He would deliver a nation from slavery)! And speaking of that man, our text now turns to the example of Moses.

A Great "Cloud of Witnesses" Teaches Us How to Live This Life of Faith: Moses

In verses 24–28, we read,

> By faith Moses, when he was grown up, refused to be called the son of Pharaoh's daughter, choosing rather to be mistreated with the people of God than to enjoy the fleeting pleasures of sin. He considered the reproach of Christ greater wealth than the treasures of Egypt, for he was looking to the reward. By faith he left Egypt, not being afraid of the anger of the king, for he endured as seeing him who is invisible. By faith he kept the Passover and sprinkled the blood, so that the Destroyer of the firstborn might not touch them.

As we consider the way in which Moses's life demonstrated that he embraced the testimony of God as supreme, let's look at verses 24–26 first. Back in Hebrews 3:5, the text reads, "Now Moses was faithful in all God's house as a servant, *to testify to the things that were to be spoken later.*" Moses very evidently had insight into God's future plans and his place in those plans "as a servant" in God's house, and knowing God's plans, "he considered the reproach of Christ greater wealth than the treasures of Egypt, for he was looking to the reward." By faith in the promises of God, Moses embraced a life of suffering with His people rather than the great comforts that would come through a more worldly choice because God's promised future, and the path that leads to it, immeasurably outweighed any present benefit. This example very much reinforces the author's point to his readers in 10:32–35 when he commands them to recall how "you endured a hard struggle with sufferings, sometimes being publicly exposed to reproach and affliction, and sometimes being partners with those so treated ... since you knew that you yourselves had a better possession and an abiding one. Therefore, do not throw away your confidence, which has a great reward."

In verse 27, Moses left Egypt by faith, like his parents, "not being afraid of the anger of the king." Moses fled into a wilderness very capable of taking his life, and he fled into a space where he had no recourse for his own defense if Pharaoh, who "sought to kill Moses" (Exodus 2:15), chose to pursue him. And he was unmoved by fear "for he endured as seeing him who is invisible" or, as the Greek text reads literally, "for he endured as seeing the One who is unseen." Moses embraced great hardship because his greatest reality was the reality of the invisible God! And this same conviction toward the reality of God is in play in verse 28 where "by faith he kept the Passover and sprinkled the blood, so that the Destroyer of the firstborn might not touch them."

Here, the author bypasses all the plagues God brought upon Egypt to recount the final one that would bring death upon the firstborn in all the land of Egypt who were not covered by the blood of a Passover lamb, a plague God promised Moses beforehand would bring the ultimate victory for "afterward he [Pharaoh] will let you go" (Exodus 11:1). R. T. France writes in his commentary on verse 28, "To kill lambs and smear their blood on Israelite doorposts would seem from a human perspective no more sensible than Noah's building of a boat on dry land, *but Moses was prepared to take God at his word*" (my emphasis).[39] Moses did take God at His word, lived his life accordingly, and Moses experienced God's commendation.

Where to begin! He was delivered from the wrath of Pharaoh. He was sustained in the wilderness. God made Himself as real to Moses as one whom he could actually see! And he was delivered, along with his people whom he suffered with, from the enslaving power of Pharaoh by the matchless and awesome power of God. And in the process, as one who would "testify to the things that were to be spoken later" (3:5), Moses saw the sprinkled blood of the lamb deliver God's people from the power of death! How's that for assurance, commendation, and affirmation from God!

So then, what is the takeaway from this example of faith? Reject the temptation to worldly ways in your life, especially when they offer deliverance from the path of suffering God's ways purposefully lead you into. And when God's path brings you into the path of powerful adversaries, remember that those adversaries are ultimately powerless on the path that is eternal. There was power in the blood of *a* lamb in Moses's time; how much more power is there in the blood of *the* lamb in our time and for all time! Moving along, let's move from individual examples to a corporate example.

A Great "Cloud of Witnesses" Teaches Us How to Live This Life of Faith: The Example of the People

"By faith the people crossed the Red Sea as on dry land, but the Egyptians, when they attempted to do the same, were drowned. By faith the walls of Jericho fell down after they had been encircled for seven days" (verses 29–30). This is another one of those examples that comforts us when we feel very flawed in our life of faith. The description in Exodus 14 shows our heroes of faith at their most unheroic! When Moses fled Egypt some forty years earlier, an angry Pharaoh did not pursue him into the wilderness. This is not the case with Pharaoh 2.0 after he let the people go. And when he had tracked the people of Israel down, they were pinned against the Red Sea. What happened next?

> They said to Moses, "Is it because there are no graves in Egypt that you have taken us away to die in the wilderness? What have you done to us in bringing us out of Egypt? Is not this what we said to you in Egypt: 'Leave us alone that we may serve the Egyptians'? For it would have been better for us to serve the Egyptians than to die in the wilderness." And Moses said to the people, "Fear not, stand firm, and see the salvation of the LORD, which he will work for you today. For the Egyptians whom you see today, you shall never see again. The LORD will fight for you, and you have only to be silent." (Exodus 14:11–14)

Great speech, but Moses was, I think, less confident than he sounded for in the next verse we read "The LORD said to Moses, 'Why do you cry to me? Tell the people of Israel to go forward'" (Exodus 2:15). And ultimately the people did as God commanded Moses (put yourself in their shoes before you judge their doubts). And when the events of the night were over, "Israel saw the great power that the LORD used against the Egyptians, so the people feared the LORD, and they believed in the LORD and in his servant Moses" (Exodus 14:31).

It was a great act of faith in a mind-boggling and unprecedented demonstration of God's power, as was the felling of the walls of Jericho. And although the apparent danger of the steps God commanded His people to take at Jericho may have been less than in the Red Sea, the people were called to walk in great faith at Jericho nonetheless. This is the first great battle in the promised land, an opportunity to send a message, to set the tone for the conquest, to demonstrate Israel's skill and bravery as a mighty army. But as F. F. Bruce writes in his commentary on verse 30 and the military strategy God commanded at Jericho, "On the face of it, nothing could seem more foolish than for grown men to march around a strong fortress for seven days on end, led by seven priests blowing rams' horns. Who ever heard of a fortress being captured that way?"[40] But the people did as God commanded them through Joshua; they did "just as Joshua had commanded the people"

(Joshua 6:8). And both through the Red Sea and around Jericho, the people experienced God's commendation.

As verse 29 teaches, God eased their path through the Red Sea, miraculously making the ground dry; and in the Exodus account, He leads them through during the night, perhaps reducing some of the terror that 1.5 million people might feel walking through a sea parted with great walls of water on either side. God also provided a pillar of cloud that separated them from the pursuing Egyptians and provided a light to their path. And ultimately, as verse 29 teaches, their adversaries, the Egyptians, were destroyed as God brought the sea back in upon them after His people had safely crossed. And in Jericho, despite following a strategy that made no worldly sense, "the people shouted, and the trumpets were blown. As soon as the people heard the sound of the trumpet, the people shouted a great shout, and the wall fell down flat, so that the people went up into the city, every man straight before him, and they captured the city" (Joshua 6:20).

So then, what is the takeaway from this example of faith? It is possible, by God's grace, to walk faithfully as a community; and we need to keep in mind that His directions to us can, and often will, be like nothing we've ever thought of or done. Furthermore, in both examples, God led His people through His appointed leaders, Moses and Joshua. This leads us to an important takeaway the author will bring to our notice in 13:17: "Obey your leaders and submit to them, for they are keeping watch over your souls, as those who will have to give an account. Let them do this with joy and not with groaning, for that would be of no advantage to you." Next, and last, let's consider a remarkable woman of faith.

A Great "Cloud of Witnesses" Teaches Us How to Live This Life of Faith: Rahab

"By faith Rahab the prostitute did not perish with those who were disobedient, because she had given a friendly welcome to the spies" (Verse 31). Like Moses and his parents, Rahab risked the wrath of a king, the king of Jericho. The king had been made aware of two Israelite spies who had entered the city and directly sent word to Rahab, letting her know he was aware they had been to her house, but Rahab gave a cover story for the men and hid them in her home. Why did she do this? In Joshua 2, Rahab explains to the spies in her home that she has heard of God's mighty works in delivering His people through the wilderness and into the land, and she concludes on the basis of the testimony she has heard "for the LORD your God, he is God in the heavens above and on the earth beneath"

(Joshua 2:11). To me, this is reminiscent of Jesus telling Thomas, "Blessed are those who have not seen and yet have believed" (John 20:29). Without the benefit of seeing anything firsthand, Rahab believed in the Lord and cast her lot with His people, and in so doing, Rahab experienced God's commendation.

After the walls of Jericho had fallen and the conquest of the city had been completed, the two spies remembered Rahab and went into the city to rescue her and her family before the city was burned. "Rahab the prostitute and her father's household and all who belonged to her, Joshua saved alive. And she has lived in Israel to this day, because she hid the messengers whom Joshua sent to spy out Jericho" (Joshua 6:25). But the commendation doesn't end there, for as Matthew records in the midst of his genealogy of Jesus Christ, "And Salmon the father of Boaz by *Rahab*, and Boaz the father of Obed by Ruth, and Obed the father of Jesse, and Jesse the father of David the king" (Matthew 1:5–6).

So one last time for now, what is the takeaway from Rahab's example? God's grace overflows toward the faithful as Rahab's family was delivered along with her, just as Noah's family was and just as Lot's family was. God is good all the time and can be trusted to be good all the time. And His goodness, grace, mercy, and glory are not withheld because of your past. In God's economy, a pagan prostitute who turns to Him doesn't have her past held over her head. To the contrary, He exalts the likes of these into the line of kings and the King of Kings! If this is all true, then let your faith be courageous in every way and against all odds, just like Rahab's!

Neglect Connections

I mentioned in our study of the example of Moses's parents that God calls us to be faithful in the possible so that He can do the impossible. The obedience God calls us to demonstrate is obedience in things we can do, and more often than not, this is obedience in small things. Put your child in a basket and cast the basket on the Nile (remember, I said "small," not easy). Cast your staff upon the water, and God parts a sea. Put your toes in the Jordan at flood stage, and God parts the Jordan just like the Red Sea. Hide some spies up on your roof, and God delivers you and you alone as He destroys an entire city. March around that city and blow trumpets, and the wall falls down (and it didn't tumble or crumble: "the wall fell down *flat*," Joshua 6:20). I could go on, but let's go to the temple for a moment.

In the book of Zechariah, a remnant of the people of Judah have returned from exile in Persia into the promised land, and God commands them to rebuild the temple. It takes them many years. They lay the foundation, get discouraged for a multitude of reasons, stop the work for a long time, and then God sends prophets to give them a wakeup call. Zechariah is one of those prophets, and the message of Zechariah is predominantly an encouragement to the people to finish the work. But as they resume the work, it becomes very evident that the temple they're building will be nothing like the glorious temple the Babylonians destroyed some seventy years earlier. Some of the people even weep over the sad comparison. And it is in this context that the Lord tells the people, "For whoever has *despised the day of small things* shall rejoice, and shall see the plumb line in the hand of Zerubbabel" (Zechariah 4:10).

The Lord later tells the people they will finish the work by His grace. And although the temple won't be what it was in Solomon's day (and remember, that temple was destroyed as a judgment against the people), the work they're doing will find its ultimate fulfillment when God sends His Son, the Messiah, to rule Israel and the world from a throne in a newly built temple on the same site where, like the governor Zerubbabel, the people "shall see the plumb line in the hand of" the King as He rebuilds the temple.

In a modern church obsessed with being a church where bigger is better, numbers and "wow" factor are measures of success, and celebrity and name recognition are sought after, there is a great need to return (repent?) to the truth that our God does great things through "the day of small things" to His glory, and oftentimes we won't live to see some of His great things, but that shouldn't concern us. One day, all who are in Christ "shall see the plumb line in the hand of" the King.

23

A Great Cloud of Witnesses Part 4
(HEBREWS 11:32–40)

As we finish Hebrews 11, I'm reminded that we often refer to this chapter as the "Hall of Faith" or "heroes of the faith," but as the author wraps up this chapter, he moves from details to a summary, trusting that the details are well-known to his readers through their knowledge of the scriptures. And in the summary, there are some unlikely choices for heroes, guys with a lot of baggage. But simply because they're unlikely doesn't mean we should write them off.

Imagine that your story sounds like this. As an infant, his parents pretty much abandoned him to the care of a nanny. In grade school, he was the worst in his class with his parents receiving reports that their son seemed unable to learn anything. He was punished constantly, made no friends, and his story remained constant through his high school years, finishing dead last in his class. By every estimation, this young man was, and always was, a complete failure in every aspect of life. Who was he? An accomplished artist and author who was at the forefront of all the world staring down Nazi Germany and leading in the effort to bring it to its ultimate defeat. His name was Sir Winston Churchill. Not all our heroes are "likely." To the contrary, I suspect most of them are unlikely.

But being unlikely doesn't keep them or us from becoming, by God's grace, a part of a great cloud of witnesses! And hasn't that been the author's point all along in chapter 11? This isn't a list of impossible examples to follow but people who are just as real as we are and just as flawed as we are, and so, just as these heroes were raised to the great height of an enduring and commendable testimony from God, we can be as well. And it is God's commendation that is the focus of this passage, for the author makes a summary point in verse 39, closing the chapter when he writes, "And all these, though commended through their faith, did not receive what was promised." This passage focuses on the commendation from God, which chapter 11 teaches always comes to the person who takes God at His word and lives accordingly: in obedient faith. This commendation, this demonstrable affirmation of God's favor, comes to us through a diversity of ways, including through the victories our trials can lead to.

God Brings Commendation through Faith with Great Victories in This Life

You can tell the author is winding down his teaching through examples because he writes in verse 32, "And what more shall I say? For time would fail me to tell of Gideon, Barak, Samson, Jephthah, of David and Samuel and the prophets." He then goes on in verses 33–35 to list some remarkable accomplishments and experiences that could fit the names he lists here as well as many he doesn't. But one thing you'll notice about this list is *every* name brings to mind biblical accounts of moments when these heroes were not at their best! This is encouraging to me, and I pray to you as well. The first four names are the four judges whose stories are told at greatest length in the period following the entry into the promised land, and all of them were involved in the struggle to establish Israel's foothold among the hostile peoples of the area. Gideon is likely the person being referred to in verse 34 where it reads, "Were made strong out of weakness."

When the Lord appeared to Gideon in Judges 6, Gideon expressed his concern to the Lord about the oppression of His people and responded to God's encouragement and call to go and lead His people into battle by saying, "How can I save Israel? Behold, my clan is the weakest in Manasseh, and I am the least in my father's house." "And the LORD said to him, '*But I will be with you*, and you shall strike the Midianites as one man'" (Judges 6:15–16). We know Gideon's story. Several times he asked God for a sign to confirm his word, but the account of Gideon shows he always ultimately obeyed God's word although on one occasion, he acted in fear of the townspeople where he lived. As is well-known, God used Gideon to bring victory over the Midianites. Dealing graciously with Gideon's doubts along the way, He whittled Gideon's army down to three hundred men and had them attack at night with torches, jars, and trumpets! Gideon's life was imperfect, but he obeyed the Lord under some remarkable circumstances and God granted him a great victory over the Midianites. Great faith, great commendation.

I don't have time to cover all the examples referred to here, but I think both the flaws and the great victories brought to them by their faith despite their flaws are well known with David and Samson, for example. But let's consider one more out of this list: Jephthah. In Judges 11–12, we learn that Jephthah had a lot of baggage. Living in Gilead, he was born an illegitimate son by a prostitute and was driven away from his family and inheritance by his brothers. He went "and lived in the land of Tob, and worthless fellows collected around Jephthah and went out with him" (Judges 11:3). But the elders of Gilead clearly saw enough worth in Jephthah to ask him to be their leader in the war against the Ammonites. Jephthah was somewhat bitter over the invitation to lead but "Jephthah said to the elders of Gilead, 'If you bring me home again to fight against the Ammonites, *and the* LORD *gives them over to me*, I will be your head'" (Judges 11:9). Jephthah then demonstrated in his negotiations with the king of the Ammonites that he was well versed in God's word and its account of matters of historical significance to both Ammon and Israel to make the point that the Lord defends His people Israel and brings defeat upon their enemies. But when the Ammonite king rejected the accounts from God's word, Judges 11:29 and 32 read, "Then the Spirit of the LORD was upon Jephthah … So Jephthah crossed over to the Ammonites to fight against them, and the LORD gave them into his hand."

But as you may know, in the prelude to the battle, Jephthah made a foolish and unnecessary vow that cost him the life of his only child, his daughter. Imperfect guy. Tons of baggage. But God called him, and he was faithful in a great way. And God commended him by bringing a great victory through him. Nowhere, by the way, do we see the endorsement or exaltation of the flaws of these heroes in the biblical text. The flaws often brought lasting consequences. But in between the lines in these accounts, we see God's great grace working through the obedient faith of these heroes and affirming their faith in great victory over the enemies of His people. But this gracious affirmation of obedient faith does not always come in the form of a great and evident victory. Sometimes the victory He wins through us is by the experience of hardship and suffering.

God Brings Commendation through Faith by the Great Trials of This Life

This is vividly illustrated in verse 35: "Women received back their dead by resurrection. Some were tortured, refusing to accept release, so that they might rise again to a better life." Verse 35 shows a break in the passage. The women receiving back their dead are victorious occasions where Elijah and Elisha ministered to two different women and their sons who had died. In both instances, God worked mightily to revive these dead young men back to life. But in the second half of the verse, the text shifts to those who suffered the trial of torture, and in a comparison that only makes sense in God's eternal economy, these refused "to accept release, so that they might rise again to a better life."

Most of us would consider God's affirmation of our faith by restoring a dead son back to this life—a life destined to die again—to be a greater blessing. But here, the author is making the point that the faithfulness that leads to a resurrection to eternal life is better, and God's commendation in the lives of those who suffer in light of His great promise is better. And as you can see, the hardship and suffering endured in the hope of the promise of a better resurrection takes many forms in redemption history: mocking, flogging, slavery, imprisonment, stoning, being sawn in two (Isaiah according to tradition), and they were killed with the sword. This is great physical hardship, but in the middle of verse 37 and into verse 38, the text shifts to those who suffer from being deprived of the world's comforts: "They went about in skins of sheep and goats, destitute, afflicted, mistreated—of whom the world was not worthy—wandering about in deserts and mountains, and in dens and caves of the earth."

These seem like odd forms of commendation for our faith, but as we saw at the end of chapter 10, it's not so odd in God's economy. Remember in 10:32 the author reminds his readers to "recall the former days when … you endured a hard struggle with sufferings" and in 10:34 that "you joyfully accepted the plundering of your property, since you knew that you yourselves had a better possession and an abiding one." Enduring suffering as an act of faith and trust in God's promises brings the great reward we saw in the example of the apostles in Acts 5:41 who, after they had been beaten at the order of the Jewish supreme council, "left the presence of the council, rejoicing that they were counted worthy to suffer dishonor for the name." Notice in verse 38 that the author speaks of those who suffer in this way, as an aside, as those "of whom the world was not worthy." Not worthy to the world, but precious in the sight of God. Precious enough for God to commend us with the strength to stand in such times and to bless us with the sure promises of so great a salvation. F. F. Bruce offers a great takeaway on the nature of God's commendation for faithfulness, writing, "Faith in God carries with it no guarantee of comfort in this world: this was no doubt one of the lessons which our author wished his readers to learn. But it does carry with it great reward in the only world that ultimately matters."[41] And I would add to this point that the world that does ultimately matter is not just the world of these sometimes unlikely heroes of faith in chapter 11. It includes those who have faith today.

God Joins Us Together with "So Great a Cloud of Witnesses"

The author writes in verse 39, "And all these, though commended through their faith, did not receive what was promised." Many of these did receive the blessing of many things God promised them in this life, the promise of a son named Isaac, for example. But the promise mentioned here is singular and is written as "the promise" in the Greek text. Obviously, all of these did not receive the promise of an eternal inheritance in the only world that ultimately matters, and in verse 40, the author gives his readers a reason for this, intended to be pertinent to them … and us: "Since God had provided something better for us, that apart from us they should not be made perfect."

The conditions in which these heroes of faith flourished were lesser conditions than we enjoy today because they were still in a time where many of God's great promises were unfulfilled: the final age when the Christ would come, win for us so great a salvation, and send the Holy Spirit to dwell within us forever as God's means to bring our salvation to pass. In this sense, "God had provided something better for us." But this is also another challenge and takeaway for us from this text. If all the great men and women of faith provide us such shining examples of faith in action, even though they lived in ages prior to all this fulfillment, how much more should we thrive as examples in our own lives of faith, we who have the great benefit of all that has come as a result of Christ's life, death, resurrection, and ongoing ministry as our great high priest? But here is also a great encouragement: "Apart from us they should not be made perfect."

A day is coming when Christ will finish His work in us. As Paul writes in Philippians 3:20–4:1, "Our citizenship is in heaven, and from it we await a Savior, the Lord Jesus Christ, who will transform our lowly body to be like his glorious body, by the power that enables him even to subject all things to himself. Therefore, my brothers, whom I love and long for, my joy and crown, stand firm thus in the Lord, my beloved." Stand firm in your faith, knowing a day will come when we will not only know of these heroes of faith, but because "apart from us they should not be made perfect," we will see and know them face-to-face in glory. "Therefore, since we are surrounded by so great a cloud of witnesses [urging us on!] … let us run with endurance the race that is set before us" (Hebrews 12:1).

Neglect Connections

Our lives will not be perfect until Christ resurrects us into His likeness. Until then, "we too *might* walk in newness of life" (Romans 6:4). Our lives, like all these heroes of faith, will grow in our relationship with God yet grow imperfectly. But we should grow. Our lives should be examples for other believers to follow even when we fail, provided humble repentance faithfully follows our failures. But we should be examples. This premise of the Christian life is rooted in Jesus's own words when He says in John 13:15, "For I have given you an example, that you also should do just as I have done to you." And John 13:15 isn't Jesus telling His followers to try harder. This is Jesus telling His followers to trust in the grace that makes it so, the very life of Christ in us as Paul teaches Timothy in 1 Timothy 1:16. "But I received mercy for this reason, that *in me … Jesus Christ might display* his perfect patience as *an example* to those who were to believe in him for eternal life." So Paul could confidently say, "Brothers, *join in imitating me*, and keep your eyes on those who walk according to the example you have in us" (Philippians 3:17). And Paul's confidence wasn't unfounded because he tells the Thessalonians, "And *you became imitators of us and of the Lord*, for you received the word in much affliction, with the joy of the Holy Spirit, so that *you became an example to all the believers in Macedonia and in Achaia*" (1 Thessalonians 1:6–7).

There is a form of self-deprecation in the church that sees being worthy of imitation as proud or a "works-based" faith. Sometimes this is done by people who want to deflect from the fact that they're a Christian but not much of an example to follow. In either case, this is often a practical rejection of the Gospel by dismissing what Christ promises to accomplish in and through the life of a believer. This work He does in us is worthy of boasting of in the way Paul describes when he writes, "*In Christ* Jesus, then, *I have reason to be proud of* my work for God. For I will not venture to speak of anything except *what Christ has accomplished through me*" (Romans 15:17–18). The absence of this kind of boasting in Christ to the end that we can be exemplary is more indicative of spiritual immaturity than pride or arrogance. In Christ, we must grow to be worthy of imitation, "and this we will do if God permits" (Hebrews 6:3).

24

Run the Race Set before Us

(HEBREWS 12:1–13)

One of the many sayings a person encounters within the culture of the Marine Corps is "pain is weakness leaving the body." The purpose of the saying is to convey to young men and women aspiring to be Marines that amid the trials and struggles of boot camp, they can go beyond their perceived physical and psychological barriers to rise to the standard of discipline, professionalism, and fortitude demanded of a Marine. In other words, you're not transformed into a Marine by being left to your own comforts; the transformation only comes through purposefully designed trials to stretch you, necessarily, beyond your comfort. You see the same principle in nature.

Biosphere 2, a research facility in Arizona, was created to demonstrate the viability of closed ecological systems to support and maintain human life in outer space. Inside this self-sustaining community, a diversity of mini environments was created, and nearly every weather condition was simulated except one—wind. Over time, the effects of this windless environment became apparent as many trees bent over and even snapped. Without the stress of wind to strengthen the wood, the trunks grew weak and could not hold up their own weight.[42] Our worldly culture shuns hardship, but the culture of the kingdom of God is one where a distinct community is formed by God through the discipline of hardship He brings into our lives, not to make us miserable, but as this passage teaches, "for our good, that we may share His holiness" (12:10). And these hardships are not limited to a point in time but are stretched across the extent of our Christian lives lived like a race run from start to finish.

So then, run your race to the finish! And as we run, we run mindful of the lessons we've learned from "so great a cloud of witnesses" (verse 1) who took God at His word and lived according to it, especially in times of great hardship. We must consider the example of these great heroes of the faith because although our course will not be exactly like theirs, our experience will have parallels to their hardship. And as we run, we'll also see that we must consider the greatest example of all: our Lord Jesus Christ. And as we run, we'll see as well that we must consider the discipline our Heavenly Father exercises in our life: to have a high regard for it and to understand His purpose for it while we are experiencing it. Run your race by His grace.

Consider Jesus as You Run

The first command in this passage is to "*consider* him who endured from sinners such hostility against himself, so that you may not grow weary or fainthearted" (verse 3), and from this command, we see two ways in which Jesus helps us run our race, the first being that Jesus teaches us through His example. Jesus "endured from sinners such hostility against himself." He endured all the way to the cross, which was set before Him because that was the Father's will for His one and only Son. Jesus's course was a race marked by hostility from sinners against Him with the ultimate expression of that hostility at the finish line: the cross. And He endured because, as Jesus taught in John 6:38, "I have come down from heaven, not to do my own will but the will of him who sent me." And Jesus's example was not only one of action but also attitude. In verse 2, we see that "who for the joy that was set before him endured the cross, despising the shame."

Crucifixion was the highest form of shame, a punishment reserved for those who were deemed most unfit to live, those deemed to be subhuman. Even to be associated with one who died this way was shameful. But Jesus disregarded this shame as not worthy to consider when compared to obedience to the Father's will and what would come from His obedience: the glory of being "seated at the right hand of the throne of God" (verse 2) and His everlasting ministry as the great high priest of so great a salvation to all who believe. So then, in action and attitude, we too are to "run with endurance the race that is set before us" (verse 1) because "the race that is set before us" is the Father's will. And remember, back in 10:36, the author tells his readers, "For you have need of endurance, so that when you have done the will of God you may receive what is promised." In other words, you have need to follow Jesus's example, to endure the hardship of the cross the Savior calls you to take up as you follow His example as one who has been promised so great a salvation. But Jesus not only gives us the greatest example to follow. He also gives us the power to follow Him: He sustains us in our race.

Notice in verse 3 that we are commanded to "consider him who endured from sinners such hostility against himself" and to do so for a purpose: "So that you may not grow weary or fainthearted." Isolated from its context, verse 3 could be saying that simply following Jesus's example will keep us from growing "weary or fainthearted," but verse 2 teaches that we run, "looking to Jesus, the founder and perfecter of our faith." The NLT translates verses 1–2, "And let us run with endurance the race God has set before us. We do this by keeping our eyes on Jesus, *the champion who initiates and perfects our faith.*" Jesus is the alpha and omega of our faith, the beginning and the end and the in-between! As verse 1 indicates, there are things in our lives that cause us to stumble. There are things that may not be sinful but we need to cast off if we see our life's purpose as running "the race that is set before us." And there is the "sin which clings so closely" (and doesn't it!).

Left to ourselves, we won't recognize the things that distract us from the life Christ calls us to, and we will be powerless to peel away the power of sin in our lives that clings to us like a second skin. But a life with eyes fixed on Jesus doesn't stumble because it is a life that knows our great high priest Jesus Christ has made it possible for us to "with confidence draw near to the throne of grace, that we may receive mercy and find grace to help in time of need" (4:16) "so that you may not grow weary or fainthearted" (3). Running our race is the discipline of keeping Jesus and His ways in the unchallenged forefront of our lives, but not knowing what our challenges may be in any stretch on our course, the discipline of running requires the Father's correction and discipline in our lives that is for our best.

Highly Regard the Father's Discipline as You Run

Verse 4 reads, "In your struggle against sin you have not yet resisted to the point of shedding your blood." This verse is a transition verse in this passage as it both looks back to Jesus and His example while looking forward to the nature of those challenges that may lie along any stretch on our course, especially those challenges of hostility from sinners that may result even in violence against our persons like Jesus experienced. Verse 4 begs the question, "How could we face such hostility?" and leads us into the rest of the passage, which reveals the great importance of the Father's work of disciplining us to prepare us for "the race that is set before us," beginning with the fact that the Father disciplines us as an act of love.

Quoting from Proverbs 3:11–12, the author writes in verses 5–6, "And have you forgotten the exhortation that addresses you as sons? 'My son, do not regard lightly the discipline of the Lord, nor be weary when reproved by him. For the Lord disciplines the one he loves, and chastises every son whom he receives.'" The commands in verse 5 are "do not regard lightly the discipline of the Lord, nor be weary when reproved by him." We should highly regard the Father's discipline in our lives because it is a testimony of His love for us, but the fact that it could cause us to "be weary when reproved by him" and that it can entail chastising "every son" (verse 6) indicates the Father's discipline can be unpleasant. And so verse 7 reads, "It is for discipline that you have to endure" or as the NIV conveys more clearly, "Endure hardship as discipline."

God is going to bring hardship into our lives as an act of love to make us fit to run our race, which can entail even the kind of hostility from sinners that leads you "to the point of shedding your blood." If pain is weakness leaving the body that prepares the Marine to face the full spectrum of combat, then enduring hardship in our lives is the Father's loving way of preparing His children to run the race to whatever end Christ calls you to as you follow "the founder and perfecter" of your faith (verse 2). And this leads to a wonderful dimension of the Father's discipline in our lives.

The Father's discipline confirms that we are His children. Picking up in verse 7 and through verse 8, the author explains the beautiful reality of this act of our Father's love toward us: "God is treating you as sons. For what son is there whom his father does not discipline? If you are left without discipline, in which all have participated, then you are illegitimate children and not sons." Very simply put, the discipline of hardship the Father brings into our lives to train us and correct us is evidence we are His daughters and sons! With that understanding, the greater concern isn't the presence of hardship in our lives (especially hardship because of hostility from a fallen world), but rather *the absence of it*. We highly regard the Father's discipline in our lives because it confirms to us that we are His children, knowing that "God is treating you as sons." He disciplines us because He loves us, confirming that we are His children, and so He desires for us to become like His Son, the one who is "the exact imprint of [the Father's] nature" (1:3).

The Father disciplines us to make us holy. In verse 9, the text reads, "Besides this, we have had earthly fathers who disciplined us and we respected them. Shall we not much more be subject to the Father of spirits and live?" By analogy to our earthly fathers, even our experience of imperfect discipline from them can gain our respect. If that's true, how much more does our Heavenly Father's discipline in our lives merit our respect? And notice what's at stake: "Be subject to the Father of spirits *and live?*" We are running our race to eternal life, and our Heavenly Father knows best "for they disciplined us for a short time as it seemed best to them, but he disciplines us for our good, that we may share his holiness" (verse 10). We highly regard the Father's discipline as we run because it is "for our good," and it is "for our good" because through it, He is making us holy through hardship just as gold is refined and made pure through an intense fire. We now better understand why the Father's discipline through hardship is "for our good." It demonstrates His love for us, affirms to us we are His children, and transforms our fallen nature into the holiness of His Son. But what do we do with this understanding when times of discipline come upon us?

Understand the Father's Discipline as You Run

It is one thing to understand and another thing to live by that understanding in moments that demand it. We need to see His purpose in the moment. "For the moment all discipline seems painful rather than pleasant, but later it yields the peaceful fruit of righteousness to those who have been trained by it" (verse 11). The fact that "all discipline seems painful rather than pleasant" I think was born out not only in several examples in chapter 11 but also throughout scripture. We are rarely at our best in our first reaction to hardships of any kind, but through it, we come to see "the peaceful fruit of righteousness to those who have been trained by it," which is the manifestation of Christ's character in our lives. The word translated as "trained" here is a word used to describe the training of an athlete in the gymnasium. Just as an athlete endures hardship to compete, so are we also trained for our race. Like athletes, we are God's works in progress. You may remember hot late summer days groaning through endless drills in football practice, but without them, your time on the field in the game (which is the point of it all) would be fruitless. Knowing the Father's purpose in the moment at least helps us to have a better perspective on hardship in the moment. And when those moments come for our correction, follow His course corrections.

Verses 12–13 read, "Therefore, lift your drooping hands and strengthen your weak knees, and make straight paths for your feet, so that what is lame may not be put out of joint but rather be healed." The statements "lift your drooping hands and strengthen your weak knees" are commands. When the race wearies you, do this! But where do we turn to do this? "Consider him who endured from sinners such hostility against himself, so that you may not grow weary or fainthearted" (verse 3). The first course correction when running our race becomes disheartening or wearying is to turn back to the source that gives us "mercy and ... grace to help in time of need" (4:16 and a verse you may notice we keep coming back to). To return our gaze and hope to "the founder and perfecter of our faith" (verse 2).

The second command is to *make straight paths.* This is reminiscent of John the Baptist's call to the people to repent in light of the Messiah's coming. To turn from the "sin which clings so closely" (verse 1) and get back on the course of obedience to God's Word as you run. The danger to the Christian runner of going off course into rough ground is that "what is lame may ... be put out of joint" (verse 13). To be disabled in this way would put us out of the race, but in responding to the course corrections the Father's discipline invites us to take, we will not be disabled "but rather be healed" (verse 13) so as to reach the finish line.

Neglect Connections

What I'd like to do now is focus our consideration on the exhortation in verse 1 to "lay aside every weight, and sin which clings so closely," and I want to begin with a reminder about the danger of willful sin in our lives. Looking back to Hebrews 10:19–31, the latter part of that passage is a warning to believers who "go on sinning deliberately" (10:26), and the outcome for a believer who doesn't respond to the Father's corrective discipline can lead to the fearful outcome of the Father's judgment upon us in this life. Failing to "lay aside [the] ... sin which clings so closely," as we saw in Hebrews 10, can lead to "a fearful expectation of judgment" and God's fiery indignation (10:27), leading the author to conclude, "It is a fearful thing to fall into the hands of the living God" (10:31). That statement alone ought to move us to great fear over harboring "sin which clings so closely" and lay it aside through confession and repentance. But we're also exhorted to "lay aside every weight" (verse 1). What is "every weight"?

For the runner, it's everything not necessary for the race! In his novel *The Mysterious Island*, Jules Verne tells a story of five men who escape a prison camp by hijacking a hot-air balloon. Unexpectedly though, the wind carries them over the ocean. Watching their homeland disappear on the horizon, they wonder how much longer the balloon can stay aloft, and as the hours pass and the surface of the ocean draws closer, the men decide they must cast overboard some of the weight. Shoes, overcoats, and weapons are reluctantly discarded, and ultimately, even their food is thrown overboard. In the end, they survive because they were able to discern the difference between what really was needed and what was not.[43] The "necessities" they once thought they couldn't live without were the very weights that almost cost them their lives. I think one of the greatest and most threatening spiritual maladies in the life of Christians in our culture today is a happy indifference to many things of God because we make so many distractions "necessities" in our lives.

F. F. Bruce notes, "There are many things which may be perfectly all right in their own way, but which hinder a competitor in the race of faith; they are 'weights' which must be laid aside. It may well be that what is a hindrance to one entrant in this spiritual contest is not a hindrance to another; each must learn for himself what in his case is a weight or impediment."[44] Your "weight" is whatever causes Jesus Christ and the course He has called you to run to be anything but the foremost aim in your life. These are things that are not inherently sinful, even things that are altogether good if enjoyed as God intended them. Could be your job. Could even be members of your family! For example, over the matter of following Him, a man once told Jesus, "'Lord, let me first go and bury my father.' And Jesus said to him, 'Follow me, and leave the dead to bury their own dead'" (Matthew 8:21–22); and in Matthew 10:37, Jesus says, "Whoever loves father or mother more than me is not worthy of me, and whoever loves son or daughter more than me is not worthy of me." Jesus wasn't dismissing the importance of family in God's eyes; He was addressing the very prevalent danger (both in His day and ours) where faithfulness to family rises above faithfulness to Him—job, family, or maybe it's our hobbies.

Do your hobbies bring you times of needed rest and joy, or do they set the rhythm of your life? I'll close this chapter with a confession to make the point. I used to be an avid boater. Before we moved up to the Hudson Valley in New York, I owned a beautiful (and fast) Four Winns Horizon 240, and apart from the often-forgettable moments of getting it in and out of the water, I enjoyed very few things more than being on the water in that boat. As I was sending out résumés to churches back in 2015, *following Christ's call in my life* to serve Him as pastor after seminary, I came to the realization one day that I was picking churches near bodies of water suitable for boating. That "weight" kind of crept up on me; and when I realized what I was doing, I resolved to sell the boat and did so before we moved up to New York, ironically to a guy in Albany, New York! (God has an amazing sense of humor.) I was getting off course. My "hobby" was dictating the terms of Christ's calling for me. Thankfully, by God's grace, the Spirit's conviction led me to lay it aside. So then, whatever your weight, whatever the sin, "let us also lay aside every weight, and sin which clings so closely." Run your race to the finish!

25

Run Like We're Heirs to the Kingdom

(HEBREWS 12:14–29)

Have you ever driven with folks who are hopeless speeders, driving at excessive speeds although they know the threat of the law is present? And when the radar detector goes off, rather than moving them to change their ways, they slow down as a panicked reaction to the warning and then go right back to speeding when they feel the threat of detection has passed. Wouldn't life be more peaceful if they simply drove somewhere near the speed limit? The panic in these instances is the result of the fear of an authority who can bring consequences to bear, and this is a healthy fear when it influences our actions for the better, but not so much when we live in fear without changing. In a sense, that's one of the messages in this passage.

The fear of the Lord should be "the beginning of wisdom" (Psalm 111:10), but when it doesn't produce this effect, our lives can become fear filled. But imagine you're a young person new to the driving experience and, instead of a police officer in your rearview mirror, you see your dad and a healthy kind of fear, one filled with love and respect as well, which moves you to be obedient to the traffic laws. You know Dad cares as he follows you and has your best in mind. He's trying to help you develop good habits, and knowing he's there comforts you as you know you're not alone as you drive. In a sense, this thought hews closely to this passage as well.

As God's children through faith in Christ, how do we respond to who He is and all that

He has done, is doing, and will do for us? Do we do our own thing on "the race that is set before us" (12:1), or do we run like we're heirs to the kingdom? If we run like heirs, then as we'll see in this passage, we have certain obligations as kingdom citizens. If we run like heirs, then we will strive to be people of peace and holiness. We will be obedient to live the life the Gospel calls us to live. We will be thankful for all that God gives us in this life as His kingdom citizens and all He promises to give us in an eternity when the only thing left standing will be His unshakeable kingdom. And we will come before Him in worship, not out of the kind of fear inspired by a lawless life, but out of the healthy fear one has when they know and love their heavenly Father: that He is good, kind, merciful, and compassionate and just and righteous and a consuming fire. Our God who never changes once told Moses, "Do not come near; take your sandals off your feet, for the place on which you are standing is holy ground" (Exodus 3:5). In Christ, we do so as well for a holy God dwells within us.

The Heirs to the Kingdom Must Strive to Guard Peace and Holiness

In verse 14, we are commanded to "strive for peace … and holiness." Your translation may say "pursue" or "make every effort" to do this, and with respect to peace, we do this with "everyone" or, as Paul teaches, "if possible, so far as it depends on you, live peaceably with all" (Romans 12:18). This is a command for God's people to actively seek to extend the peace we have with Him to everyone we have contact with and to never take the initiative to stir up strife in any setting including His church. This is peace that is both the absence of conflict and the presence of harmony, and there are few greater lessons today's church needs to learn and live as we are, in many ways, bitter and angry and vindictive toward the world around us and so no different than the ways of the world around us. We need to repent of this and discover a passion to be His agents of peace in the world, for "blessed are the peacemakers, for they shall be called sons of God" (Matthew 5:9).

And as we pursue peace "with everyone," we are commanded to strive, with equal zeal, "for the holiness without which no one will see the Lord." Holiness is God's own character, and as we saw in 12:10, God "disciplines us for our good, that we may share his holiness" and it is only those who "share His holiness" who can "see the Lord." The fact that we can share His holiness, His character, should not surprise us because this is the work of His grace in us who are born again through faith in Jesus Christ. Let me explain further this nature of His grace from the scriptures.

Once again from Hebrews 4:16, we know that Jesus Christ has made it possible for us to "find grace to help in time of need," and we know from Titus 2:11–12 that this "grace of God" is *training us* to renounce ungodliness and worldly passions, and to live self-controlled, upright, and godly lives in the present age." In other words, it is by God's grace that we are being made holy, that we are being given the ability to live "godly lives." And we know from the example of Enoch in Hebrews 11 that we walk with God as "those who earnestly seek him" (Hebrews 11:6 NIV). In essence, the command here to "strive ... for holiness" is a command to earnestly seek His grace that helps and trains us to live godly lives. And when we who are born again share His holiness, we can see the invisible God in very real ways and will see Him ultimately in His presence forever in glory. And so Jesus says in John 3:3, "Truly, truly, I say to you, unless one is born again he cannot see the kingdom of God." And as we strive for holiness, we do so as a *redeemed community* He is making holy.

We must "see to it that no one fails to obtain the grace of God; that no 'root of bitterness' springs up and causes trouble, and by it many become defiled" (verse 15). Here once more is the great degree and importance of tending to one another's walk within the church. As I've already shown, to fail "to obtain the grace of God" is to fail to enlist the power of His grace in our lives to make us holy. And to allow a "root of bitterness" to spring up and cause trouble is to allow a spirit that is hostile to peace to arise within the church, which must not be allowed to happen because by such a spirit, "many become defiled."

At this point, I feel burdened once again to share the message the author gives the church in 10:24–25 (NRSV) when he writes, "Let us consider how to provoke one another to love and good deeds, not neglecting to meet together, as is the habit of some, but encouraging one another, and all the more as you see the Day approaching." And if you remember in that passage, this direction was given as a prelude to a warning against the sin that crouches at the door of our lives when we neglect this zealous work we're called to in one another's lives. Here in this passage, very similarly, we're commanded to undertake this zealous life-on-life work for the sake of our peace and holiness, both individually and corporately, to guard the peace and holiness of a faithful community in Christ's kingdom—your faithful local church—for our own sake and, above all, for His name's sake.

Sisters and brothers, we must be those who strive, who earnestly seek, to honor His name as holy; and we can't do this when our time together in our church is a secondary consideration for so many within the body as indicated by the investment of our time to it. We express a timeless practical truth when we say, "What we pay attention to is an indicator of what we care about." We have to honestly ask ourselves, "Are we committed to the work Christ has called His church to or are we neglecting it?" As the author closes this part of the passage, he makes the point that an heir to the kingdom must not neglect their inheritance of so great a salvation by shifting to the example of Esau.

Much can be said about Esau and what is said of him in verses 16–17, but the primary focus is on the fact that Esau "sold his birthright for a single meal." Esau's "birthright" was his status as Isaac's heir, which was his due as the firstborn. And as the account in Genesis 25:29–34 teaches,

> Esau came in from the field, and he was exhausted. And Esau said to Jacob, "Let me eat some of that red stew, for I am exhausted!" … Jacob said, "Sell me your birthright now." Esau said, "I am about to die; of what use is a birthright to me?" Jacob said, "Swear to me now." So he swore to him and sold his birthright to Jacob. Then Jacob gave Esau bread and lentil stew, and he ate and drank and rose and went his way. Thus, Esau *despised* his birthright.

Esau despised his birthright, yet the author writes in verse 17, "For you know that afterward, when he desired to inherit the blessing, he was rejected, for *he found no chance to repent*, though he sought it with tears." The phrase "he found no chance to repent" in the Greek text is literally "he found no *place* to repent." At this point, Esau's spirit was "unholy" (verse 16) for although he sought the blessing of his inheritance with tears, "Esau said to his father, 'Have you but one blessing, my father? Bless me, even me also, O my father.' And Esau lifted up his voice and wept … Now Esau hated Jacob because of the blessing with which his father had blessed him, and Esau said to himself, 'The days of mourning for my father are approaching; then I will kill my brother Jacob'" (Genesis 27:38, 27:41). Esau's heart was beyond repentance as Paul teaches in 2 Corinthians 7:10. "For godly grief produces a repentance that leads to salvation without regret, whereas *worldly grief* produces death."

Esau neglected his inheritance because he despised it. He saw no worth in it. His god was a worldly god, the god of his passions and appetites, and so Esau is an example that is the polar opposite of holiness and peace because his neglect of something priceless drove his spirit in a direction away from the God who could make him holy. And all this should remind us of an earlier warning in 2:3 where the author writes, "How shall we escape if we neglect such a great salvation?" And it is to the matter of "such a great salvation" that the author now turns as he makes the point that our inheritance in Christ is incomparably great by way of a contrast between two covenants.

We Are Heirs to a Majestic Kingdom because of a Better Covenant

We now see the author appeal to vivid and powerful imagery to make this point in verses 18–24. I'm going to cover these verses fairly quickly, but as we move through them, I want you to keep in mind that three things are happening here, which we've seen in the book of Hebrews already. The contrast between the covenants is meant to convey that (1) the new covenant is better; (2) that the old covenant is a shadow of the new, which points us to things in the new covenant that we find in the old, but now in a better and greater way; and (3) that there are some aspects of the old covenant that remain true to a new covenant people today. Now then, engage your imaginations and listen as we learn in a whole new way how, under the old covenant, God's presence prompted intense fear and separation.

> For you have *not* come to what may be touched, a blazing fire and darkness and gloom and a tempest and the sound of a trumpet and a voice whose words made the hearers beg that no further messages be spoken to them. For they could not endure the order that was given, "If even a beast touches the mountain, it shall be stoned." Indeed, so terrifying was the sight that *Moses* said, "I tremble with fear." (verses 18–21)

Notice he begins by saying, "For you have *not* come to." This is not a description of the state of the relationship of the author's readers with God. As we'll see in a moment, they come to something very different, but for those tempted to turn from Christ to seek God through the law, this is a stark reminder of what seeking God under the old covenant was like. Even Moses, whose place before God was highly personal, was terrified by the sight and sound manifestation of God at Sinai. This account of God's establishment of His old covenant relationship with Israel symbolizes, for the author, a covenant marked by terrifying fear and separation, which is the extreme opposite of the confident approach to God that Christ has won for His people like we see in 10:19–23 ("we have the confidence to enter the holy places by the blood of Jesus" 10:19).

Under the new covenant, the heirs can draw near to God with confidence. Emphasizing the stark contrast between the old and new covenants, verses 22–24 read,

> *But* you have come to Mount Zion and to the city of the living God, the heavenly Jerusalem, and to innumerable angels in festal gathering, and to the assembly of the firstborn who are enrolled in heaven, and to God, the judge of all, and to the spirits of the righteous made perfect, and to Jesus, the mediator of a new covenant, and to the sprinkled blood that speaks a better word than the blood of Abel.

"But you have come!" For those who are in Christ, this is where we are! But if you're unfamiliar with this passage, you may never have known how awesome and majestic this place is where we draw near to Him with confidence! He begins with the place! The New Jerusalem. The dwelling place of God, which is in heaven and which we know from Revelation 21, will come down to the new earth to be God's dwelling place with us in eternity. This is who and what we come to as we worship, and the author paints a picture for us working from the outside to the center. Can you imagine the "innumerable angels in festal gathering" witnessing our worship when we come together on Sunday mornings (or the day when your church comes together)? And can you imagine their rejoicing when someone turns to Jesus Christ and is saved when we gather?

And among this great cloud of witnesses is "the assembly of the *firstborn* who are enrolled in heaven." This word *firstborn* is used of Jesus in 1:6 as the one who is the heir of all things, and it is used here of the faithful of all ages who are joint heirs of all things with Him. These are the faithful who have gone before us "who are enrolled in heaven," and we can rejoice in the hope that we will join them as Jesus taught His disciples in Luke 10:20 when He commanded them to "rejoice that your names are written in heaven."

Moving now to the center, we see "God, the judge of all"; and as if to assure us that His judgment toward us is favorable, the author comes back to the saints, saying, "And to the spirits of the righteous made perfect." Remember, we learn in Hebrews that this is God's aim in the life of His people: to make us perfect. In this life, "perfect" entails the spiritual maturity He desires for us in Christ and that His grace makes possible in this life. I believe the picture here, however, is the full perfection of our spirit. That this is, in essence, an assurance to us that His holiness, which we strive for in this life, will be brought to perfection in our spirits in heaven. From there, we look to the day when God will complete this perfect work in our whole persons when our perfected spirit is rejoined with our resurrected body as a fit and perfect tent for a perfected spirit. And what makes this possible?

The picture returns to the center where "the founder and perfecter of our faith" (12:2) is shown in the role the author has taught us exhaustively of throughout this book: "And to Jesus, *the mediator* of a new covenant, and to the sprinkled blood that speaks a better word than the blood of Abel." We've seen this word *better* throughout the book, and here we see it for the last time. Because of Jesus Christ, "we feel sure of *better* things ... that belong to salvation" (6:9). We have "a *better* hope ... through which we draw near to God" (7:19) because Jesus is "the guarantor of a *better* covenant" (7:22) and He "has obtained a ministry that is as much more excellent than the old as the covenant he mediates is *better*, since it is enacted on *better* promises" (8:6). And all because "the sprinkled blood" of our great high priest "speaks a *better* word than the blood of Abel." This is what we come to in Christ: the full majesty of heaven and the full promise of eternity. An inheritance of all things as joint heirs with the Savior who "upholds the universe by the word of his power" (1:3). A "better word" indeed! Such a great salvation that we must not neglect! And "Jesus Christ is the same yesterday and today and forever" (13:8).

God Has Always Been Worthy of Our Obedience, Gratitude, and Reverence and Awe

I wrote earlier that the teaching on covenants here shows, once again, the new covenant to be better, but that it also shows us how the old covenant points to the new and how some things never change, regardless of the covenant by which we live in relationship with Him. We see this in verse 25. "See that you do not refuse him who is speaking. For if they did not escape when they refused him who warned them on earth, much less will we *escape* if we reject him who warns from heaven." The people of Israel suffered God's judgment in the wilderness for refusing to heed His word, and if that was true, how much more so will it be true if we refuse to obey the "better word" of the Gospel? The word *escape* here is the same one used earlier in 2:3 when he writes, "How shall we *escape* if we neglect such a great salvation?" Obedience to His Word is His standard of faithfulness under any covenant with the Lord, and if the consequences for disobedience were great under the old covenant, how much greater will they be for us who are under the new? Maybe verses 26–27 are meant to get our attention and impress this point upon us.

At that time his voice shook the earth, but now he has promised, "Yet once more I will shake not only the earth but also the heavens." This phrase, "Yet once more," indicates the removal of things that are shaken—that is, things that have been made—in order that the things that cannot be shaken may remain.

At Sinai, the mountain shook and terrified everyone present. Imagine what it will be like when the whole universe is shaken when God removes everything from it, which will not be part of the eternity of "all things" He will soon make forever new and forever good! Those "things that cannot be shaken" and so will "remain."

"Therefore, let us be grateful for receiving a kingdom that cannot be shaken" (verse 28), which is our eternal inheritance! But whether at Sinai or in the presence of the majesty of heaven and all who are in it, God is worthy, not only of our gratitude, but of that which proves our gratitude is genuine, that we "offer to God acceptable worship, with reverence and awe" (verse 29) or, as the NLT translates, "with holy fear and awe." This is not the fear that brought terror as we see in verse 21, but the holy fear that comes before Him in worship, mindful that we do so with a deep sense of the majesty and holiness of the God we worship. And lest we become prone to being too lax or casual in our worship, the author closes by reminding His readers—and us—of one important thing about our great God and Savior that never changes: "For our God is a consuming fire" (verse 29).

Neglect Connections

What is your vision or sense of God in your heart and mind when you worship? Is it reverence and awe? I once visited a church with my wife after we had moved to a new location. I showed up in dress slacks and shoes and a long-sleeved button-down shirt—but no tie. I hate ties. Every man in the church was wearing a suit and tie, and I greeted the first one I saw by extending my hand and introducing myself. He looked me over from head to toe then turned around and walked away without saying a word. We never visited this church again. I know the mindset. "You wouldn't visit the president in jeans and a polo shirt, so don't come before God dressed that way. Give Him your Sunday best!" In this church we visited, this was "reverence and awe" to them. But is God the president? Does He look at our attire/appearance when we come to worship Him? "Do not let your adorning be external—the braiding of hair and the putting on of gold jewelry, or the clothing you wear—but let your adorning be *the hidden person of the heart* with the imperishable beauty of a gentle and quiet spirit, *which in God's sight is very precious*" (1 Peter 3:3–4). One way to neglect a great salvation through worship is to attribute holiness to superficial things. Don't do this "for the Lord sees not as man sees: man looks on the outward appearance, but *the Lord looks on the heart*" (1 Samuel 16:7).

In the scriptures, the act of worship is often associated with the posture of bending low before the Lord. This is the posture of submission. This is also the posture of trust because in this posture, you're defenseless—in the presence of a God who is "a consuming fire." We can take the problem of associating holiness and acceptability toward God in our worship with our appearance to the other extreme from what I mentioned above, but both extremes are indicative of an inward reality. If worship for you is hanging out in your worship service sipping a latte and checking your text messages during the sermon, then odds are your god is not "a consuming fire." But if your God is one whom you love with a healthy fear that He is God (and "a consuming fire") and you are not, then odds are the posture of your heart before Him is as Paul describes in Romans 12:1. You come before Him "by the mercies of God" found by your earnest seeking of His blessings through the power of the Gospel of His Son. You "present your bodies as a living sacrifice." Your life is a constant offering to Him for His good will and pleasure. And by His grace as you present yourself to Him in this way, you are "holy and acceptable to God": "The holiness without which no one will see the Lord" (12:14). And as Paul concludes in Romans 12:1, this "is your spiritual worship," a worship where we come before Him with "reverence and awe."

26

Brotherly Love Must Continue

(HEBREWS 13:1–7)

I once read a story of a man who had an uncle with cerebral palsy named Greg. Uncle Greg was a believer who found contentment in life despite his disability and lived an inspiring life of ministering to others in the ways that he could. One summer, Uncle Greg attended a "handi-camp" week at a Christian retreat center, and a member of the church of Uncle Greg's nephew—a man named John—was serving as a volunteer at the camp that week. For four days, twenty-four hours a day, John fed Uncle Greg every bite of his food, gave him every drink, slept on a concrete floor on an air mattress beside Uncle Greg's bed, took him to the bathroom, cleaned him up as well as everything else Greg needed, including helping Uncle Greg swim for the very first time in his life! According to camp tradition, on the last day of camp, each volunteer comes before the group with their camper to recap all the different things they did and then they ask the campers one question: "What was your favorite thing of the week?" The campers always say the same thing—swimming.

But when John and Uncle Greg came up and John was finished recapping Uncle Greg's week, John then turned to Uncle Greg and asked, "What was your favorite part of the entire week?"

Uncle Greg said, "You."

John said, "Oh, there had to be something else. Was it the swimming? Was it the snack time?"

Greg once again simply said, "You."

Love is who *you* are and what *you* do!

The NET of Hebrews 13:1 reads, "Brotherly love must continue," and I chose the NET's translation of verse 1 as the title for this chapter because it better conveys that verse 1 is a command to us as well as the fact that the command "Brotherly love must continue" sets the tone for the rest of this passage. In other words, this passage is the author's teaching to his readers of what brotherly love looks like. Now the particular concerns he draws attention to were likely matters of specific concern for his original audience, but these particular concerns point to three dimensions of how we show brotherly love that are always applicable to us, even if the particular issues he addresses aren't things we're presently struggling with.

In Romans 12:10, Paul writes, "Love one another with brotherly affection. Outdo one another in showing honor." He then continues in Romans 12 to flesh out brotherly love in actions, things we should do and refrain from for the sake of others. In this Hebrews 13 passage, we see this same framework of what we must do and what we must refrain from as an act of love toward others. And as verse 1 indicates, we must continue to love in this way: to act in such a way that we are used by God to bring His best into the lives of others. But in another sense, verse 1 is not only a command to love in this way, but also a declaration of what love is. "Brotherly love must continue" because as Paul teaches in 1 Corinthians 13:8, "Love never ends." Love will remain as a manifestation of God's nature in His people from now into eternity. It "must continue"; therefore, we must love in this way now and participate in something that is truly eternal! And what does something truly eternal look like now?

Love One Another through Our Genuine Care for Those in Need

Although it's not as common in our day as it was in the first century, the author focuses first on our care through hospitality, writing, "Do not neglect to show *hospitality to strangers*, for thereby some have entertained angels unawares" (verse 2). Travelers in the first century were often at risk as inns in the Roman Empire were often places where guests were exploited and even put in danger by their stay. Showing hospitality, therefore, was a great act of loving care; and for traveling believers who were often strangers to their hosts, the hosts were held to a high standard. In 3 John 5–8, John writes, "Beloved, it is a faithful thing you do in all your efforts for these brothers, *strangers* as they are, who testified to your love before the church. You will do well to send them on their journey *in a manner worthy of God*. For they have gone out for the sake of the name, accepting nothing from the Gentiles. Therefore, *we ought to support people like these*, that we may be fellow workers for the truth." Our hospitality, even today, meets the great needs of those traveling in their ministry and joins us with them as partners in their ministry. And in doing so, we sometimes entertain "angels unawares" not unlike how both Abraham and Lot did so in Genesis 18–19, and in Abraham's case, he entertained the Lord Himself as well! In essence, every guest ought to be treated by us as those whom heaven has sent! But not every lodging is hospitable.

The author commands his readers to "remember those who are in prison, as though in prison with them, and those who are mistreated, since you also are in the body" (verse 3). This ought to sound very familiar to us as he had previously commanded them to remember their testimony of caring for those who were afflicted and in prison back in 10:32–34. And as he did in chapter 10, the command here isn't to simply recollect past faithfulness *but to persist in it*. I suspect many of us have a can of WD-40 around the house, but have you ever wondered what WD-40 stands for? The WD stands for "water displacement," but you might ask, "What in the world does the '40' stand for?" That's how many times they tried to develop an effective formula. They failed thirty-nine times but succeeded on the fortieth try! I think sometimes in ministry we harbor a sense that "we've met our quota" or "I've done enough," but again, as Paul teaches in 1 Corinthians 13:8, "Love never ends." Whether it is hospitality or care for those suffering imprisonment or affliction for their faith, in any way, our loving care has no quota because loving care has no end in the life of God's people. Brotherly love must continue, not only in the outward deeds of loving care, but also in our care for one another *through what we keep ourselves from*.

Love One Another by Guarding Our Lives from Destructive Temptations

This is an extremely interesting shift in the teaching focus because we're now charged with tending to the purity of what is mostly private, not only for our own sakes, but especially for the sake of the church. In verses 4–5, the author challenges his readers on matters of infidelity in marriage and the love of money: the two areas where Christian ministry fails and brings great harm to the church far more frequently than through any other form of moral failure. "Let marriage be held in honor among all, and let the marriage bed be undefiled, for God will judge the sexually immoral and adulterous. Keep your life free from love of money, and *be content* with what you have, for he has said, 'I will never leave you nor forsake you'" (verses 5–6). In essence, the key to being faithful both in matters of marital fidelity and finances is expressed in what the author writes at the end of verse 6: "Be content with what you have, for he has said, 'I will never leave you nor forsake you.'"

Be content with what the Lord has given you, especially with respect to your spouse and your material means. Paul addresses this in Philippians 4:11–13 when he writes, "I have learned in whatever situation I am to be content. I know how to be brought low, and I know how to abound. In any and every circumstance, I have learned the secret of facing plenty and hunger, abundance and need. I can do all things through him who strengthens me." "I can do all things through" the one who promised, "I will never leave you nor forsake you." Brothers and sisters, pick anyone who has a faithful testimony within your church and ask yourself, "If that sister or brother fails morally due to infidelity or greed, what would be the impact on all of us?" I can assure you the impact would be great. So what are some practical steps to guard our lives from destructive temptations?

To begin with, don't isolate yourself from the Christian community. The author has emphasized the dangers of sin overtaking our lives when we do this on two occasions. Stay committed to your life within the church, and as you do, stay accountable to someone. Make sure someone in your life knows what's going on in your life and in your *thought* life. Live transparently with a handful of people who know you well and can be trusted with knowing you well.

Second, confess your sins. Do this before God daily; and when you do, repent of them, whether they are sins in thought, word, or deed. Where your sins have offended another, confess them to the one offended and seek their forgiveness. And as a matter of self-examination, ask yourself right now when you last confessed your sin before God and before another.

Third, think of the consequences. When you sin, you're focused on the desire, not the consequences, but sin always has consequences that are oftentimes horrible, especially when you consider all the people your sin affects. Now you might be embarrassed to admit to yourself and to God that you have sinful desires that can have horrible consequences. But if you have people in your life that you're accountable to, I'm certain that if that friendship is authentic, you'll discover you're not alone! Let's get real and admit there's a mess still living inside of us just as the Lord taught Cain when He said, "Sin is crouching at the door. Its desire is contrary to you, but you must rule over it" (Genesis 4:7). Keeping the consequences in mind can be a very healthy practical deterrent to sin as you imagine having to explain to your wife, your kids, the elders of your church, and dozens of others how you betrayed their trust because of infidelity, greed, or some other sin. The fear of having to have those conversations can be very healthy and quite motivating. It *should* be motivating because we should never want to betray the trust of the people we love the most and would hurt the most by our moral failure.

Lastly, and most importantly, let your desires always be rooted in your relationship with the Lord. Sin is a powerful force that prompts powerful desires that are not for our good, but when our conversations with ourselves begin to go down the road that we can trade our spouses for a better model, or that our money is best used to gratify our desires (which always prompts a demand for more), then we're in essence telling God that what we want is better for us than what He gives us *and* that we trust what we want more than we trust Him! But when the Lord remains at the forefront of our desires, we are content with all that we have as the author teaches in verse 5. Consequently, we can confidently say, "The Lord is my helper; I will not fear; what can man do to me?" (verse 6) or as Paul taught in Romans 8:31, "If God is for us, who can be against us?" Sometimes, the main person who is against us is ourselves!

Coming back to Romans, Paul cries out in desperation over himself, "Wretched man that I am! Who will deliver me from this body of death?" (Romans 7:24) and then proceeds to thank God that Jesus Christ gives wretched men such deliverance. And so Jesus taught us to pray *daily* to the Father, "Lead us not into temptation, but deliver us from evil" (Matthew 6:13). Why? Because, short of glory, there is a wretched man, a wretched woman, crouching within each of us as the enemy of love for one another. But with the Lord who is both our helper and is for us, we can prevail in love.

Love One Another by Finishing Your Race Well

The last two commands in this passage are to once again remember and to imitate. "Remember your leaders, those who spoke to you the word of God. *Consider* the outcome of their way of life, and *imitate* their faith" (verse 7). The author will refer to his readers' leaders two more times in chapter 13: both in the present tense in verses 17 and 24. But here he refers to them in the past tense as "those who *spoke* to you," and "the outcome of their way of life" is likely a reference to their life as a finished work. These are leaders his readers knew and whose example they can remember as examples of those who ran well in the race the Lord set before them all the way to the finish. But again, this is purposeful reflection: "Consider the outcome of their way of life, and imitate their faith." But how is finishing your race well an act of love?

Remember, love is the sacrificial giving of what we have been given for the sake of another's physical or spiritual needs, and we have perhaps no greater gift to give to our brothers and sisters in Christ than the testimony of a life surrendered to Jesus Christ and transformed by Him. Think of the people in your life who have finished their race well, those whom you know ran their race "looking to Jesus, the founder and perfecter of our faith" (12:2) and you're confident they were received by their Lord and Savior with a "well done good and faithful servant" (Matthew 25:21). Think of the great need we have that is met by the power of an example—another one of the great cloud of witnesses—which inspires us to follow it. Our need *for* love and our need *to* love is great, to care for those in need, to guard those we love from our own temptations to destructive sin, to love by leaving a faithful legacy as an example worthy of imitation to the ones we love.

Neglect Connections

What is brotherly love? I pray we have a better sense of it now after considering this passage. Our culture is woefully misguided on what love is, and that flaw in the culture's understanding of love infects the church in insidious ways. I think John gives us the clearest and most concise picture of love in 1 John 3:16 when he writes, "*By this we know love*, that he laid down his life for us, and we ought to lay down our lives for the brothers." Jesus surrendered His life fully to meet our greatest needs; *to love is to follow His example.* To lay down our lives for others so that God's best may come into their lives through us. And if we're at all uncertain about what that looks like, John paints that picture for us as well in 1 John 3:17–18: "But if anyone has the world's goods and sees his brother in need, yet closes his heart against him, how does God's love abide in him? Little children, let us not love in word or talk but in *deed* and in *truth*."

Love is real action to meet the needs of others in accordance with the truth, with what God's Word calls good. And it is the giving of our whole selves, our whole lives, which is why, as this passage teaches, love is not only the actions that show care by what we do, but love is also the very essence of who we should be. To allow sin to entrench itself in our lives is profoundly unloving because it ultimately will devour people we love and care about. In contrast, to live an exemplary life in Christ is profoundly loving since such an example does more to "stir up one another to love and good works" (10:24) than perhaps anything else we do. So then, let me close for now with where we began this chapter. "Let brotherly love continue," for by God's unfailing grace, it must continue.

27

Is My Cross in His Camp?

(HEBREWS 13:8–13)

s my cross in His camp? It's a curious question with an intensely personal application. It's a question, I believe, which challenges us in our convictions as Jesus's followers more than any other. Let me start to show you how this is so through a story.

As a Christian pastor in Iran, Mehdi Dibaj spent nearly ten years in prison for his faith. Converting from Islam in 1955, Dibaj was given every opportunity by the authorities to regain his "freedom." First, he was asked to sign a paper admitting he was wrong and that he wanted to return to Islam. For refusing, he was beaten, tortured, and put through mock executions. In the process, his wife succumbed to the pressure, converted to Islam, and married another man. The Iranians continued pressuring Dibaj to renounce his faith, but Dibaj refused and remained in prison. He was freed only after a fellow pastor named Haik sent an open letter to Western media publicizing Dibaj's plight, but soon after, Haik was murdered; not too long after that, Dibaj met the same fate. These stories can be countlessly told of Christians in Iran over the past half century or so, but it begs the question, Is it worth it? Is there any meaningful point in suffering for Jesus Christ? Would any of us endure such suffering for His name's sake today? In 1977, there were only two thousand seven hundred evangelicals in Iran out of a population of forty-five million people. Of these, only three hundred were former Muslims. Today, there are close to fifty-five thousand believers in Iran, of whom twenty-seven thousand are from Muslim backgrounds.[45] Is it possible, perhaps, that the kingdom of heaven and its citizens are called to work in ways very different than this world?

But am I willing to work in these very different ways? Is my cross in His camp? More importantly, would Jesus say my cross is in His camp? And if He would, on what basis would He confirm this? What truth would He see in my life that would lead Him to affirm me in this way? One way to view this passage is as a litmus test for what Jesus must see to say, in accordance with the truth of the scriptures, "Yes, your cross is in My camp." So then, let's take a look at Jesus's camp.

In Jesus's Camp, He Is Our *Soul* Provision

Yes, this is a bit of a play on words for He is our "sole provision." And as such, He is ever-faithful. Jesus is always trustworthy to follow for "Jesus Christ is the same yesterday and today and forever" as we read in verse 8. This verse is an abrupt declaration about Jesus that serves to look back and forward in the text. Looking back, it follows on the heels of verse 7 where we're commanded to consider the way of life of our faithful leaders and imitate them. Exemplary leaders are a great blessing to God's people as chapter 11 teaches us, but remember the author followed chapter 11 with the greatest example of all: our Lord Jesus, "the founder and perfecter of our faith" (12:2). In verses 7–8, the author calls each of us to remember the great examples of faith in your life and imitate them, but most importantly, remember and imitate the greatest example in your life who, unlike all other examples, is always with you. He never changes, and He "will never leave you nor forsake you" (13:5). The Greek text distinctly separates verse 8 between the phrase "the same yesterday and today" and the phrase "and forever" as if to teach us that Jesus has proven Himself faithful to us "yesterday and today" and, therefore, can be trusted to be faithful to us "forever." Jesus is always trustworthy to follow, and in a world so full of voices to follow that do not have our best in mind, we must follow Jesus exclusively because the grace of Jesus's life and teaching is our greatest benefit.

Verse 9 reads, "Do not be led away by diverse and strange teachings, for it is good for the heart to be strengthened by grace, not by foods, which have not benefited those devoted to them." At first glance, the nature of the "diverse and strange teachings" referred to here seems a bit mysterious, but the author narrows things down to teaching about "foods." Even still, it's difficult to precisely pinpoint what was being taught about foods that might cause believers to "be led away." But given that his readers are likely dealing with temptations to embrace old covenant Judaism, this may well be the ritual practices of Judaism with respect to foods making inroads into the church. But whatever the source or kind of teaching about foods, they offer no benefit to "those devoted to" such teaching. The NEB translation of verse 9 makes this point emphatically, saying, "It is good that our souls should gain their strength from the grace of God, and not from scruples about what we eat, *which have never done any good to those who were governed by them.*" Paul likewise makes this point very plainly in 1 Corinthians 8:8: *"Food will not commend us to God. We are no worse off if we do not eat, and no better off if we do."* This is actually very relevant for us today because all sorts of "diverse and strange teachings" about the spiritual benefit of foods are working their way into the church in our day.

One website titled Original Christianity and Original Yoga (and the title should be enough warning, but sadly, in the church today, it's not and many are "led away") claims that "a fundamental truth of the cosmos" is that

> diet is a crucial aspect of emotional, intellectual, and spiritual development. This is presented to us immediately in Genesis. The first sin of the human race involved eating. "And when the woman saw that the tree was good for food, and that it was pleasant to the eyes, and a tree to be desired to make one wise, she took of the fruit thereof, and did eat, and gave also unto her husband with her; and he did eat. And the eyes of them both were opened, and they knew that they were naked" (Genesis 3:6–7). Moreover, it was only after eating that Adam and Eve perceived their nakedness. *This dramatically demonstrates that diet and consciousness are interrelated.* (my emphasis)[46]

The website proceeds to twist a few other scriptures in support of its point then concludes, saying, "The *spiritual traditions* of all ages, *whose purpose is the freeing of the human being through conscious evolution*, have been unanimous in stating that the basic requisite of the path to enlightenment is purification. According to the Beatitudes it is purification which results in the Divine Vision: 'Blessed are the pure in heart: for they shall see God'" (Matthew 5:8).[47]

I'm going to go out on a theological limb and assert that there is nothing about food or diet of any kind that purifies our hearts and transforms our spirit in a way commendable to God. Rather, "it is good for the heart to be strengthened by grace" (verse 9). Jesus Christ and the vital ongoing eternal life-giving relationship we have with Him is our true and lasting food. Jesus taught this very plainly to a crowd clamoring for free bread like Moses gave their forefathers, telling them, "Your fathers ate the manna in the wilderness, *and they died*. This is the bread that comes down from heaven, so that one may eat of it and not die. I am the living bread that came down from heaven. If anyone eats of this bread, he will live forever" (John 6:49–51). The grace of Jesus's life and teaching is our greatest benefit, the only kind of food that brings growth to an eternal life. And this is an exclusive benefit.

This beneficial grace of Jesus is exclusive to His followers for "we have an altar from which those who serve the tent have no right to eat" (verse 10). The reference to "those who serve the tent" is likely a reference to God's direction for His people under the old covenant such as what we see in Deuteronomy 12:17–18. The people were commanded to "not eat within your towns the tithe of your grain or of your wine or of your oil, or the firstborn of your herd or of your flock, or any of your vow offerings that you vow, or your freewill offerings or the contribution that you present, but you shall eat them before the LORD your God in the place that the LORD your God will choose." Writing very metaphorically here, the author essentially declares that we eat from a different altar with a right to do so denied to those who partake of the sacrifices they bring to the place the Lord directed them to.

Speaking equally metaphorically (and graphically but still absolutely true), Jesus continued to tell the crowd in John 6:53–54, "Truly, truly, I say to you, unless you eat the flesh of the Son of Man and drink his blood, *you have no life in you*. Whoever feeds on my flesh and drinks my blood has eternal life, and I will raise him up on the last day. For my flesh is true food, and my blood is true drink." To clarify His point, Jesus then told His disciples, "It is the Spirit who gives life; the flesh is no help at all. The words that I have spoken to you are spirit and life" (John 6:63). "It is good for the heart to be strengthened by grace" (verse 9), the grace and power of the Holy Spirit working in us by the very power of the life and teaching of Jesus Christ. For the author, I believe his concern for people being tempted to find sustenance at a lesser table led him to remind his readers that access to "the throne of grace, that we may receive mercy and find grace to help in time of need" (4:16) comes only to those who have embraced Jesus Christ, their great high priest and the founder and perfecter of their faith, by grace through faith alone. "Those who serve the tent" are of a different camp who lack an important share of Christ.

Those in Jesus's Camp "Bear the Reproach He Endured"

In verses 11–12, the author narrows his focus on the many old covenant sacrifices alluded to in verse 10 down to the sin offering of the Day of Atonement, writing, "For the bodies of those animals whose blood is brought into the holy places by the high priest as a sacrifice for sin are burned *outside the camp*. So, Jesus also suffered *outside the gate* in order to sanctify the people through his own blood." Very much like the sin offering of the Day of Atonement was "burned outside the camp," Jesus died on the cross outside the city walls of Jerusalem, outside the gate of those walls. And unlike most other offerings, the sin offering of the Day of Atonement was not allowed to be eaten even by the priests. But as Jesus and the author of Hebrews teach, followers of Jesus Christ do have the benefit of doing so, of truly partaking of the one truly effective sin offering, Jesus Christ, who "suffered outside the gate [i.e., outside the camp] in order to sanctify the people through his own blood."

The point the author continues to make here is the distinction God makes between people through faith in Jesus Christ. For the author, the distinction he was making to his readers is that they are no longer in the camp of old covenant Judaism. He could have very well used one of his favorite adjectives here by reminding them "you're in a *better* camp" with better sacrifices and better promises enjoyed under a better covenant! Why even think about drifting back into a far lesser camp? *But here's the rub for the author of Hebrews readers and for us.* What does life in a "better camp" look like? Read verse 13. As with many teaching points in chapter 13, the author is driving home a main point with force one last time. Let's trace the point of verse 13 in light of the previous few chapters.

> But recall the former days when, after you were enlightened, you endured a hard struggle with sufferings … For you have need of endurance, so that when you have done the will of God *you may receive what is promised*. (10:32, 10:36)

> By faith Moses, when he was grown up, refused to be called the son of Pharaoh's daughter, choosing rather to be mistreated with the people of God than to enjoy the fleeting pleasures of sin. He considered the reproach of Christ greater wealth than the treasures of Egypt, *for he was looking to the reward*. (11:24–26)

Women received back their dead by resurrection. Some were tortured, refusing to accept release, *so that they might rise again to a better life*. (11:35)

Consider him *who endured from sinners such hostility against himself,* so that you may not grow weary or fainthearted. In your struggle against sin you have not yet resisted to the point of shedding your blood. (12:3–4)

And as we consider our Lord Jesus "who endured from sinners such hostility against himself" as the example for us to follow, consider Paul's words in Romans 8:16–17, where he writes, "The Spirit himself bears witness with our spirit that we are children of God, and if children, then heirs—heirs of God and fellow heirs with Christ, *provided we suffer with him in order that we may also be glorified with him*." And so the author writes in verse 13, "Therefore let us *go to him outside the camp* and *bear the reproach he endured*."

Good newsflash. This entire narrative of suffering for faithfulness to Jesus Christ's commission to His church as the essential pathway in this life to a victorious eternity is thoroughly lost on the church in America today. We do everything in our power to be protected and delivered from the very thing that establishes us as fellow heirs with Jesus Christ of all things in eternity. What we are called to as followers of Jesus Christ is exactly what the Lord taught in Matthew 10:38 when He said, "Whoever does not take his cross and follow me is not worthy of me." Our cross is to "go to him outside the camp and bear the reproach he endured." So then, is your "cross" in His camp?

Neglect Connections

When the author wrote in 12:4, "In your struggle against sin you have not yet resisted to the point of shedding your blood," he was clearly indicating this was within the realm of the possible in God's will for our lives as those who are in Christ's camp. And this holds true today. In an article on Christian History Institute's website titled "Persecution in the Early Church," the article states, "It is estimated that more people have been martyred for Christ in the past 50 years than in the church's first 300 years."[48]

Clearly, Christ still calls His people to bear such a cross, but I don't think this spiritual reality sinks in to most of us from Western cultures. This is powerfully illustrated by an encounter one man shared with Christian doctors ministering in the Arab world. He writes,

> I think the most vibrant missionaries I have met are medical doctors serving in lonely outposts of the Arab world. These physicians and nurses are aware that in winning a Muslim to Christ, they condemn their converts to ostracism and persecution; even martyrdom. One doctor said to me, "How do you think I feel in longing to lead people to Christ, knowing that the moment my patients receive Christ they face a life-and-death contempt in this culture?" The man replied "It must seem pointless."[49]

And herein lies our spiritual problem. If our cross is in Christ's camp, is this "pointless"? If our cross is in His camp, is this even "tragic"? Or is it "precious in the sight of the LORD is the death of his saints" (Psalm 116:15)? The contrast between our perspective and the truth is even starker in Revelation 14:12–13, where, in the great persecution at the end of the age, John writes this: "Here is a call *for the endurance of the saints*, those who keep the commandments of God and their faith in Jesus. And I heard a voice from heaven saying, 'Write this: Blessed are the dead who die in the Lord from now on.' 'Blessed indeed,' says the Spirit, 'that they may rest from their labors, for their deeds follow them!'"

This isn't pointless or tragic. This is the manifestation of God's grace in our lives of the highest order and to His glory! This is blessing and rest and eternal reward! Coming back to the conversation between the man and a missionary doctor in the Arab world, after the man said, "It must seem pointless," the doctor replied, "Pointless? This is the point of the gospel. The cost and consequence of receiving Christ is the entire point of … 'Take up your cross and follow me.'"[50] Folks, this isn't pointless. It is *the* point. "*Let us go to him outside the camp and bear the reproach he endured.*" Is this where you're at? Is your cross in His camp?

28

Seek the City that Is to Come

(HEBREWS 13:14–25)

In Hot Springs, Arkansas, you'll find the Morris Antique Mall. Nothing on the inside distinguishes this antique store from dozens like it in town. There's a musty smell and dusty relics from the past. But if you look closely at the outside of the Morris Antique Mall, you'll see something that makes it distinct: before it was an antique store, it was a church building.[51] A focus on the future prevents a church from becoming a resting place for dusty relics. The tendency to confine a church's ministry to its past rather than releasing that ministry to the future Christ is calling it to is widespread, and no local church is immune to this tendency.

Neither was the body of believers the author was writing to, for he gave them this exhortation in verse 14: "For here we have no lasting city, but we *seek the city that is to come.*" As Christians, we find ourselves in an unusual place in this world. We're called to walk in this world along the way to a destination that is not in this world. Therefore, we're called to "travel" very differently. Seeking a city that is to come entails living life in this world and in the church that does not follow the pattern of this world. It is the life of a kingdom citizen that previews the life of a kingdom that is coming and is already here in the sense of the lives of its citizens. But it is not yet here in the sense the author describes when he writes in 12:27–28 that this coming kingdom will be accompanied by "the removal of things that are shaken—that is, things that have been made—in order that the things that cannot be shaken may remain. Therefore, let us be grateful for receiving a kingdom that cannot be shaken." And what cannot be shaken is what we seek, what we run for, and evidently so.

Seek the City that Is to Come through a Life of Sacrifices Pleasing to God

"For here we have no lasting city, but we seek the city that is to come." Life on earth for Christ's church must be a life of looking forward and not to something "better" that this life on earth can offer, but to something *truly* better that God promises us in eternity through Jesus Christ. As with most of what the author teaches in chapter 13, this future focus is not a new point but an emphasis on a point of life in Christ he has already taught, particularly in Hebrews 11.

For example, in 11:8–10, we learned that Abraham walked by faith in this life "for he was *looking forward to the city* that has foundations, whose designer and builder is God" (11:10). The author then explains how those who walk by faith live in this world as if "they are *seeking* a homeland" (11:14) because "they desire a better country, that is, a heavenly one. Therefore, God is not ashamed to be called their God, for *he has prepared for them a city*" (11:16). And then there's Moses who "considered the reproach of Christ greater wealth than the treasures of Egypt, *for he was looking to the reward*" (11:26). Moses showed us that walking by faith shuns the blessings this world can offer, and in 11:35, saints of old taught us that walking by faith embraces the curses of this world as "some were tortured, refusing to accept release, *so that they might rise again to a better life.*" Looking forward, shunning worldly blessings, and embracing worldly curses. Citizens of "the city that is to come" live in a very particular way now, including, as verses 15–16 teach, offering sacrifices that "are pleasing to God."

Verses 15–16 read, "Through him then let us continually offer up a sacrifice of praise to God, that is, the fruit of lips that acknowledge his name. Do not neglect to do good and to share what you have, for *such sacrifices* are pleasing to God." The readers of this book of Hebrews have already been taught in 10:8–9 that the sacrifices offered according to the law have been done away with. But here we see that the new covenant comes with new kinds of sacrifices to "continually" offer God, including sacrifices of praise, which verse 15 explains are "the fruit of lips that acknowledge his name." This is our act of declaring God's greatness and expressing our commitment to Him.

Another kind of new covenant sacrifice that is pleasing to God is in the offering of our very lives to Him as Paul teaches in Romans 12:1, "To present your bodies as a living sacrifice, holy and acceptable to God, which is your spiritual worship." And in verse 16, we learn that what is holy, acceptable, and pleasing to Him is "to do good and to share what you have." The sacrifice God wants is us—body, heart, mind, soul, strength, and will—surrendered to Him so that He can work in and through us according to His good will and pleasure. To cling to the past rather than to surrender to the future He is leading us to is to rob Him of His due. But to surrender the entire road ahead to Him is to give Him glory, honor, and praise. As F. F. Bruce writes in his commentary on verse 16, "Christianity is sacrificial through and through; it is founded on the one self-offering of Christ, and the offering of his people's praise and property, of their service and their lives, is caught up into the perfection of his acceptable sacrifice, and is accepted in him."[52]

The charge "to do good and to share what you have" in verse 16 applies to our lives without exception. We're not to narrow it because everyone is our neighbor in this world, and we have been placed among them so that God, by His grace, may reach them through the Gospel and become our *forever* neighbors we welcome "into the eternal dwellings" as Jesus teaches in Luke 16:9. But in verses 17–22, the author narrows the focus for us who "seek the city that is to come" to how we live in the here and now through our relationships within the church, particularly with respect to the church's leaders.

Seek Faithful Relationships between the "Shepherds" and the "Flock"

In 1 Peter 5:1–5, Peter addresses this "shepherd-flock" dynamic. He exhorts the elders to "shepherd the flock of God" (1 Peter 5:2) willingly and eagerly with godly motives, leading foremost by example while refraining from being domineering over the flock. Peter then commands the flock to be humbly "subject to the elders" while warning them that "God opposes the proud but gives grace to the humble" (1 Peter 5:5). Herein then is a constant rub of sinful human nature. As leaders, we are tempted by ambition and power, and as followers, we are tempted by pride and rebellion. A church seeking the city that is to come rejects these worldly passions so that among the flock, the church strives to obey its leaders and submit to them as we see in the beginning of verse 17.

But the author doesn't simply give this command. He gives a rationale as well, writing, "For they are keeping watch over your souls, as those who will have to give an account." The verb "keeping watch" conveys these leaders are always on the alert for danger, not unlike how Jesus describes the good shepherd in John 10. And the account that will one day have to be given by these leaders *keeping watch* is to God. This verse makes the positive assumption that the leaders of a church are serving in this way, but given this standard, leaders of a church are charged with a great and weighty purpose, their ministry held to the highest account by the highest authority. If we are commanded to obey our leaders and submit to them, it must be for a good purpose Christ has designed into His church. And so to frustrate the ministry of the leaders within the church, especially on the basis of personal pride while knowing they bear a burden you do not, is not a mark of a life sacrificed to God and pleasing to Him nor is it beneficial to the church.

This is evident in the remainder of verse 17, which reads, "Let them do *this* with joy and not with groaning, for *that would be of no advantage to you*" where "this" refers to the work of "keeping watch over your souls." In Acts 20:28, Paul tells the elders of the church at Ephesus, "Pay careful attention to yourselves and to all the flock, in which the Holy Spirit has made you overseers." To rebel against the command to obey your leaders and submit to them never confers an advantage to the church and is, in essence, a rebellion against the Holy Spirit who has appointed them to their roles. But when leaders serve well, it confers great advantage to the church. Therefore, pray for your leaders to serve well.

Verses 18–19 read, "*Pray* for us, for we are sure that we have a clear conscience, desiring to act honorably in all things. I urge you the more earnestly to do this in order that I may be restored to you the sooner." Notice the author appeals to his readers to "pray for *us*" (lumping himself in with the leadership of the church) but then narrows it down to a personal appeal "that *I* may be restored to you the sooner." This gives us a hint at the nature of the relationship the author has with his readers (he may be part of their leadership), but the fact that he urges them to pray "more earnestly" that he be restored to them conveys that he believes this would be advantageous to them, beneficial for them. And it would be because he and his fellow leaders "have a clear conscience, desiring to act honorably in all things." In other words, these leaders are serving well, and he urges his readers to pray that they will continue to do so. This ought to be a great longing of the church, but the implicit challenge to the leaders of a local church is to embrace the high calling of our ministry: to keep watch over the souls under our care as those who will have to give an account to the Lord, such that we have a clear conscience and are thoroughly honorable in our convictions and actions. And part and parcel of this high standard is to have the highest longing for the spiritual well-being of the flock.

Shepherds must pray for the flock to serve well. This is exactly what the author does after he appeals to the flock to pray for their leaders when he writes in verses 20–21, "Now may the God of peace who brought again from the dead our Lord Jesus, the great shepherd of the sheep, by the blood of the eternal covenant, *equip you with everything good that you may do his will,* working in us that which is pleasing in his sight, through Jesus Christ, to whom be glory forever and ever. Amen." Notice what serving well entails in this prayer.

1. First and foremost, the shepherd of the flock for all to follow, obey, and submit to is "our Lord Jesus, the great shepherd of the sheep."
2. It is God who equips us with everything good that we may do His will.
3. When God holds such sway over a local church, the works it does is pleasing in his sight.
4. The means by which this gracious work of God is done in us is "through Jesus Christ." This reminds me *again* of a very key verse in Hebrews, which teaches us that through Jesus Christ our great high priest, we can "with confidence draw near to the throne of grace, that we may receive mercy and find grace to help in time of need" (4:16).
5. Lastly, this gracious work of God in us who live our lives as living sacrifices, holy, acceptable, and pleasing to Him, seeking the city that is to come, glorifies Jesus Christ, "the founder and perfecter of our faith" (12:2) "forever and ever." The city of this world moves according to the passions of the sinful nature. The city of God moves according to His grace and is worth seeking.

Seek the City that Is to Come by the Grace of God

In these last four verses, there are plenty of clues over which we can spend a lot of time speculating about who the author of Hebrews is, who he's writing to, and where they live, but I'm going to humbly confess that I'm not going to be the first person in church history to definitively answer those questions. Sorry 😊. But in verse 22, we do see an important closing point when the author writes, "I appeal to you, brothers, bear with my word of exhortation, for I have written to you briefly." The phrase "word of exhortation" is typically associated with a sermon or message. The book of Hebrews is a message of one with a pastor's heart toward his readers, and the author is pleading with his readers to bear with his message. To give it a fair hearing. He hasn't burdened them with too much.

He's written to them "briefly." And although verse 25—"Grace be with all of you"—might simply be seen as a typical benediction, it is also a very concise summary of all he's written.

You see, his readers are being tempted to not go to Christ outside the camp. They're being tempted to find a lasting city here. The life of seeking the city that is to come comes with hardship, and so he reminded them that they have need of endurance. Why? Because the race set before them that leads to the city that is to come demands endurance. It demands endurance because doing the will of God in this fallen world comes with a hard struggle with sufferings, public exposure to reproach and affliction, and the plundering of their property. It entails bearing the reproach Jesus endured.

It's a hard calling in this life, and as if sensing they desired deliverance from it, the author chastised them in 12:4, saying, "In your struggle against sin you have not yet resisted to the point of shedding your blood." Escaping all of this by turning from Christ and retreating to a life of seeking a relationship with God through the old covenant law was tempting. The hardship of following Christ would surely subside if they did. In their own right, they were a church tempted to look back to a past God had done away with, a course Christ was not part of. In contrast, Abraham, the great biblical example of genuine faith, was looking forward to the city that is to come and so should we, anticipating that Christ will lead us forward along a course we've yet to encounter. You've heard me cite F. F. Bruce's commentary several times over the course of this book, and so ever so appropriately, I'd like to close this book with a benediction of sorts with a quote at length from Bruce's exceptional closing comments on the book of Hebrews.

Benediction

> Christians are Christians by virtue of certain acts of God which took place at a definite time in the past, but these acts of God have released a dynamic force which will never allow Christians to stick fast at any point short of that divine rest which in this life is always a goal to be aimed at and never a stage which has been reached. The faith once for all delivered to the saints is not something which can be caught and tamed; it continually leads the saints forth to new ventures in the cause of Christ, as God calls afresh. It was Abraham's firm faith in the unchanging God that made him so ready to go forth at God's bidding, not knowing whither he might be led. To stay at

the point to which some revered teacher of the past has brought us, out of a mistaken sense of loyalty to him; to continue to follow a certain pattern of religious activity or attitude just because it was good enough for our fathers and grandfathers—these and the like are temptations which make the message of Hebrews a necessary and salutary one for us to listen to. Every fresh movement of the Spirit of God tends to become stereotyped in the next generation, and what we have heard with our ears, what our fathers have told us, becomes a tenacious tradition encroaching on the allegiance which ought to be accorded only to the living and active word of God. As Christians survey the world today, they see very much land waiting to be possessed in the name of Christ; but to take possession of it calls for a generous measure of that forward-looking faith which is so earnestly urged upon the readers of this epistle. Those first readers were living at a time when the old, cherished order was breaking up. Attachment to venerable traditions could avail them nothing in this situation; only attachment to the unchanging and onward-moving Christ could carry them forward and enable them to face a new order with confidence and power. So, in a day when everything that can be shaken is being shaken before our eyes and even beneath our feet, let us in our turn give thanks for the unshakable kingdom which we have inherited, which endures forever when everything else to which men and women may pin their hopes disappears and leaves not [even a ruin] behind.[53]

And may the Lord bless you and keep you by the mercy and grace of His countenance ever shining upon you as you *look forward* to an eternal weight of glory beyond compare. Amen.

Endnotes

1. "J.R.R. Tolkien Quotes," Goodreads, accessed March 1, 2024, https://www.goodreads.com/quotes/137661-it-s-a-dangerous-business-frodo-going-out-your-door-you.

2. F. F. Bruce, *The Epistle to the Hebrews*, rev. ed., New International Commentary on the New Testament (Grand Rapids, MI: Wm. B. Eerdmans Publishing Co., 1990), 50.

3. Joseph Loconte, *The Searchers: A Quest for Faith in the Valley of Doubt* (Thomas Nelson, 2012), 98–99.

4. Steve Turner, "The Ballad of John and Jesus," *Christianity Today*, June 12, 2000, 86.

5. D. A. Carson, "Natural Drift from Holiness," quoted from "Reflections," *Christianity Today*, July 31, 2000, https://www.preachingtoday.com/illustrations/2001/february/12857.html.

6. William Arndt et al., *A Greek-English Lexicon of the New Testament and Other Early Christian Literature* (Chicago: University of Chicago Press, 2000), 52.

7. F. F. Bruce, *The Epistle to the Hebrews*, rev. ed., New International Commentary on the New Testament (Grand Rapids, MI: Wm. B. Eerdmans Publishing Co., 1990), 68.

8. Sara Germano, "Yoga Poseurs: Athletic Gear Soars, Outpacing Sport Itself," *The Wall Street Journal*, August 20, 2014, https://www.wsj.com/articles/yoga-poseurs-athletic-apparel-moves-out-of-the-gym-to-every-day-1408561182.

9. F. F. Bruce, *The Epistle to the Hebrews*, rev. ed., New International Commentary on the New Testament (Grand Rapids, MI: Wm. B. Eerdmans Publishing Co., 1990), 81.

10. Philip Yancey, *Prayer* (Zondervan, 2006), 88.

11. Kaushik Patowary, "The Lighthouse That Wrecked More Ships Than it Saved," *Amusing Planet*, Oct 17, 2018, https://www.amusingplanet.com/2018/10/the-lighthouse-that-wrecked-more-ships.html.

12. Kevin DeYoung, "Who Do You Say That I am?," *The Gospel Coalition*, November 20, 2014, https://www.thegospelcoalition.org/blogs/kevin-deyoung/who-do-you-say-i-am.

13. F. F. Bruce, *The Epistle to the Hebrews*, rev. ed., New International Commentary on the New Testament (Grand Rapids, MI: Wm. B. Eerdmans Publishing Co., 1990), 94.

14. F. F. Bruce, *The Epistle to the Hebrews*, rev. ed., New International Commentary on the New Testament (Grand Rapids, MI: Wm. B. Eerdmans Publishing Co., 1990), 105–106.

15. ABC7.com staff, "Knott's Berry Farm ride stuck 148 feet in air; 21 riders rescued," December 31,2016, https://abc7chicago.com/knotts-berry-farm-ride-stuck-sky-cabin-rescue/1680029.

16. Randy Alcorn, "Your Suffering Can Be the Pathway to Greater Godliness," *Eternal Perspective Ministries*, August 6, 2018, https://www.epm.org/blog/2018/Aug/6/suffering-pathway.

17. Jeanna Bryner, "Temptation Harder to Resist Than You Think, Study Suggests," *Live Science*, August 3, 2009, https://www.livescience.com/10556-temptation-harder-resist-study-suggests.html.

18. Bill Thrall, Bruce McNicol, and John S. Lynch, *TrueFaced* (NavPress, 2004), 152–153.

19. F. F. Bruce, *The Epistle to the Hebrews*, rev. ed., New International Commentary on the New Testament (Grand Rapids, MI: Wm. B. Eerdmans Publishing Co., 1990), 130.

20. Sean Woods, "Anthony Bourdain on Writing, Hangovers, and Finding a Calling," *Men's Journal*, June 25, 2019, https://www.mensjournal.com/food-drink/anthony-bourdains-life-advice-20140919.

21. Tim Keller, *Making Sense of God*, (Viking, 2016), 153.

22. David Finch, "Minnesota firefighter leaves his own wedding to battle a blaze," *The Week*, last updated September 27, 2018, https://theweek.com/speedreads/798406/minnesota-firefighter-leaves-wedding-battle-blaze.

23. Warren Wiersbe, "Is God in it?", *Preaching Today*, accessed May 27, 2024, https://www.preachingtoday.com/illustrations/1995/august/1053.html.

24. John Claypool, "The Future and Forgetting," *Preaching Today*, accessed March 1, 2024, https://www.preachingtoday.com/sermons/sermons/2010/july/thefutureandforgetting.html.

25. Max Tegmark, *Life 3.0: Being Human In The Age Of Artificial Intelligence* (Alfred A. Knopf, 2017), 29.

26. Reflections, "Heroes are Different from Superstars," *Christianity Today*, October 2, 1995, https://www.christianitytoday.com/ct/1995/october2/5tb048.html.

27. Cision PR Newswire, "2018 Edelman Trust Barometer Reveals Record-Breaking Drop in Trust in the U.S." January 21, 2018, https://www.prnewswire.com/news-releases/2018-edelman-trust-barometer-reveals-record-breaking-drop-in-trust-in-the-us-300585510.html.

28. F. F. Bruce, *The Epistle to the Hebrews*, rev. ed., New International Commentary on the New Testament (Grand Rapids, MI: Wm. B. Eerdmans Publishing Co., 1990), 173.

29. Tullian Tchividjian, *Surprised by Grace* (Crossway, 2014), 182.

30. F. F. Bruce, *The Epistle to the Hebrews*, rev. ed., New International Commentary on the New Testament (Grand Rapids, MI: Wm. B. Eerdmans Publishing Co., 1990), 182.

31. R. T. France, *Hebrews*, rev. ed. The Expositor's Bible Commentary: Hebrews–Revelation (Grand Rapids, MI: Zondervan, 2006), 111.

32. F. F. Bruce, *The Epistle to the Hebrews*, rev. ed., New International Commentary on the New Testament (Grand Rapids, MI: Wm. B. Eerdmans Publishing Co., 1990), 209.

33. Evan Allen, "Marathon provides a lesson: Inspiring guys can finish last," *Boston Globe*, April 22, 2015, https://www.pressreader.com/usa/the-boston-globe/20150422/281509339726042.

34. Lee Strobel, *The Case for Christ* (Grand Rapids, MI: Zondervan, 1998), 13.

35. William Arndt et al., *A Greek-English Lexicon of the New Testament and Other Early Christian Literature* (Chicago: University of Chicago Press, 2000), 827.

36. Dr. Steven R. Cook, "Walking with God," *Thinking on Scripture*, November 25, 2014, https://thinkingonscripture.com/tag/marcus-dods/,

37. F. F. Bruce, *The Epistle to the Hebrews*, rev. ed., New International Commentary on the New Testament (Grand Rapids, MI: Wm. B. Eerdmans Publishing Co., 1990), 295.

38. Ninie Harmon, "Jesus, I'm Coming Home," *The Southeast Outlook*, May 12, 2005, https://www.preachingtoday.com/illustrations/2005/may/15954.html.

39. R. T. France, *Hebrews*, rev. ed. The Expositor's Bible Commentary: Hebrews–Revelation (Grand Rapids, MI: Zondervan, 2006), 160.

40. F. F. Bruce, *The Epistle to the Hebrews*, rev. ed., New International Commentary on the New Testament (Grand Rapids, MI: Wm. B. Eerdmans Publishing Co., 1990), 317.

41. F. F. Bruce, *The Epistle to the Hebrews*, rev. ed., New International Commentary on the New Testament (Grand Rapids, MI: Wm. B. Eerdmans Publishing Co., 1990), 329.

42. Jay Akkerman, "Wind Makes Us Strong," *Preaching Today*, April, 2006, https://www.preachingtoday.com/search/?query =Biosphere.

43. Ed Haynes, "Learning to Discard 'Necessities'", *Preaching Today*, September 1997, https://www.preachingtoday.com/ search/?query=Jules%20Verne.

44. F. F. Bruce, *The Epistle to the Hebrews*, rev. ed., New International Commentary on the New Testament (Grand Rapids, MI: Wm. B. Eerdmans Publishing Co., 1990), 335–36.

45. Michael G. Maudlin, "Have You Seen Jesus Lately?", *Books & Culture*, May/June 2002, 14.

46. "Spiritual Benefits of a Vegetarian Diet," *Original Christianity Original Yoga*, accessed 19 February 2024, https://ocoy.org/original-yoga/how-to-be-a-yogi/spiritual-benefits-of-a-vegetarian-diet.

47. Ibid.

48. "Persecution in the Early Church," *Christian History Insitiute*, accessed 19 February 2024, https://christianhistoryinstitute.org/magazine/ issue/persecution-in-the-early-church.

49. Calvin Miller, *Jesus Loves Me: Celebrating the Profound Truths of a Simple Hymn* (Warner Books, 2002), reprinted in "Quick Takes," Christian Reader (March/April 2002).

50. Ibid.

51. Michael A. Howes, "Rest Makes Rust," *Preaching Today*, May 1996, https://www.preachingtoday.com/search/?query= Morris%20Antique%20Mall.

52. F. F. Bruce, *The Epistle to the Hebrews*, rev. ed., New International Commentary on the New Testament (Grand Rapids, MI: Wm. B. Eerdmans Publishing Co., 1990), 384.

53. F. F. Bruce, *The Epistle to the Hebrews*, rev. ed., New International Commentary on the New Testament (Grand Rapids, MI: Wm. B. Eerdmans Publishing Co., 1990), 392.

Printed in the United States
by Baker & Taylor Publisher Services